John Updike

Revised Edition

Twayne's United States Authors Series

Warren French, Editor

Indiana University, Indianapolis

TUSAS 481

JOHN UPDIKE
Photo © Jill Krementz

John Updike

Revised Edition

By Robert Detweiler

Emory University

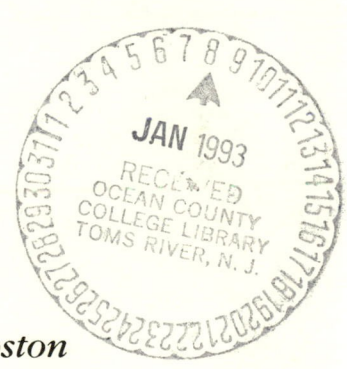

Twayne Publishers • *Boston*

John Updike

Robert Detweiler

Copyright © 1984 by G. K. Hall & Company
All Rights Reserved
Published by Twayne Publishers
A Division of G. K. Hall & Company
70 Lincoln Street
Boston, Massachusetts 02111

Book Production by Linda L. Smith

Book Design by Barbara Anderson

Printed on permanent/durable acid-free
paper and bound in the United States of
America.

Library of Congress Cataloging in Publication Data.

Detweiler, Robert.
    John Updike.

    (Twayne's United States authors series ; TUSAS 481)
    Bibliography: p.
    Includes index.
    1. Updike, John—Criticism and interpretation.
I. Title. II. Series.
PS3571.P4Z64   1984   813'.54   83–18472
ISBN 0-8057-7422-X
ISBN 0-8057-7429-7 (pbk.)

In Memory of My Father: My Chiron

Contents

About the Author

Robert Detweiler earned his Ph.D. in English at the University of Florida and taught there from 1961–65. After that he taught at Hunter College and Florida Presbyterian College, and from 1974–82 was director of the Graduate Institute of the Liberal Arts at Emory University. He has been visiting professor of American Studies at the University of Salzburg, University of Hamburg, and University of Regensburg, and is now Professor of Comparative Literature at Emory University.

Mr. Detweiler is author and editor of books on modern fiction, literary criticism, and literature and religion, among them *Story, Sign, and Self* (1978), *Derrida and Biblical Studies* (1982), and *Art/Literature/Religion: Life on the Borders* (1983). He has translated fiction and criticism from German into English for American publication and has published widely in European and American literary and religious studies journals.

Preface to the Revised Edition

The first editon of this study, published in 1972, interpreted the fiction of John Updike that had appeared through 1971: six novels and four short-story collections—ten texts in thirteen years. Updike's productivity in the ensuing decade remained prodigious: four more novels and three more short story collections (a fourth, *Too Far to Go*, consists mainly of stories previously collected elsewhere). These eight new texts I treat in three new chapters in this second edition.

My emphasis in the first edition was not, of course, on Updike's prolificness, nor is it in this one. I was, and am, concerned mainly with writing an appreciative analysis of his narrative art that also remarks on his social-cultural significance. Since Updike is recognized primarily as an accomplished stylist, I have examined most thoroughly the texture and structure of his writing and have paid special attention to the metaphoric language, above all the image patterns, that mark his style. In my preface to the first edition I described Updike as writing an "elaborate, texture-conscious, structurally balanced, highly controlled, mythically resonant fiction," and I still think that this characterization is accurate. Since he is, however, regarded more and more as a literary chronicler of American marital-sexual mores and trends, I have in this new edition commented more extensively on this dimension of his novels and stories.

Restrictions of space have dictated that I limit my study to considerations of Updike's narrative prose fiction. Hence I have for the most part ignored his poetry, essays, and reviews. I am not sorry to miss the opportunity to discuss his verse, for I do not think that he is a particularly skilled poet, although he is certainly a clever composer of light verse. I do, however, regret that I could not work with his discursive prose, for he is a first-rate essayist, and it would be a pleasure to comment on the occasional pieces gathered into three published collections.

Three book-length studies of Updike had come out prior to the publication of my own in 1972. Since then Updike criticism has become something of a minor industry. I call attention to representative critical texts in a revised bibliography, and I have cited other Updike interpreters here and there, but, again, space restrictions prohibit any extended dialogue with them. I have shortened and tightened the original eleven chapters, which covered Updike's fiction from *The Same Door* through *Rabbit Redux,* and besides the appended chapters on Updike's fiction since 1971, I have included a brief Updike biography.

I am indebted to the Twayne editors, and especially to Warren French, editor of the Twayne United States Authors Series, for their patience and forbearance during the years it took me to attend to this revised edition.

Robert Detweiler

Emory University

Acknowledgments

Permission has been granted to reprint the poem "Mirror" from THE CARPENTERED HEN AND OTHER TAME CREATURES by John Updike. Copyright © 1957 by John Updike. Originally appeared in *The New Yorker* as "Reflections," and reprinted by permission of Harper & Row, Publishers.

Permission has also been granted by Harper & Row, Publishers to quote from the poems "Tao in the Yankee Stadium Bleachers" and "Room 28," which appear in THE CARPENTERED HEN AND OTHER TAME CREATURES by John Updike. Copyright © 1956, 1957 by John Updike.

Permission has been granted by Alfred A. Knopf, Inc., to quote from "Suburban Madrigal," "Earthworm," "Thoughts While Driving Home," "Shillington," Movie House," "Seven Stanzas at Easter," and "Erotic Epigrams." These poems appear in TELEPHONE POLES AND OTHER POEMS by John Updike. Copyright © 1958, 1959, 1960, 1961, 1962, 1963 by John Updike.

Permission has been granted by Alfred A. Knopf, Inc., to quote from the poem "Fireworks," which appears in MIDPOINT AND OTHER POEMS by John Updike. Copyright © 1964 by John Updike.

Permission has been granted by Alfred A. Knopf, Inc., to quote from the book reviews "Creatures of the Air," and "More Love in the Western World" which appear in ASSORTED PROSE by John Updike. Copyright © 1961, 1963, by John Updike.

Permission has been granted by John Updike to quote from "The Dogwood Tree: A Boyhood," which appears in ASSORTED PROSE by John Updike. Copyright © 1962 by Martin Levin.

Permission has been granted by Alfred A. Knopf, Inc., to quote from "Dream and Reality," "Tossing and Turning," and "Phenomena." These poems appear in *Tossing and Turning* by John Updike. Copyright © 1977 by John Updike.

Chronology

1932   John Updike born in Shillington, Pennsylvania.

1936–1950   Attends Shillington public schools.

1945   Moves with family to a farm in Plowville, Pennsylvania.

1950   Enters Harvard University

1953   Marries Mary Pennington.

1954   Is graduated *summa cum laude* (with a major in English) from Harvard; sells first story ("Friends from Philadelphia") to *The New Yorker.*

1954–1955   Attends the Ruskin School of Drawing and Fine Art in Oxford, England, on a Knox Fellowship. Daughter Elizabeth born.

1955–1957   Works as a staff writer for *The New Yorker* and writes some of "The Talk of the Town" columns.

1957   Son David born; moves with family to Ipswich, Massachusetts.

1958   Collected poems, *The Carpentered Hen.*

1959   Son Michael born; *The Same Door, The Poorhouse Fair.*

1960   Daughter Miranda born; *Rabbit, Run.*

1962   *Pigeon Feathers and Other Stories.*

1963   *Telephone Poles and Other Poems; The Centaur.*

1964   Receives National Book Award for *The Centaur;* elected member of the National Institute of Arts and Letters; *Olinger Stories, A Selection.*

1964–1965   Travels to Russia, Rumania, Bulgaria, and Czechoslovakia as part of the U.S.S.R.–U.S. Cultural Exchange Program.

1965   *Of the Farm* and *Assorted Prose.*

1966   *The Music School;* receives First O. Henry Prize for "The Bulgarian Poetess."

1968   *Couples.*

1969   *Midpoint and Other Poems.*

1970   *Bech: A Book.*

1971   *Rabbit Redux.*

1972   *Museums and Women and Other Stories.*

1973   Travels and lectures for three weeks as Fulbright lecturer in Ghana, Nigeria, Tanzania, Kenya, and Ethiopia.

1974   *Buchanan Dying* (play); separates from his wife Mary and moves to Boston; subsequently divorced.

1975   *A Month of Sundays* and *Picked-Up Pieces.*

1976   *Marry Me;* moves to Georgetown, Massachusetts.

1977   *Tossing and Turning;* new edition of *The Poorhouse Fair* with introduction by Updike; marries Martha Bernhard.

1978   *The Coup.*

1979   *Problems and Other Stories* and *Too Far to Go; Too Far to Go* produced as television drama.

1981   *Rabbit Is Rich;* it receives Pulitzer Prize and American Book Award; awarded Edward MacDowell Medal for literature.

1982   *Bech Is Back.*

1983   *Hugging the Shore*

Chapter One

John Updike: Out of the Ordinary

> The spirit has infinite facets, but the body
> confiningly few sides.
>
> —from "Tossing and Turning"[1]

John Updike was born on 18 March 1932 in Shillington, Pennsylvania. The only child of Wesley and Linda Grace Hoyer Updike, he spent his early years in the Shillington parental home, which was shared with his mother's parents John and Katherine Hoyer, the inspiration for the fictional grandparents in narratives such as *The Centaur.* These were lean years for the Updikes, and the time came when they could no longer afford to inhabit the Shillington house. Hence they moved, when their son was thirteen, to the farm in Plowville, ten miles outside of Shillington, where Mrs. Updike had been born. His father, a high school mathematics teacher for thirty years of his life, supported his family, including the senior Hoyers, in this early 1800s house (like the Kern house in "Pigeon Feathers," it had no indoor plumbing) on a poor salary and commuted with his son to the Shillington public schools.

Updike's mother had literary aspirations for herself, and her reading and writing created an atmosphere in which her son's creative talents could grow. Influenced by *The New Yorker* magazine, Updike determined to become a cartoonist, and as a youth drew for the school papers. He also wrote articles and poems, kept a journal, sent pieces out for publication and had them rejected. This evidence of an adolescent literary apprenticeship has been carefully saved and stored by Updike himself and is now in the care of his mother, who lives in the Pennsylvania farmhouse (his father died in 1972).

A good student in his small-town high school, Updike entered Harvard, on a full scholarship, in 1950. He majored in English, became editor of the Harvard *Lampoon,* and was graduated *summa cum laude* in 1954. During his sophomore year he met Mary Pennington, a Radcliffe fine arts major two years older than he and the daughter of a Unitarian pastor. They married in 1953 while Updike was a junior. In 1954 he sold his first story, "Friends from Philadelphia," to *The New Yorker* and thus launched a career that would make him one of the most prolific literary artists in the history of American letters.

Updike and his wife spent a year during 1954–1955 at the Ruskin School of Drawing and Fine Art in Oxford, financed in part by a Knox Fellowship. During this time their first child Elizabeth was born. While the Updikes were in Oxford, they were visited by the prominent editor and writer E. B. White, who offered John a position as a staff writer with *The New Yorker.* This was exactly the job that he had wanted, and he accepted the offer. Returning to the United States and settling with his small family in a Riverside Drive apartment, he wrote, among other things, the "Talk of the Town" column, exhibiting an urbanity, wit, and polished style (although he was just twenty-three) that made him just right for *The New Yorker* ambiance. He also worked on a long autobiographical novel called *Home* but abandoned it after writing some six hundred pages. He gradually became disillusioned with the social-literary climate of New York, however, and feared that it would inhibit the development of his career as an author, remarking that his stories could hardly compete with the frenetic real life of the city. Hence he left *The New Yorker,* and in April of 1957 the family moved to Ipswich, Massachusetts, a town close to the coast and an hour's drive north of Boston, where he would reside for the next seventeen years. A second child David was born that same year.

This move, which cut him off from the immediate New York literary scene, appeared to be a risky one for a neophyte author, but it began to pay off quickly. Renting an office above an Ipswich restaurant, he wrote there on a daily schedule, sold stories to *The New Yorker* as well as an occasional "Talk of the Town" column, and worked on longer fiction. In 1958 his first book, a collection of poems called *The Carpentered Hen,* was published, and in 1959 his second, *The Poorhouse Fair,* a mildly futuristic novel about an old people's home set in a fictionalized version of Shillington. The poetry collection was largely ignored by reviewers, but the novel was favorably received by such critics as Mary McCarthy and won the Rosenthal Award. Nineteen-fifty-nine also saw the publication of *The Same Door,* Updike's first short story collection, and the birth of his second son Michael—a productive year in every respect. Yet along with this lively artist's activity, Updike also took vigorous part in Ipswich community life. He involved himself in local civic matters and was a member of the Democratic Town Committee. Reared as a Lutheran in Pennsylvania, he joined the Congregational Church in Ipswich—the setting which inspired scenes of church-going in *Couples* and *Marry Me*—and became a faithful attendant there. He contributed reviews to the town newspaper, played poker with friends regularly, and devoted serious practice to his golf game.

As James Atlas puts it, "To ward off the perils of celebrity, Updike followed Flaubert's advice that in order to be a great writer one must live like a bourgeois."[2] Yet at this point he was less bothered by the corrupting potential of fame than by the symptoms of a religious-philosophical crisis in his life. He himself identified this malaise, which persisted for a number of years during his late twenties, as a feeling of hopelessness prompted by his recognition of the inevitability of death. Reading the works of existentialist-oriented thinkers such as Kierkegaard and the Swiss neoorthodox theologian Karl Barth helped him realize, he says, the strategy of taking a leap into faith that would allow him to function effectively against the knowledge of death's certainty.

The lurking sense of death has figured strongly in Updike's fiction. It is prominent in recent narratives such as *Rabbit Is Rich* and *Bech Is Back* but was already central in *Rabbit, Run,* the first novel of what is now his Rabbit trilogy, written during his crisis and published in 1960, the year also in which Updike's last child, Miranda, was born. *Rabbit, Run* brought Updike considerable attention, and notoriety, as a gifted young writer who could—and would—deal candidly with sexuality in the context of serious literary art. The novel also began his reputation as a novelist of American middle-class marital mores. Two years later his second collection of short fiction, *Pigeon Feathers,* appeared, and a year after that both *Telephone Poles and Other Poems* and the novel *The Centaur* were published. Although *The Centaur,* a mythic-nostalgic evocation of adolescence in Pennsylvania, mystified some reviewers and received a mixed reception, it won its thirty-two-year-old author the prestigious National Book Award and led to his election to membership in The National Institute of Arts and Letters—the youngest man ever to receive that honor.

During 1964–1965 Updike travelled to Eastern Europe as an American representative in a United States-Soviet Russian cultural exchange program. Experiences from that tour were translated into fiction such as "The Bulgarian Poetess," winner of an O. Henry award, and other short stories comprising the *Bech: A Book* collection published in 1970. But meanwhile, in 1965, he brought out *Of the Farm*, an exquisitely fashioned novel of domestic frustration and adjustment, and his first collection of nonfiction entitled *Assorted Prose*, which collection disclosed to those who had not already read his discursive prose (mainly in *The New Yorker*) what an accomplished essayist and reviewer he was. Indeed, this collection and two subsequent ones lead to conjectures that had Updike devoted his energies to full-time academic and semischolarly writing, he might well have established himself as a major social-cultural critic of the stature of an Edmund Wilson. In 1966 he published *The Music School*, his third collection of short stories.

Living the middle-class suburban life in Ipswich did not prevent Updike's involvement in a network of erotically charged friendships among a group of young married pairs there, like those depicted in the 1968 novel *Couples*. How much of that narrative is autobiographical remains open to speculation, but Updike himself and friends from that era in Ipswich grant that it reflects the intimacy within that circle. *Couples* became a best seller and at least a qualified literary success; it also earned Updike approximately a half-million dollars for the screen rights, although a film was never made from the book. Not least, in connection with the publication of *Couples*, Updike was presented in *Time* and *Life* as an important chronicler of American bourgeois morality—and of its excesses—and thus was propelled further along his way toward achieving status as a major literary-cultural force.

Following the appearance of the largely autobiographical and quirky *At Midpoint and Other Poems* in 1969, *Bech: A Book* came out in 1970—a witty collection of stories featuring the middle-aged "blocked" Jewish novelist Henry Bech. Like most writers, Updike professes unconcern with his critics' judgments yet is obviously irritated by what he considers wrongheaded responses to his work. In a mock bibliography appended to *Bech: A Book*, Updike satirized some of his detractors, such as Norman Podhoretz, by linking their names to ludicrous titles.

The early seventies, one recalls, were the waning years of the "counter-cultural revolution," which era Updike treats in *Rabbit Redux,* the second book of the Rabbit trilogy, published in 1971. The novel is an account of extreme marital discord in the context of a chaotic period of our national life. The story collection *Museums and Women* published the next year confirmed that Updike's interests were focusing more intently on marriages in various stages of difficulty and disintegration; particularly the five Maple stories gathered here dramatized the ominous signs of dissolving marital bonds. This emphasis on the dynamics of marriages in distress and on infidelity clearly derived in good part from the increasing pressures on the Updikes's own union. After fifteen years, their marriage had developed severe strains; in 1974 they separated, and he moved to an apartment in Boston. Later that year they were granted one of the first no-fault divorces in Massachusetts.

Such personal problems did not seem to slow down Updike's literary production. In 1974 he published *Buchanan Dying,* a dull closet drama and to date his only play, and in 1975 he brought out *A Month of Sundays,* featuring the irascible midwestern clergyman the Reverend Tom Marshfield, and his second book of discursive prose, an impressive work of some five hundred pages entitled *Picked-Up Pieces.* In 1973, meanwhile, he had taken an extensive trip under State Department sponsorship to a number of developing nations, among them Ghana, Tanzania, and Kenya, impressions from which journey found their way into stories eventually published in *Bech Is Back* but above all into *The Coup.* In 1976 his "romance" (as he identified it) *Marry Me* appeared, possibly his poorest longer work of narrative; and in that year he also moved from Boston back to the North Shore area, this time to the village of Georgetown. In 1977 he brought out his fourth volume of verse, *Tossing and Turning,* like his newer fiction marked by a sexual frankness verging on the confessional, and also a new edition of *The Poorhouse Fair* for which he composed an introduction.

In the fall of 1977 Updike married Martha Bernhard, seven years his junior and ex-wife of a Boston law executive. Years earlier, members of the same social set as the Updikes, they had bought the Updikes's house when Updike and family moved to a less populated area in the Ipswich vicinity. John and Martha Updike now live with her children in a large and handsome Georgetown house overlooking the Atlantic Ocean, while his first wife, who has also remarried, has remained in the Ipswich house.

In 1978 Updike published *The Coup*, his "Africa novel," and a year later two short story collections: *Problems* and *Too Far To Go*, the last of which brought together all seventeen of the Maple tales in one volume. It was now manifest through both of these collections that Updike's fictions of nostalgia for youthful innocence had been transformed into evocations of nostalgia for happy—or at least durable—marriages. That tone persists in Updike's two works published since then, both of them sequels: *Rabbit Is Rich*, the third book of the Rabbit trilogy, and *Bech Is Back*. These two volumes generated a new round of public curiosity over Updike and resulted in pieces such as a 1981 *Saturday Review* essay on him, "Turning Sex and Guilt Into an American Epic," and a 1982 *Time* cover story—the second—on him.[3] They also won high praise for their literary quality, *Rabbit Is Rich* earning Updike an American Book Award, a Pulitzer Prize, and a commendation from the National Book Critics Circle.

The interest of the news and entertainment media has not been limited to Updike's writing per se. Although *Couples* was never filmed, and although the Hollywood film version of *Rabbit, Run* from the late sixties turned out to be remarkably bad cinema, the television dramatization of *Too Far to Go*, produced in 1979 (with Blythe Danner and Michael Moriarty playing Joan and Richard Maple), was a popular and critical triumph which demonstrated how good television, on occasion, can be.

The nature and effects of that production can be described to situate Updike today in the context of American society and letters: it was a film that dealt responsibly, skillfully, and positively with infidelity and the end of a marriage—hardly happy themes—and it resonated well among the American public; one suspects that we may even have been instructed by it. Updike himself must strike Americans who care about their artists as an anomaly: he is a millionaire who earns his wealth by writing on the middle class and by applying the middle class virtues of industry and discipline to his profession. He is an example of the American success story, yet one who has, in his fiction, characterized mainly American failures.

He is a respected and prize-winning author, many of whose texts would be considered objectionable, because of their sexually oriented language and content, for reading and discussion in various educational and religious circles. He is judged by a majority of critics, probably, to be a major novelist of the twentieth century, and yet by some others as a lightweight composer of precious prose hardly worth taking seriously. His third book of essays and reviews, *Hugging the Shore,* published in 1983, will do little to alter these opinions. This massive collection (over 900 pages) consists of many brilliant and imaginative pieces on an astonishing range of subjects literary and otherwise, but it is also comprised of negligible ones that do not deserve inclusion.

As this study will show, I believe that Updike has established himself on the basis of his fiction as a formidable and influential literary-critical force—not without some troubling flaws, as full of contradictions as America itself and reflecting both its genius and immaturity, yet as a writer whose imagination can be trusted and followed in its explorations of problematic living in our time.

Chapter Two
The Same Door:
Unexpected Gifts

We have one home, the first, and leave that one.
The having and leaving go on together.

—from "Shillington"

Grace and Epiphanies

The Same Door, published in 1959, is a collection of sixteen short stories written over a period of five years and originally published, some in different form, in *The New Yorker.* Certain aspects of casual unity are created by a consistent authorial attitude toward life and by a recurrent structural technique. Updike himself articulates the attitude in the foreward to a later collection called *Olinger Stories.* Answering the complaint that one of those stories seems to have no point, he comments "The point, to me, is plain, and is the point, more or less, of all these Olinger stories. *We are rewarded unexpectedly.* The muddled and inconsequent surface of things now and then parts to yield us a gift."[1] This point is the one made as well, if sometimes negatively so, in the *The Same Door;* and it expresses a conviction of the author that becomes more determinative as the body of his fiction grows. Updike is a Christian, if not a "religious" writer in the accepted sense, and the centrality of grace in the Protestant experience finds its way into his art through the expression of the gift or the reward.

The particular unifying technique is similar to the construction of the Joycean "epiphany," at least according to the way in which that much-debated term has been generally understood. Somewhat as in Joyce's *Dubliners, The Same Door* stories, instead of attempting the brutal surprise or the psychological shock, concentrate on producing the gradual revelation—the culminating knowledge-plus-emotion that dawns upon the protagonist following his crucial experiences and upon the reader after he has finished the story. Also, as in Joyce's stories, Updike's epiphanies, while they do not depend upon an overt religious context (except in "Dentistry and Doubt"), translate fundamentally religious or at least moral experiences into artistic imagery and action. The revelatory moment does not result from any sensational conflicts or climactic scenes, for these are not stories of deep passion, violence, or death. They occur in the midst of daily life, mixing with the stuff of the mundane; and the insight slowly materializes through a fine fusion of memories, reflexes, and some subtle catalyst of the unexpected. Against the wonted beat of familial or vocational being, a counterpoint insinuates itself in these stories that at last upsets the rhythm and forces the characters and reader to pause and then to reconsider the whole composition.

"Friends from Philadelphia"

Although the sixteen stories span a period from the very beginning of Updike's career to his establishment as a respected young artist, one finds little difference in the quality of the fiction. "Friends from Philadelphia," the first tale, shows some evidence of a neophyte author in search of a style; but the result is not a weak story by any means: it is, at its worst, a narrative that does not sound like the later, familiar Updike. The sentences are often short and choppy, dialogue predominates, and very little of the metaphoric interplay that marks the later fiction is present. The story succeeds, however, along other lines. Through careful characterization via dialogue, Updike reveals the sensitive uncertainty of late adolescence in contrast to the bluff confidence of adults who have located their secure little niches in society.

The tale is simple enough. Fifteen-year-old John Nordholm, who lives a mile outside Olinger, hikes into town to buy the wine that his parents need to entertain expected guests from Philadelphia. Since he is too young to buy alcohol, he stops by the Lutz home and asks if the father will buy it for him. Mr. Lutz himself arrives home later slightly drunk and agrees to drive John and the teenage Lutz daughter to the liquor store. He allows John (underage) to drive the new family car to the store, takes John's two dollars, and soon reappears with the wine. When they arrive at the Nordholm house, John asks hesitantly for his change and receives it along with the bottle. As Lutz and his daughter drive away, young John Nordholm discovers that the wine is Château Mouton-Rothschild 1937.

The charm of the story, along with the semi-sophisticated banter between the teenagers and the description of the television-addicted Mrs. Lutz in her darkened room, is in the ambivalent kindness of Mr. Lutz. His is an unexpectedly gracious act, for the wine obviously cost much more than the innocent boy anticipated; and the man does not humiliate him in front of the snide daughter by refusing to give change or by divulging the quality and price of the wine. But his gesture is also a patronizing one that increases Mr. Lutz's self-esteem at the expense of the Nordholms. John's schoolteacher-father can't afford good wine or a new car as the uneducated but prosperous Mr. Lutz can, and young John is left with the ironic reward. He is gifted for his family's poverty but suffers condescension for it as well. The revelation of the story, therefore, is that kindness has its price, perhaps, and that receiving grace demands its own kind of maturity.

"Ace in the Hole"

The second narrative, "Ace in the Hole," could be a preliminary sketch for *Rabbit, Run*. Fred "Ace" Anderson, like Harry Angstrom, is a twenty-six-year-old ex-high school basketball star, married, father of a small child, and the sad product of maternal domination. On the particular day of the story, he has been fired from his job— not for the first time—as a used-car salesman; and he returns home to await the arrival of his working wife and to appease somehow her anticipated anger at his latest failure. The story is packed with the complications and baggage of young American marriage. Evey, the wife, is Roman Catholic; and Ace is Protestant—a sore point between them. Their life is saturated with TV, pop music, beer, and the omnipresent cigarettes. They appear to have married directly out of high school when they were too young and when they had developed no skills; and they survive in a precarious financial state. Evey has matured, but Ace has not. He lives in the illusion of his teenage glory and is a childish egotist.

That evening Evey takes rather stoically the news of the firing (Ace's mother has already told her), but the irresponsible young husband soon irritates her into bitter recriminations. Then Ace turns on his charm. He distracts her by applauding their baby daughter's antics, then persuades her to dance with him to the sound of dinner music on the radio. The tale ends with the two of them, everything unresolved, dancing a quickening swing step in the isolation of the drab apartment, trying pathetically to relive the popularity of their carefree high school days.

Updike has, amazingly, already found his métier in "Ace in the Hole." The story offers less in terms of plot and action than "Friends from Philadelphia" but much more in terms of pure mood created out of sheer verbal craftsmanship. It is, much like *Rabbit, Run,* a sustained metaphor of nervous movement and a tension of opposites. Ace is always in motion: driving the car, smoking hastily, tapping a foot in rhythm, running home from his mother's house with the small daughter in his arms—still shifting restlessly on life's basketball court, trying to score and to be the hero again with the effortlessness of the natural. But Ace is not a natural in the workaday world. An indulgent mother and cheap early fame have spoiled him, and he is already a clearcut failure at the approaching prime of life. The antagonistic characters, his opposites, make his plight the more obvious. The prowling high school youths who insult him at the traffic light only show him (like the boys playing back-alley basketball at the start of *Rabbit,Run*) the reckless innocence that he has lost. His weary and dispirited wife, with her dogged common sense, makes him seem more of a loser.

Apart from a sexual innuendo, the title has a double sense. The protagonist is Ace "in the hole": jobless, unprepared to be a man, and threatened with a spouse nearly ready to leave him. But he also *has* his ace in the hole: his animal charm and his instincts that will help him to survive even if he ruins others in the process. The story is an inversion of the maturation pattern, for the events that should jolt the initiate into growing up at last only cause him to fight reality with a wasteful nervous energy. "Ace in the Hole" seems authentic because it fashions a modern American type, the teenage hero seduced by quick success into thinking that the adult world is easy to conquer but who soon suffers disillusion and the gradual degeneration into bumhood. Olinger can be too kind, the family-community can be too generous, when it offers its sons what they should strive a lifetime to deserve—and then permits grace to turn quickly into judgment. Updike has forced more news about one dead end along the American way of life into one brief story than many writers manage to report in a whole novel. It is no wonder that he returned to the theme and the place and expanded the microform into *Rabbit, Run.*

"Tomorrow and Tomorrow and So Forth"

In this tale (the third in the collection), young Mark Prosser is teaching *Macbeth* to a class of restless eleventh-graders; the narration is third-person, from Prosser's point of view. Updike's later familiar blending of the lofty and the trivial (on which *The Centaur* is based) appears here for the first time with clarity. It is carried in the title: "Tomorrow and Tomorrow and So Forth" joins the beginning of the famous Shakespearean soliloquy with the callous teenage disregard for highflown language, just as the inane teenage paraphrases of the speech clash with the quite incisive analysis that Prosser gives the bored students—and that is lost, of course, on them. That incongruity, introduced by the pupils' barbarizing of a classic, is deepened and then justified and resolved in the central action of the story.

Just before the period is over, Prosser intercepts a note passed from the provocative Gloria Angstrom to a boyfriend in which she confesses that "He's heavenly with poetry. I think I love him. I really do *love* him," Prosser detains the girl after class and lectures to her firmly but kindly about the dangers of using love's vocabulary too lightly; she leaves on the verge of tears. Immediately after, while Prosser is enjoying this surprising evidence of his professional-masculine charm, another teacher enters to tell him the gossip of the day: Gloria has written the same sort of note about two other faculty members and had them purposely discovered. Prosser has obviously been duped, and he is angered by the girl's duplicity; but he also comprehends that the trick has backfired on her: "The girl had been almost crying; he was sure of that."

Updike manages to project, in the unpredictable extremes of a youthful mind, a pettiness and a potential nobility that contribute together to the imaged truths of the story. As Prosser discovers, "a terrible tenderness" marks adolescents; and that oxymoron contains the power of the narrative. A young girl can use her budding sexuality to play an irritating trick on her instructors, but she will also respond to an honest encounter. The experience holds a gift for pupil and teacher. He takes her seriously, in their private discussion after class, in spite of her immaturity; and she answers with an acknowledgment of respect for him that was hidden hitherto behind the façade of mischief. "This petty pace from day to day" is quickened and made worthwhile by the occasional spontaneous meeting of two momentarily unmasked selves.

"Snowing in Greenwich Village"

"Snowing in Greenwich Village," the seventh of *The Same Door* series, is one of the most impressive performances in the collection. It shifts from the Olinger setting to Manhattan and introduces Richard and Joan Maple, a young married couple who appear repeatedly older and unhappier in later collections. Richard (in the advertising trade) and Joan have just moved to West Thirteenth Street in the Village and have invited an old acquaintance over for the evening, Rebecca Cune, a girl with "a gift for odd things."

The three drink sherry and converse, but the talk is dominated by Rebecca's wry recollections of the strange people she has known. Joan, who has a cold and has not been at all witty in the conversation, is roused by the clatter of the horses of mounted policemen. She rushes to the window, sees snow falling outside, and hugs her husband in a moment of unguarded intimacy while their guest watches blandly. When Rebecca leaves, Richard walks her home and follows her upstairs, aroused, to see her apartment. At her door as he prepares to leave, they are poised to embrace; but Richard destroys the critical moment with a joke that misfires, and departs.

The undertone of sexual competition pervades the tale. Joan and Rebecca are at cautious odds from the start, and Updike contrasts them graphically: Joan's angular "Modiglianiesque" features give her an air of simplicity, but Rebecca is a da Vinci type whose constant enigmatic smile reminds one of the mystery of the tantalizing Mona Lisa portrait. Beneath the purposefully casual conversation, one is made to feel the unnamed struggle. Richard is the prize, Joan the defender of her property, and Rebecca the predator. Joan's weapon is her defenselessness; Rebecca's, her cool and cryptic reserve that promises a hidden excitement. Richard is caught between loyalty toward his wife, who is put at a disadvantage by the off-beat discussion, and Rebecca's novel attractiveness. The chatting remains discreet, but the adultery motif accompanies it through the repeated references to beds: in the first paragraph, Richard lays

Rebecca's coat and scarf on his marriage bed; Rebecca relaxes on the floor in the living room with her arm on the Hide-a-Bed (while Joan sits straightbacked on a chair); Rebecca tells about the bedroom troubles she had in sharing her apartment with a pair of lovers; and, when Richard at the end visits her apartment, he is surprised to see the double bed that dominates the room.

Rebecca's knack for comic recitation gradually emerges as the extent of her substance. She achieves her unique personality at the expense of others, exaggerating their foibles to fit the style of her performance. That Rebecca is a predator in every way Richard suddenly grasps after his wife's impulsive embrace, as he sees Joan and himself from Rebecca's viewpoint. She will twist the moment of tenderness into a joke when she narrates the scene to other friends; the simple wife with the sniffles who hugs her husband in ludicrous joy because it happens to be snowing. But Richard's discovery does not make her less desirable; for when Richard escorts her home (at Joan's insistence—a smart if risky strategy, since it forces her opponent's move), they hold an embarrassed dialogue that masks the tension of presexual encounter and that continues inside her apartment. The crucial moment, exquisitely described, occurs at the door when Richard acts to leave; and the result could go either way. Rebecca, very close to him in the shadows, is waiting for him to make the move. If he does, he betrays his wife; if he doesn't, he becomes the ridiculous male. He tries a joke and stutters; the timing and the situation are ruined. He is free but at the expense of his pride.

Since this is Richard Maple's story, one must inquire what unexpected gift he receives. It may be, in part, the thrill of the just-missed extramarital adventure; but, more likely, it is that he does *not* become intimately involved. He has had the quick glance into the tantalizing maze of illicit romance but also the luck, or the grace, to avoid its penalties—emotional, social, and moral. A fine line may exist between lust and love, but the libido need not always incite to sexual consummation; it can produce other kinds of knowledge as well. Lust can teach.

"A Gift from the City"

The thirteenth story, "A Gift from the City," employs the technique of inversion. James and Liz are a well-to-do young couple with a baby daughter who live in Greenwich Village. Liz telephones her husband at work on a Friday afternoon to tell him that a poor Negro from North Carolina has been at her door asking for work and that she has given him ten dollars and sent him away. But the man wants to come back on Saturday evening to thank the husband as well for their generosity. That prospect upsets James; and, when the Negro actually does appear the next evening, James in his embarrassment gives him twenty dollars more. James and Liz are afraid now that they have a permanent dole on their hands and are not sure if they should believe his story. When James returns home from work on Monday evening, Liz informs him that the Negro has been there once more, and that she sent him away without any money. He does not appear again, and the equilibrium of their life is restored.

The title signifies the inversion that gives the story its rationale. James tells the Negro to accept the thirty dollars from them "as a gift from the city." What he and his wife do not see, in their genteel materialist pride, is that the Negro himself is the real gift from the city to them. Whether he is a small-time swindler or someone in genuine need, he is involved in a struggle for survival; and he is offered to them as a unique introduction to the destitution that characterizes the other side of metropolitan living. But James and Liz, for all their humanitarian impulses and notions of decency, do not really want to *know* the Negro. James is insulted when the black man refers to them as his only friends in New York. The scene in which James sees a similarity between the Negro's head and a new shaver he has designed is revealing. James is immersed in a world of things, and philanthropy must remain nicely objective and distant in that schema.

James thinks twice of magic circles around his wife and child that would protect them from the hundred daily dangers of Manhattan living. In the first reference, he is sorry that love is too immaterial to protect his dearest ones; but, by the end of the story, in his frustration over the resilient Negro, he believes that he has "sold his life, his chances" for his wife's sake and that she should make her own enchanted circles. But love in this story is too dependent on the modern symbols of affluence for its effectiveness and is perhaps more a matter of egotistic possession than of shared affection. In any case, James and Liz are in a charmed circle that they have unwittingly drawn around themselves and from which they cannot escape. Because of their economic and social success, they are separated from much of the real humanity of the city. In spite of their broadmindedness, they are morally narrow; they have chosen not to help; and, through their wealth, they are made spiritually poor. To be able to give graciously is also a gift; and the couple, by refusing to meet the Negro in all his potential, are denying themselves the gift they most need.

"The Happiest I've Been"

If "A Gift from the City" concludes with an ironic word about peace of mind and moral compromise, "The Happiest I've Been," the final story of the collection, returns with considerable nostalgia to the context of a fading moral innocence. John Nordholm (as Updike states it in the foreward of *Olinger Stories*), having taken his turn as protagonist in "Friends from Philadelphia," narrates the story in the first person as a nineteen-year-old college student who is home in Olinger for the Christmas vacation. The tale is stylistically different from the others in *The Same Door*. It is essentially plotless and has the form of a reminiscence, a series of smoothly connected vignettes that one would guess to be transposed autobiography— Updike's personally experienced Shillington into the fictive Olinger of 1951. Yet the story evokes a mood that marks a transitional stage in one's maturing rather than a specific history and geography. It is the period of the end of youthful innocence, when one practices the rites of adulthood half-willingly to demonstrate sophistication, yet lingers with the more familiar and less complicated habits of late adolescence.

John is picked up in the evening by Neil, a friend of his, to drive to a girlfriend's New Year's party in Chicago, seventeen hours distant; but, once beyond parental ken, they decide to attend first in Olinger a party given by former high school classmates. They stay at the party until three in the morning and then take two girls home to nearby Riverside. Margaret, one of the girls, invites the others into her parents' home for early coffee; while Neil and the other girl pet in the darkened house, John and Margaret sit and talk until she falls asleep in his arm. As dawn breaks, the two boys finally leave for Chicago. Neil has John drive the car and sleeps beside him as the trip begins.

Except for "A Gift from the City," this is the longest story of the collection and one of Updike's favorites. John tells the story in a retrospective late-teenager style, but the angle of vision is not therefore wholly a teenager's; it is a double view that tempers the precious hours of the youthful past with the increased wisdom of the present. The result is a certain discrepancy of moods and tones that creates the sense of loss now beginning to invade Updike's fiction. This mood is indicated in the adverbial superlative of the title ("The *Happiest* I've Been") and in the shadow of sadness that lingers over the careful description. Updike quotes Henri Bergson in the preface to *The Same Door:* "How many of our present pleasures, were we to examine them closely, would shrink into nothing more than memories of past ones!" That realization, which applies exactly to this story, is also Wordsworthian: with increasing self-consciousness comes the loss of natural, spontaneous joy, so that the stylizing mind must reconstruct its pleasures artificially out of the past.

"The Happiest I've Been" broadens into a modern maturation ritual, replete with the archetypal accoutrements, that does not simply dress up the old forms of twentieth-century art but also adds a new interpretive dimension. The season, the party, and the trip embody and symbolize the transitional nature of the experience that introduces a new stage of maturity. It is nearly New Year (the classmates pretend that it *is* New Year's Eve), the time to begin formally a fresh kind of existence; and the trip has echoes of the *rite de passage.* John leaves the old farm and his gnarled grandmother and aging parents for young, robust Chicago and the girlfriend awaiting him there; and, of course, the actual journey begins at the pristine moment of dawn. It is an emphatic moment of separation from family and home and the start of the independent journey through adult life.

The party particularly has ritual elements. It is a last meeting in youthful irresponsibility; less a reunion than a final celebration of oneness; still held in a parental home, but in one from which the parents are absent. The games, the alcoholic drinks, the dancing, all combined with a constant awareness of *the time,* blend the playfulness of adolescence with the growing sophistication of impending adulthood. When at midnight "everyone" tries to kiss the only married girl of the group, the concentrated ritual duality becomes most apparent; it is an embracing of the new state of being attempted through a playful gesture.

The new relevance of the maturation pattern appears after the party among the privacy of the two couples. The movement is from the group to individuals, from the tribe to self-conscious formal structures. For John Nordholm, the revelation of beginning maturity that promises goodness for the future and that makes him the happiest he's been comes through the double incident of demonstrated faith that others have in him: "There was knowing that twice since midnight a person had trusted me enough to fall asleep beside me." The nostalgia for an irretrievable carefree past is balanced by a pride in the assumed responsibility of adult relationships. One trusts one's sexual being, one's safety, with the other person; and there is joy in accepting the burden of that faith.

Variations on the Themes

The other stories in the collection present variations on the themes and motifs already described. "Dentistry and Doubt" concerns an American divinity student at Oxford who, plagued by Luther-like struggles with the devil, finds solace in a visit to an English dentist when the man working on his teeth prompts him into recalling a faith-restoring quotation. The story ends with an apt natural metaphor: as the student watches birds through the window, he sees two wrens snatch a crumb from a blackbird—like a pair of weak humans outsmarting Satan.

"Who Made Yellow Roses Yellow?" contrasts the suave Manhattan playboy Fred Platt with his old Ivy League classmate Clayton Clayton, the middle-class plodder who has made good as a big business executive. Just returned from France, Platt wants a job with Clayton's firm but is too proud to ask directly. When they meet for lunch, Fred offers hints that Clayton, still dazzled by his friend's worldly wise front, doesn't take seriously. Frustrated by his failure, Fred insults the bewildered Clayton with school-primer French as they separate. Fred Platt is one of Updike's thoroughly unpleasant character creations (Freddy Thorne in *Couples* is a more recent one), but he is also pathetic. Caught in the web of his own perverse personality, he cannot really meet anyone else on honest terms; and he seems doomed to isolation in his shallow social superiority. Even the last name (Platt is German for "flat" or "low") reinforces the sense of underlying failure.

"Sunday Teasing," in turn, is a subtly cruel story of a marriage relationship; and Updike uses in it the trick of fiction within fiction to impose the effect. The young couple Arthur and Macy, after a discussion about family affection with their Sunday dinner guest, retire for the evening; and Macy reads a depressing French short story that she passes on to her husband. He explains its essence to her—it concerns a "perceptive man caged in his own weak character"—and he then defends the hero's apparently harsh treatment of the heroine. When Macy begins to cry in confusion, Arthur humors her and puts her to bed. One realizes gradually that Arthur is also very aware but very weak, and the skillfully placed aspects of the story fall into line. Unamuno's *The Tragic Sense of Life* (which Arthur is reading), Arthur's distorted understanding of Protestant individuality, his playful demand that Macy mimic the Garbo line, "You're fooling me."—all these assume a terrible irony. Arthur does not, perhaps cannot, love his wife; but he doesn't have the courage to tell her. Instead, he keeps them both suspended in a painful illusion of communion. Behind his self-righteous Christian pose, he is sinning against her and himself.

In "His Finest Hour," George and Rosalind Chandler intervene in a bloody marital quarrel in a neighboring Manhattan apartment. A month later, they receive an extravagant gift of flowers from the neighbors "to show that everything was right between our families." The Chandlers move to Arabia; homesick for America, George's first vision is always of a profusion of flowers in the shabby West Side rooms. This is a story of the unexpected and unrecognized reward, but George Chandler's "finest hour" is not when he ends the quarrel but when he and his wife are the surprised recipients of the flowers from the people they had thought to despise.

In a "Trillion Feet of Gas," a young New York couple are enduring the lengthy visit of a mildly obnoxious British houseguest. At a party, the three meet a windy Texas businessman, "a States' Righter, a purchaser of Congressmen, a pillar of reaction," who entrances them all with his blunt, crude power. His vulgarity finally puts the carping Englishman on the defensive; and in his quasicapitulation, before so much "gas," to America's "hideous vigor," he enters into a kind of comradeship at last with his hosts.

"Incest" begins with the description of a titillating dream that Lee, a young husband, relates to his wife at supper; and it ends with him asleep and dreaming again. In between, he plays with his spoiled baby daughter while his exhausted wife rests; and he manages to lull the child to sleep with a bedtime story. As the title suggests, the story probes the complexity of a marriage involvement from the male perspective. In a sense, Lee is married not just to his wife but to her aggressive mother, whom she resembles, and also to his demanding child. The dream of the other woman, then, illustrates the familiar wish-fulfillment of basic Freudianism; but it also shows the husband's acceptance of his actual situation. In the end of the dream, he finds himself washing the mysterious blonde girl with a garden hose. She could be his daughter grown up, his secret ideal woman, his mother-in-law, or all three merged. In any case, "the task, like rinsing an automobile, was more absorbing than pleasant or unpleasant"; and such a reaction, Updike would say, is the reality of most of our experiences.

In "The Alligators," which returns to the Olinger setting, Joan Edison is the new girl from Baltimore who enters the Olinger fifth grade in mid-semester. The class taunts her about her city ways; but Charlie (the protagonist), although he takes part in the perse-cution, secretly loves her and determines to confess it to her and become her champion against his classmates' torment. But, by the time he is ready to make his move, Joan has become "queen of the class." Charlie, an only child, has misinterpreted the strange man-ifestations of adolescent affection; he understands too late that the others all along teased her to make her one of them. As the eternal outsider, Charlie does not comprehend the rites of initiation; and, because he is so young, his alienation is all the more pitiful.

Conclusion: Behind the Doors

"The same door" as a metaphor of communication is physically or figuratively present in all of the stories of the collection. It can function literally, as with Richard and Rebecca frozen in the tension of sexual attraction at the door of her darkened walk-up, or the poor Negro waiting outside the Village apartment for help from strangers, or George Chandler entering timidly to intervene in the neighbors' marital battle. Or it can be the symbolic door between husband and wife, between old friends, or between chance acquaintances. Some doors are opened quickly and gladly, others are opened only to be slammed shut, some are quietly closed, and some are never opened at all. The image of the door, a familiar object of ordinary life, is fitting and effective for Updike's purpose: to show that the formative events of one's being occur within the framework of the common, and that the common moments can be redeemed or lost through the quality of one's response to others.

Chapter Three

The Poorhouse Fair: The Godless City of God

No windows intrude real light into this temple of shades.

—from "Movie House"

The Shape of a First Novel

The Poorhouse Fair is the story of life in one sterile corner of the future welfare state: among the inhabitants and administrators of a New Jersey old people's home. But the novel in its mythical leanings is also an ironic portrayal of the realized modern City of God, ironic in that the new order has been achieved mainly by men of fervent social vision who long ago (from the vantage point of the novel) removed God from their universe and replaced him with the ideal of the perfect state. Doubly ironic, then, is that—within the institution of the old people's home, where all is tidiness and comfort and where all apparent needs are satisfied—the "senior citizens" of the model state are dissatisfied and await their deaths with the static boredom of those from whom science has taken away the hope of immortality. That elemental dissatisfaction excites the eruption of basic instincts which forms the incongruous climax of the novel.

The book has many of the earmarks of a *tour de force.* A novel about the aged, largely and convincingly from the perspective of the aged, it was written by a twenty-six-year-old young man. It dares to project itself into the future for time and setting—usually the domain of science fiction—and yet it maintains an essentially realistic tone. A first novel, it shows few signs of apprenticeship. The unique spatial and temporal setting, the strategy of perspective, the tension of age discrepancy in characterization, the subtle dimensionality of nearly plotless action, and the elaboration of language fuse to embody and to project the irony of the godless-City-of-God myth that provides, in turn, the thematic profundity of the story.

The Poorhouse Fair is a relatively short, three-part novel fashioned out of over forty vignettes. The events of the story transpire from morning to evening of a single day—the day traditionally set aside in late spring for the aged wards of the state to display outdoors and to sell to the public the quilts, the hand-carvings, and other wares they have made throughout the year for this event. In the first part, the old people casually prepare for the fair, setting up booths and stringing colored lights in spite of the threat of imminent rain; and their aimless busyness is interrupted only by such minor excitements as the appearance of a horribly crippled cat on the poorhouse grounds and the arrival of the soft-drink truck bringing refreshments for the day. The young driver, bedeviled by some of the old men, backs his truck into the poorhouse wall, demolishing a sizable section of it. At that moment, the rain begins to fall; and the old people disappear into the house for lunch.

The second part is dominated by the sitting-room discussion that occurs among various aged inhabitants and that is then interrupted and dominated by the prefect of the home. Since the rain appears to have ruined the plans for the fair, some of the old people gather after lunch in the sitting room to pass the time conversing and reading. The interchange begins with political reminiscences by old Hook, a ninety-year-old ex-schoolteacher who is the unacknowledged leader of the inhabitants. Conner, the prefect, who makes an unprecedented and not very welcome entry midway in the conversation, compulsively shifts the talk to the level of a political-religious argument. Against Conner's own better judgment, he systematically destroys whatever religious faith and hope for immortality may have survived in the old people, substituting for them his own belief in the perfectibility of the socialized welfare state. In particular, he attempts to back old Hook into an intellectual corner and manages at least partially to shake the old man's trust in a benevolent natural universe.

The third part introduces an abrupt, brief, and violent action— the only action to speak of in the whole novel. With his obsession for order and since the rain has stopped, Conner has instructed the old people to help him repair the damaged wall on the poorhouse grounds before the fair begins. While they are carrying stones to

mend the damage, Gregg, a malicious old man who is slightly
drunk at the moment, purposely throws a stone at the prefect and
hits him on the leg, then another that strikes him in the back.
Conner, both puzzled and frightened, begins a nervous retreat. Like
excited savages, some other old people join Gregg in following
Conner and pelting him with stones and dirt. The attack ceases as
suddenly as it began; Conner has not been hurt, only humiliated.
Hook has not participated in the stoning, yet later he is accused by
Conner of instigating the attack and is insulted by the prefect and
by his young aid.

The rest of the novel treats the fair itself, as various visitors mingle
with the old people and as a sense of the interinvolvement of un-
related persons develops. The concluding vignette has old Hook
waking up in the night following the fair, troubled by the vague
feeling that there is something he must tell Conner, but what it is
he cannot recall.

Autobiography and Fiction

The poorhouse itself figures in Updike's own adolescent past. In
"The Dogwood Tree: A Boyhood," which recalls his Pennsylvania
childhood home, Updike writes: "The town was fringed with things
that appeared awesome and ominous and fantastic to a boy. At the
end of our street there was the County Home—an immense yellow
poorhouse, set among the wide orchards and lawns, surrounded by
a sandstone wall that was low enough on one side for a child to
climb easily, but that on the other side offered a drop of twenty or
thirty feet, enough to kill you if you fell."[1] In retrospect, Updike
sees the hollow in which the poorhouse stood from a Dantean perspective; he describes it as "a dreadful pit of space congruent with
the pit of time into which the old people (who could be seen circling
silently in the shade of the trees whose very tops were below my
feet) had been plunged by some mystery that would never touch
me."[2]

In Updike's childhood memory, apparently, one finds the experiential core of *The Poorhouse Fair*. The childish fascination with
the incomprehensible fact of death becomes the creative impetus for
the young artist who describes life on the verge of its encounter
with death. The sensation of Limbo that held the boy achieves
necessary articulation, then intellectual transformation, in the ironic

City-of-God vision of the adult novelist. Such transformation of personal past into problematical fiction is characteristic of Updike's novelistic strategy. His novels and stories sometimes depend upon autobiographical experience, and he has not at all attempted to conceal that relationship from his audience. To the contrary, the candid descriptions of childhood and youth in the "First Person Singular" recollections of *Assorted Prose* allow the reader to mark the similarities. Certainly, all novelists draw in some degree from a personal, historical past; but Updike persistently plumbs his past, constantly produces new variations upon a few key experiences, and creates dramatized meanings for the present out of those soundings. The poorhouse of Updike's boyhood is one of those tangible realities that he mythologizes for the present.

The Futurist Setting

Actual dates are never mentioned, but the year seems to be about 1975. Otherwise, the aura of the future is established throughout the novel by descriptions of ultramodern technical devices and of political and social situations. Automobiles are "run by almost pure automation"; increasing longevity is making the welfare state itself more and more necessary; and race problems have disappeared. Above all, international political and social conditions are changing radically according to what Updike introduces as the "well-publicized physical theory of entropia, the tendency of the universe toward eventual homogeneity, each fleck of energy settled in seventy cubic miles of otherwise vacant space. This end was inevitable, no new cause for heterogeneity being, without supernaturalism, conceivable." He speaks familiarly of the Americas as constituting "the Free Hemisphere" and as coexisting through "the London Pacts" with "the Eurasian Soviet" in an enervating stalemate. A President Lowenstein is chief of state, a playful allusion to the benevolent Eisenhower image (Eisenhower was in office at the time of the novel's composition). and also a hint at the phenomenon of a Jewish president, as the associations of the name Lowenstein might suggest.

In describing the future, Updike runs the risk of all would-be prophets—that of having his vision checked by history as time catches up with his projection. But such fiction need not be evaluated in terms of its detailed historical accuracy, only in terms of the efficacy of the use of the future as a metaphor of the present. Like most serious futuristic novels (Aldous Huxley's *Brave New World;* George Orwell's *1984*), *The Poorhouse Fair* is prophetic not in the sense of literal prognostication but as it warns against dangerous contemporary trends by envisaging the fearful excesses of their unchecked fulfillment.

Time and Space

The elapsed time of the narrative is only twelve to perhaps fifteen hours, but these hours are packed so full of diverse action and shared from so many perspectives that one feels a true dimension of temporal scope and depth. The narrow framework of time is expanded as well through repeated backward glances. As one would expect among the aged, their significant thoughts in *The Poorhouse Fair* are mainly memories; the past for them is more vital and more actual than the present. As a result, the time structure of the novel could be compared to a pyramid, of which the apex representing the immediate present of the narrative, rises out of the broad base of recollection and reminiscence that ranges all the way back to Hook's hazy memories of the late nineteenth century and then—up the pyramid—through the twentieth century to the lucidity of the disillusioning modern focus. Updike creates the effect of temporal depth by placing his characters in situations that stimulate the aged memory and then allowing the individual consciousness to take over; he has his old people move back and forth easily in their thoughts over a half-century and more of activity; and, through that technique, the basic framework of fifteen hours convincingly absorbs literally lifetimes of experience.

A similar twofold intensification of spatial setting develops in the novel. The actual narrative remains steadily anchored in the physical environs of the poorhouse itself; no action takes place anywhere else, yet the constant variation of happenings in the house and on the grounds and the sheer rapid shifting of scenery within the circumference of the home assure sustained reader involvement. Then, as in the temporal dimension, the geographical setting (though not as thoroughly) expands through the memory. Hook particularly envisions his former Pennsylvania home that lies beyond the Delaware River, and in his musing he provides the novel with a certain longing for a desirable "beyond" that is physically based but, at the same time, is a state of mind. Conner acts as an illustration of the inverted process. Instead of visualizing the idealized past, Conner pictures the achieved utopia of the future for himself in graphic terms: "grown men and women, lightly clad, playing, on the brilliant sand of a seashore, children's games. . . . triangles and rhomboids flashingly formed by the intersection of legs and torsos scissoring in sport, and the modulated angles of nude thoracic regions, brown breasts leaning one against another, among scarves of everlasting cloth, beneath the sun." Conner's vision has no locale: it is the baseless dream of a spiritually orphaned idealist.

Sensuous Image and Extravagant Metaphor

When Buddy, the prefect's young aid, shoots the crippled cat, the following portrayal, with its quick emphasis on the visual, tactile, olfactory senses, is deftly sketched: "The animal dropped without a shudder. Buddy snapped back the bolt; the dainty gold cartridge spun away, and the gun exhaled a faint acrid perfume. . . . Going up to the slack body he insolently toed it over, annoyed not to see a bullet-hole in the skull. Chips of wood adhered to the pale fluff of the long belly. The bullet had entered the chin and passed through to the heart."

However adept Updike may be at creating such sensuous images, his stock in trade is the extravagant metaphor. His elegant control of the delicate tension between the tangible and the fanciful allows him to rely on the poetically wrought metaphoric analogy to carry the mood and tone (the emotional and intellectual temper) of his story. In the first part of *The Poorhouse Fair,* one finds a description of the doctor's eyes: "his green irises rode a boat of milk, under the white sky. Thus his eyes were targets." At the end of the novel as two town boys are watching their girl friends parade naked in the shine of the automobile headlights, this subtly phallic description appears: "Above, the stars were not specks but needles of light suspended point downward in a black depth of stiff jelly."

In this approach to the depiction of spatial setting, through the elaborate metaphor, Updike demonstrates his departure from the dominant traditions of twentieth-century American fiction. It is true that he follows the Naturalistic mode now and again, but he seldom bothers with the transparent symbolic ciphers that our post-Naturalists have delighted in. He economizes on the actual presentation of setting and avoids the detailed and exhaustive effort of the

Naturalists, but still achieves the desired mood and tone in his settings through the evocative quality of his metaphors.

The Nonprotagonist Strategy

The two persons most attentitively followed throughout the narrative are Hook and Conner; and the antithesis that they form is the working, thematic antithesis of the novel. Hook represents the outmoded generation with its lingering absolute spiritual values, a waning but necessary belief in the supernatural and in the dignity of man's individuality. Conner, in contrast, is of the new scientific humanist breed; he believes only in the empirically established and in the technologically possible. Skeptical of human nature itself, he preaches the coming perfection of machinery and bureaucracy but not of the human spirit.

But neither Hook nor Conner is, in the usual sense, the protagonist. One discovers in *The Poorhouse Fair* no protagonist at all. The danger always exists that the absence of a strong central character will also negate reader involvement—that traditionally vital element of identification or vicarious experiencing (or with the antihero, a perverse fascination) that draws the reader to the novel. But Updike has taken that chance and succeeded. One recognizes and accepts the truth of his total fictional environment in a strangely unmediated manner, for it emerges directly instead of through this or that character as mouthpiece or even as symbol. The reader, in other words, becomes the protagonist in Updike's novel, although not in the sense of the *nouveau roman* reader participation, where the reader must solve compositional puzzles; Updike does the basic work himself, just as he must finally provide the culminating point of view. Even though Updike's theme is social and moral, he has written an artistic novel that stands or falls not on the power of message but on the strength of form.

Updike's will to experiment is not the only reason for the strategy of the heroless story: the theme itself happens to function best without a protagonist. In the new welfare state, homogeneity is the byword; therefore, a strongly individualistic, colorful hero or even antihero would be out of place. Where some sort of focus is necessary for purposes of contrast, Hook and Conner provide it. Hook (and most of the other old people) in his helpless, harmless disagreement with the smothering sameness of the accomplished society, and

Conner in his flaccid compliance are the best possible substitutes for actual protagonists. The weak old man and the state's flunky are accented enough to project negatively the ironic theme but not enough emphasized to dominate the novel. The City achieves perfection at the cost not only of God but also of humanity; and its saints, therefore, must merge with the scenery.

Action and Substance

The vignette nature of the novel already preempts the possibility of strong central action, but more important is the ironic vision that Updike has in mind: nothing happens in the novel because nothing happens in the realized City of God. The key word in *The Poorhouse Fair* is boredom: Conner is bored, the inmates are bored, society outside is bored; and, if the inmates are the least bored, it is because they have the relative richness of pre-utopian memories to dwell upon. In the state where homogeniety is the ideal, little conflict can exist. Where technological perfection is close at hand, there can be little anticipation, little chance of climactic action. The chief irony of the secular utopian dream is that, once it is actualized, it turns deadly and ruins its creators not through demonic execution but through sheer tedium. The lotus-eaters have subverted the space age.

Against this background, then, the single climactic action that occurs, the stoning of Conner, assumes greater meaning. The scene becomes a last desperate, pitiful gesture of defiance against the inevitable victory of the technological generation; and Updike's imagery evokes such an interpretation. The vignette for a moment becomes uncharacteristically laden with near-Expressionistic symbolism. Conner, the exacting, efficient agent of the new generation, demands order; the damaged wall around the poorhouse must be rebuilt for appearances' sake, so that visitors to the fair will not receive a bad impression. The old, male inmates are ordered to repair it. They look and function like primitives, with stooped shoulders and long-hanging arms, as they clumsily and slowly handle the heavy rocks. An instinctual savagery erupts among them, one strangely incongruous with the civilized supersociety which cares for them and which Conner represents. Like wild animals sensing fear in their prey, the old men are excited by Conner's manner into attacking him.

The onslaught, of course, is as ineffectual as it is brief; Conner cannot be seriously hurt by stones that the old men throw. What counts, literally and symbolically, is the spirit of the action. The attack by the aged is simultaneously brutal and hopelessly weak, a final wild protest by the last vitally *human* generation before life succumbs to the impersonal, collectivist monotony of the future. Cursing, screaming, and throwing earth, joined by the old women cackling obscenities, the old men of the old era have their final ecstatic moment. Before the incident is over they are laughing, ridiculing Conner and amused, apparently, at the absurdity of their own actions.

Paradoxically, the most positive note of the novel may be in that violent, primitive action, if one wishes to understand it as a sign that, beneath the hypnotic sameness of the utopian civilization, a disruptive quality still lurks. There may be a crack in the wall that surrounds the modern City of God, through which persons may escape into a wilderness of potential bestiality where life is tragically imperfect but where one can at least still find an individual identity.

Language and Substance

As prolific essayist and reviewer and as novelist, short-story writer, and poet, Updike has consistently displayed versatility in three areas: discursive, analytical prose; narrative fiction; and the image, metaphor, and rhythm of verse. Because his employment of language has always been spectacular in these three areas, he is regularly praised or damned for what his language does or does not accomplish. Part of the condemnation very likely involves guilt by association; Updike's tenure with *The New Yorker* has opened him to suspicion of sharing and perpetuating the image of glibness and sophisticated but superficial cleverness that marks the magazine. Regarding the majority of his poems and a good part of his essays, such as those that constituted "The Talk of the Town" column, the charge may be true: the pieces are elegant, knowledgeable, often playful, and easily forgotten—exactly what they are supposed to be. Whether or not one wants to consider Updike's *New Yorker* years his apprenticeship or not, he was hardly writing for posterity at the time. Apart from the lack of serious purpose or the absence of depth, the language of his verse and prose of that period is, if anything, remarkable for its consistency of polish and urbane correctness—in other words for its creation of wit in an extension of the eighteenth-century sense; and it is unfair to fault him for a missing profundity.

Updike's creation of dialogue in *The Poorhouse Fair* is superb; he has a good ear, one in tune with the modulations of the American voice: the lyric tones of the visionary, the antiquated echoes of the retired educator, the worried speculations of the middle-class wage-earner and his spouse, the inane mouthings of the prejudiced, the reflective vulgarities of the deprived and depraved are all notes on the novel's resonant scale.

It is almost refreshing to find an occasional awkward passage in Updike's fiction. He overextends himself, for instance, in the following sentence about Conner: "And the aura of holiday . . . infected him, and he began the flights of stairs, but not so suddenly Buddy did not communicate, through the simple pink oval of his face caught in the corner of Conner's eye as he seized the doorknob, amazement." The marooned word "amazement" following the long modifying clause produces an effect like Mark Twain speaking German. But such failings are rare in Updike; when they do occur, they are all the more obvious against the backdrop of general excellence, but they are always compensated for by scores of superior metaphoric designs.

Updike is not a victim of his style. His fiction is marked by a certain humility for which there exists no satisfactory term in the literary critical vocabulary. Whether it is the Pennsylvania Dutch honesty combined with the Harvard sophistication or some other chemistry that gives Updike his artistic singularity, his fiction is never snobbish or condescending. Nor, in spite of the total transformation of the autobiographical backgrounds, is Updike ever a *poseur*. What removes the chill from the ironic and cynical *The Poorhouse Fair* is the presence of compassion—a compassion that is the result of humility and talent—that renders the most negative situation affirmative by a sympathetic study of even the unlovable characters. That trait becomes even more marked in the following novels and stories, and it has led to the frequent charge that Updike wastes his craft by expending it on worthless types. But he seeks only to understand the modern world by comprehending the variations of the human species. He does not therefore write "confessional exercises" in the American tradition but artistic confession in the Goethean sense—as a compassionate record of mankind's struggles for meaning and being, which, constituted as it is from autobiography and knowledgeability, is more convincing than the American legacy alone.

The prefatory quotation to *The Poorhouse Fair* is the conclusion of an apocalyptic prophecy attributed by Luke the Evangelist to Jesus; "If they do this when the wood is green, what will happen when the wood is dry?" The question, of course, is appropriate to the theme of the generations in the novel: maturity does not necessarily bring wisdom and righteousness. Applied to Updike's ironic utopia, it means, simply, that the perfection of technological achievement is not the solution to most human ills. Jesus' words are spoken as part of an eschatological vision that anticipates the advent of the Kingdom of God with all its cataclysmic trappings. But in *The Poorhouse Fair* one sees that the cataclysm has not arrived and never will. This novel about the future, in a final irony, compels one to acknowledge that there is no future for a humanity that delimits itself by a surrender to officialdom and to the machine. The price of perfection is no less than the human spirit itself.

Chapter Four

Rabbit, Run: The Quest for a Vanished Grail

> How promiscuous is the world of appearances!
>
> —from "Suburban Madrigal"

Morality in Motion

The Poorhouse Fair is an achievement of tightly controlled microcosmic focus by a relatively inexperienced writer. *Rabbit, Run,* the first novel of what has become the Rabbit trilogy, maintains the discipline, accelerates the power, broadens the scope, and popularizes the interest. It is extremely sensual, clinically sexual, cynically middle-class, and insistently moral. A few book reviewers have implied that Updike composed his second novel as a purposely sensational shocker to capture the American mass audience, but Updike sacrifices no integrity whatsoever in *Rabbit, Run.* It is not to his career at all what *Sanctuary,* say, was to Faulkner's. In the relaxing of censorship standards and in the ensuing flood of explicitly sexual novels that have appeared since the publication of *Rabbit, Run* in 1960, Updike's book has largely lost its capacity for shock, and it can now be appraised much more objectively in terms of its artistic qualities.

The novel is not deficient in the fictional risks that one learns to expect from Updike. In *The Poorhouse Fair,* Updike moves dangerously close to gimmickry in depicting a proximate science-fiction future; in *Rabbit, Run,* he displays a similar fascination with time that leads him into a more difficult experiment. He composes the whole novel in the historical present to provide a precarious dramatic immediacy—a short-story technique that functions very well in this long narrative. In addition, if *The Poorhouse Fair* is a *tour de force* of sorts as the accomplishment of a young man composing a sensitive and empathetic novel about the aged, *Rabbit, Run* is no less so as a story that runs along archetypal heroic lines, yet is utterly devoid of heroic characters and situations. Updike gives himself practically nothing to create from: not a colorful setting but just a common, conventional, slightly squalid Pennsylvania suburban town; not even an antihero but just a nonhero with still less potential for tragedy than Arthur Miller's salesman.

The enveloping ironic myth in *The Poorhouse Fair* is the godless City of God; one could call the archetype of *Rabbit, Run* the futile quest for the nonexistent Holy Grail. Although Updike never mentions it as such, the futile quest is present in the sheer nervous movement, in the ceaseless search of the protagonist for a Something that he himself cannot identify. The nonhero runs compulsively but aimlessly through an industrialized wasteland, dogged by a lust that distorts his relationships with all others but that at least blots out the pain of the archetypal wound: the deadly boredom of daily life. Even the Chapel Perilous does not offer a decisive experience but instead, as the edifice of modern Protestantism, becomes a kind of spiritual spa which protects the best-kept secret: that men are all, behind their conditioned reflexes, nonbelievers; and that the quest has no goal.[1]

Rabbit, Run, like *The Poorhouse Fair,* is divided into three sections: two equally long initial and middle parts and a short climactic conclusion. The opening scene shows the central character, Harry "Rabbit" Angstrom, twenty-six-year-old ex-basketball star of Mt. Judge High, as he pauses on his way home from work for a game of alley basketball with some half-willing teenagers. Arriving home late to Janice, his pregnant, tippling, and TV-entranced wife, he is overcome by disgust as he considers how shallow and false his daily life has become. He leaves with no explanation and on impulse spends the night driving his car in the direction of the United States southland, teased by romantic visions of an easy life there. He gets as far as West Virginia, turns around, and returns during the early morning through eastern Pennsylvania to Mt. Judge—not to his home but to the apartment of Tothero, his old high school coach. Tothero takes him in; that evening on a double date, Rabbit meets Ruth Leonard, a prostitute, achieves an immediate sexual rapport with her, and moves into her apartment. The rest of the section treats the growing affair between Ruth and Rabbit and the efforts of Eccles, the young Episcopalian minister, to make Rabbit face the responsibility of his marriage.

The second section resumes the narrative two months later. Rabbit is still living with Ruth; Janice with their small son has moved into her parents' home and is waiting to have her baby. In two major scenes from the section, the point of view, which has been exclusively Rabbit's, shifts briefly to Eccles and his painful discussions with the parents of Rabbit and Janice, then to Ruth's stream-of-consciousness musings about her unwitting slide into prostitution. The story then moves back to Rabbit. On a double date with Ruth and another couple, he learns details of Ruth's former sex life that anger him; and that night he asks her to perform fellatio, a humiliating act for her that undermines whatever genuine love may have been between them.

The same night he learns that Janice is in labor, rushes full of guilt and contrition to the hospital, and resolves to redeem their marriage. He lives at home with Nelson their son while Janice recovers; when she returns, they share a satisfying life for nine days. Then on a Sunday he attends the Episcopalian service and returns home aroused by a suggestive post-church encounter with Lucy Eccles, the minister's young wife. He tries awkwardly to make love with Janice that afternoon; when she rejects him, he leaves and stays away all night. Janice, in despair, drinks herself into a near stupor; on Monday, the next day, she inadvertently drowns their new baby daughter while bathing her.

In the third and final section, Rabbit learns from Eccles of the death of his daughter and returns to Janice and his in-laws. They prepare numbly for the funeral on Tuesday afternoon. After the chapel service and in the cemetery, Rabbit has an ecstatic, reconciliatory religious experience that turns into a breakdown after the burial. He suddenly tells the horrified mourners that the baby's death was not his fault and, in the same breath, tries to console his wife. Then he runs away with Eccles in pursuit. Eccles cannot catch him. That evening Rabbit slips back into town and goes to Ruth's apartment. He learns from Ruth that she is pregnant with his child. When he cannot bring himself to consider a divorce from Janice, Ruth throws him out. The novel ends with Rabbit's running aimlessly and in panic through the night.

Images of the Nonhero

The complexity of Harry Angstrom's personality, which is metaphoric of the complexity of experienced reality, is apparent in the
nature and objects of his quest. The ironic search for the nonexistent
Grail may serve as the guiding myth, but the dimensions of his
quest are, on the one hand, more primitive than that and, on the
other, more specifically modern. The quest reaches into the reflexive,
instinctual depths of his animal being, out into the social context,
and blindly toward a spiritual realm that is barely conceivable in
this skeptical age. Updike shapes image and scene to fashion, therefore, a novel that is a unique blend of the cerebral and the biological.
Without exaggerating the protagonist's self-understanding (Rabbit
is not stupid, but neither is he self-consciously perceptive), Updike
develops, largely from the perspective of the central character, an
acutely analytical study of personality.

In terms of the most obvious image, Updike prompts the reader
to see in Harry the qualities, mainly liabilities, that his nickname
implies. First, he looks something like a rabbit: "the breadth of
white face, the pallor of his blue irises, and a nervous flutter under
his brief nose as he stabs a cigarette into his mouth partially explain
the nickname." Throughout the novel, such physical hints are
dropped: "His upper lip nibbles back from his teeth in self-pleasure";
"Rabbit stealthily approaches his old home on the grass, hopping
the little barberry hedge"; "Today was payday. Fingering so much
lettuce strengthens his nerves."

The implicit qualities are just as fitting. Harry, like his animal
namesake, is mild in nature and openly harmless, even a frightened
creature; but if he is allowed to roam unchecked, he can do damage
through his constant and voracious appetites. In line with the ironic
quest motif of the novel, he is always ready for flight, always poised
to escape when life threatens him, and is indeed often on the run
and in hiding. Even when secure, he is afflicted by a twitchiness,
a nervous agitation that upsets those around him. More important,
he shares the rabbit's reputation for reproduction; in a few month's
time, he has impregnated two women and automatically considers
women in terms of sexual encounter. The fundamental image thus
fixes the dominant element of characterization in the novel: Rabbit
is a dangerous man, and all the more so because of the deceptively
bland façade; the reverse side of his good-naturedness is a fatal

weakness of character, the inability to check his animal lusts and his visceral impulses that leads to pure irresponsibility.

A second image that gradually assumes an archetypal form is that of the modern sports hero. The nervous motion that marks the rabbit imagery is also part of the basketball game. Rabbit, a county basketball star eight years before the story begins, has difficulties because he has known adulation and success in his immaturity and has made them an impossible ideal for his adulthood. Basketball is not really a game for him but a model for existence. When, for example, he assesses his marriage against the feeling that basketball gave him, he finds it lacking. As he tries to explain to Eccles, "I once played a game real well. I really did. And after you're first-rate at something, no matter what, it kind of takes the kick out of being second-rate. And that little thing Janice and I had going, boy, it was really second-rate."

The rabbit image is appropriate for guiding the characterization in the novel, while the image of the basketball game directs the action. Therefore, it is not by accident that Updike begins *Rabbit, Run* with the alley basketball scene. Harry Angstrom, pushing his way into a casual teenagers' game, is nostalgically and pathetically trying to recapture the fame of his faded high school career. Only half-mindful of the resentment he fires in the outclassed boys, he loses himself briefly in the illusion of his past minor glory: Rabbit sees himself as an ex-hero. The whole novel, in a sense, is his restless, mindless necessity of trying to become all over again the county high scorer, the champion, the darling of the crowds.

Since basketball has been his model for life, life itself is ultimately just a game. Marriage, fatherhood, job, religion are all somehow play; he still believes in the platitudinous mouthings of his old coach ("the will to achieve," "giving our best") as the magic formulas for success—just as he heeds the banal preachings on television of Jimmy the Mouseketeer. Conversely, Rabbit's sporadic attempts to escape his marriage and his town and his shifting from job to job represent his desire to quit the game, to get off the court. His frustration and his resultant panic grow from the knowledge that he must keep on playing when the playing no longer produces sensual pleasure or egotistical satisfaction.

Rabbit is not, it should be emphasized, an antihero, Existentialist or otherwise. He is not a radical individualist asserting his total freedom as he challenges the mores of his society. Nor is he an

ultimately lovable and forgivable picaresque rascal who disguises a
stellar nature behind the scrapes that involve him. The antihero has
qualities that society may not value, but they are at least of the
kind that give him individuality and identity and that provoke
unwilling admiration. Irresponsible, undependable, and gutless,
Rabbit is the quintessence of the nonhero. That Updike has not
made him an entirely despicable man but has instead cast him in
the ironic mold makes the portrayal all the more effective.

The Quest

The quest is always a flight away from something and a search
for something else. Both the opening scene (after the basketball
game) and the closing one exemplify the flight-search dimension.
In Rabbit's initial night drive to West Virginia, he is escaping a
suffocating marriage and chasing an impossibly romantic vision:
"He wants to go south, down, down the map into orange groves
and smoking rivers and barefoot women." The trip is rife with ironic
illusion and allusion. He drives through such towns as Bird in Hand,
Intercourse, and Paradise, Pennsylvania. He listens on the car radio
to Connie Francis and Mel Torme torching their tributes to American pop erotica, and he considers (stimulated, of all things, by
Wilmington, Delaware) the unique thrills of making love to a Du
Pont woman. Rabbit is the modern knight roaming the countryside
in his 1955 Ford, crooning "Ev, reebody loves the, cha cha cha";
and he ends alone, womanless, and lost in a backwoods lovers' lane.
His journey is pathetic and sordid—pathetic, because the only adventures along the way are the cheap offerings of manufactured
music, bad roadside food, and vicarious sex; sordid, because, of all
the chivalric qualities, the only one that Rabbit seems to possess is
the capacity for adultery. It is a revival of the cliché to remark that
in all of this flight and search Rabbit is looking for himself, but it
is true nevertheless. The tragedy is that he never learns. So, at the
end of the story, having alienated absolutely everyone but the long-
suffering Eccles, Rabbit is in flight once more as he tries to escape
the chaos of himself through the sheer physicality of running.

Updike renders the mythic underpinnings of the quest unmis-
takably clear in his images of the Grail as its culmination. Rabbit
himself in his dialogic joustings with Eccles returns time and again
to oblique queries about this undefinable thing he is hunting. Trapped

into thought by the young minister, Rabbit says inanely, "I *do* feel, I guess, that somewhere behind all this . . . there's something that wants me to find it." Eccles' retort is laconically to the point: "all vagrants think they're on a quest. At least at first." In their continuing encounters, the Grail becomes an algebraic "X" that substitutes for the missing element in Rabbit's marriage, in his sex life, and in his religion. While playing golf with the runaway husband (Eccles functions better on the golf course than in the pulpit or pastorate), Eccles starts a line of conversation that goes like this:

Harry, . . . why have you left her? You're obviously deeply involved with her."
"I *told* ja. There was this thing that wasn't there."
"What thing? Have you ever seen it? Are you sure it exists?"
. . . . "Well if you're not sure it exists don't ask me. It's right up your alley. If you don't know nobody does."

Eccles does not know, yet paradoxically, Rabbit senses what *he* is after. Still on the golf course and arguing pointlessly with Eccles, Rabbit hits a beautiful drive from the tee that fills him with the emotional-esthetic purity of his basketball days. " 'That's *it!*' he cries and, turning to Eccles with a smile of aggrandizement, repeats, "That's it!' " Eccles' last words before the feat have been, significantly, "You don't care about right or wrong; you worship nothing except your own worst instincts." Rabbit does worship—at least trusts in—his own instincts; but such worship is a reaction to a dominant Puritanism that dictated his religious training and that still controls his environment.

For Rabbit and the romantic tradition he unwittingly adopts, natural depravity yields to the potential divinity of one's own being; and the old search for redemption becomes the romantic search for the infinite. Both concepts fit perfectly the ironic pattern of Rabbit's life as imaged in the Grail hunt; according to the legend, only the pure in heart have hope of finding the elusive Grail. Rabbit, for all of his perversity, incredibly sees himself in terms of that purity, for he has been duped by the hero reflex into believing his instincts, and they tell him consistently that what he feels good in doing must *be* good.

Rabbit often experiences remorse—he is still too much the Puritan not to—but it fades in the exhilaration of instinctive action.

In the absorption of animated emotion, in the sublimation of the spirit to the sensations of the flesh (Rabbit, like all romantics, still accepts that dichotomy), he comes closest to the fulfillment of the second concept: that reaching for the infinite in order to satisfy some appetite or psychological need originating in the here-and-now. The ironic circularity is apparent: inspired by the grandness of his quest Rabbit is at last pitifully content to identify his Grail with the sex act, the athletic success, the ambiguous praise of a friend, so that, despite all his wandering, he ends up where he began.

The pathos of the novel that results from an application of the archetypal Grail-quest configuration lies in the melancholy revelation that Rabbit, despite his suffering, never becomes the initiate. At one point, it appears, however, that he will: living alone with little Nelson while Janice is recovering from the birth, Rabbit, willing to make a new start, "feels the truth: the thing that had left his life had left irrevocably; no search would recover it. No flight would reach it." But through the seductive ecstasy of an emotionalized religious experience at the graveyard ceremony he loses the truth that could ripen and mature him. When the others misunderstand the experience, he reverts to form—the form of the nonhero who does what is most natural for him: he runs. Because Rabbit has lived by his reflexes, he becomes, finally, no more than a reflex.

Oedipus in Pennsylvania

The inner parallel to Rabbit's mythic quest for the Grail is his obsessive need for the ideal mother and lover. One hesitates to revive once more the subject of the Oedipus complex, overworked as it has been in modern literature and in criticism since the advent of Freudianism; but one need not really apologize for its appearance in *Rabbit, Run*. Updike uses it with subtle vitality as a unifying focal image that magnifies the motivations, the desires, and the destinies of the protagonist and those who are bound up in his existence.

Rabbit's *angst* (his surname contains the term) forces him to a dual reaction that involves the two faces of the Oedipal dilemma. He gropes toward the innocent past (life with the mother) and fumbles with sex (life with the lover), and he unconsciously strives to use both as security and anodyne. The backdrop of his struggle is the void of his meaningless present which asserts itself as boredom and as a paralysis of the will. Against that terrible blank he draws security from the past as he attempts to return to the womb; on the night of his daughter's birth, he even sleeps in the foetal position. But the past, the prenatal home in the womb, is also an anodyne as it offers the false hope of vegetable comfort, just as the sex act invites to momentary forgetfulness through the consuming sensual pleasure of physical indulgence.

Rabbit is the *son-sun* with all of the metaphysical connotations of the pun, and the female characters are the satellites in orbit around him: Janice; Ruth; his mother; Lucy Eccles; Mim, his sister; and even old Mrs. Smith his employer, and Becky, his fated baby. A good part of Rabbit's frustration is that he seeks fulfillment of an ideal nearly as impossible to realize as his vague religious search: he wants to find in one woman the security of the mother and the excitement of the lover. His society being what it is, he could feasibly find each in separate women, but that will not do for Rabbit because he is temperamentally monogamous, a family man at heart for all his rabbity excursions. Here the connection between his hero neurosis on the general level and his Oedipal problem on the particular one becomes clear: his need to be loved by the crowd, which includes the comfort and excitement of adulation, is but the broad expression of what he desires in the marriage relationship. The woman who accepts him in bed must not only pat him on the head but also dry his tears. He has been spoiled by his parents and his society into believing that a wife should exercise both functions for him, and he is disillusioned when reality proves otherwise.

His rejection of Janice, therefore, and the attraction of the prostitute Ruth are for him psychologically predictable. Rabbit and Janice have never experienced anything approaching a genuine marriage relationship. The original rapport was sexual, beginning as a series of secret assignations in a girlfriend's bedroom and culminating in a hasty wedding when Janice's pregnancy became apparent. The recurring vision of Janice that Rabbit wants to recapture is not of his wife as mother but as the naked and eager lover, and that vision is based on one experience alone that catches Janice out of character. After the marriage, their sex life has degenerated, as if it needed the stimulus of the clandestine. Rabbit is caught with the sloppy, listless, and pregnant (now for the second time) ex-high-school student; and all he can do about her is to hope pathetically (one

notices the teenage idiom) "that tomorrow she'll be his girl again."
Far from satisfying Rabbit's desires for a mother and a lover in one,
Janice is no longer even the lover.

If Janice is neither, Ruth seems to hold the promise of becoming
both. As a prostitute, she has the sexual sophistication that Janice
lacks; but she also possesses the motherly nature and attributes that
are alien to Rabbit's wife. She cooks very well and likes it; she keeps
a clean apartment; she even takes a legitimate job to help support
the two of them when Rabbit moves in with her. Above all, once
Rabbit has cracked the toughness of her professional veneer, she
caters to him with her maternal instincts and gives him the emotional protection he needs. It seems that to solve the predicament,
Rabbit should divorce Janice and marry Ruth. But he is much too
entangled in the knots of his personality, too vacillating in his
capricious sense of obligation, to carry through a divorce and a
remarriage. Instead he does—typically—nothing; and he loses Ruth.

Updike provides enough details of Rabbit's relations with his
parents to show that his trouble began with them. The scene in
which Eccles visits the senior Angstroms (an incident balanced by
the discussion with Mrs. Springer, Janice's mother) places much of
the blame on Rabbit's rearing. Mrs. Angstrom, the dominant parent, is the strong-willed wife whose bitterness at the weaker husband
who has not fulfilled her expectations she sublimates into overlove
for her son. In the conversation with the minister, she defends Harry
("Hassy," she still calls him, like the German *Hase*—"rabbit"); but
the husband condemns him. For her, Rabbit is the victim; and
Janice is the manipulator who managed "to get herself pregnant so
poor Hassy has to marry her when he could scarcely tuck his shirttail
in." Her husband's reaction is quite the opposite: "He's become the
worst kind of Brewer bum. If I could get my hands on him, Father,
I'd try to thrash him if he killed me in the process." When the
discussion deteriorates into mutual accusations about the parents'
marriage, Eccles hears and sees enough to guess at the almost transparent causes for Rabbit's confusion: the "rumpus" scenes (as Rabbit's father euphemizes them) between the parents have had a
cumulative and deleterious effect on the son. Mrs. Angstrom has
at least given to her son the capacity for suffering, and it increases
his humanity. His misfortune is that he cannot live his sorrow into
tragedy and gain moral stature at the end.

The Revenge of Eros

Updike, by creating an abnormal figure, forces one to realize that the abnormal has become, paradoxically, the representative of the norm. John Barth has remarked that his task in writing the modern novel is to resolve apparent contradictions into paradox. Updike is doing the same thing. If paradox is what one finally arrives at, it is at least a category of logic that imposes a measure of order—this era's substitute for Classical and Christian order—upon chaos.

Rabbit's movement is from reflexive action to an attempted self-understanding; although the attempt ends in failure, to trace it is to realize the fullness of troubled humanity that Updike's people contain. Rabbit's behavior as the Oedipal son-husband is actualized in his interrelations with his mother, his wife, and his mistress; but the other women in the story complete his pattern. Lucy Eccles is the most fascinating of these. Committed to a life of social respectability as a pastor's wife, she is actually a disciple of Freud who believes more in the power of instinctive sexuality than in transcendent divinity. She chafes under the restrictions that the parsonage places upon her and finds an immediate attraction—even a perverse delight—in defining Rabbit upon the first meeting as a "primitive" husband and father—one utterly different from her own mate, the self-conscious, dutiful Jack Eccles. Rabbit sees her as a potential "lay" (in his own vulgar idiom), as the goal of a particularly interesting sexual adventure, since her social position is what it is (perhaps a substitute for the unattainable Du Pont girl?); but it is partially her fault that she affects him that way. Although her invitations to him appear more tantalizing to his overstimulated imagination than they are intended to be, the flirtatious overtones are there; and in one sense she is to blame for the fatal sequence of events in the last part of the novel.

After Rabbit attends Eccles's church, marking another stage in his rehabilitation as husband and father, Lucy asks him to walk her home. Her conversation is daring; she asks him in for coffee. When he takes the invitation too intimately, she is insulted; but the damage is done. "Whether spurned or misunderstood, Eccles's wife has jazzed him, and he reaches his apartment clever and cold with lust." When Janice, still convalescing from the birth of their daughter, will not make love with the aroused Rabbit, he deserts her again. She takes solace in her alcohol and, in a drunken accident, drowns the baby. Ironically, Lucy Eccles has a more destructive hand than anyone in frustrating her husband's own ego-salving game of redeeming Rabbit.

Rabbit exudes an erotic magnetism. He is a sexual animal, and women respond. There is a loving sensuality to nearly everything he does, from fondling a basketball to eyeing a blossoming school girl to stroking a sex partner; as a result, he lives in a state of excited anticipation that expends energy in the drive for satisfaction. One of the main artistic achievements of the novel is the manner in which Updike indirectly marks Rabbit's obsession: he depicts Rabbit as quite unable to confront any eligible woman except in terms of her sexual desirability. Rabbit's preoccupation with breasts and pudenda is a sign of his use of sex as security and anodyne. They are the parts that fire his *angst*-deadening lust, but they also suggest the womb and the infant nurture to which he longs to return: thus the strange double attraction that pregnant women exercise over him. His final expression of desire for Ruth is typical: "If he can just once more bury himself in her he knows he'll come up with his nerves all combed." Other nuances are frequent: Rabbit insists on washing Ruth's face before making love to her, but he wants to sleep cradled in her arm; when he sees his daughter for the first time behind the window of the hospital nursery, he also studies the nurse holding her; and when he sees his mother after the baby's death, at the funeral home, Updike describes it thus: "she steps toward him with reaching curved arms. 'Hassy, what have they done to you?' She asks this out loud and wraps him in a hug as if she would carry him back to the sky from which they have fallen."

In the final pages of the novel, all of Rabbit's women are somehow present. Janice, his mother, and Mim are at the cemetery; baby Becky has been buried; and, as he runs from the grave, he wonders about Lucy Eccles: would she have had him? And he finds himself at last back at Ruth's apartment. It is as if, at the end, persons and circumstance combine to overwhelm Rabbit with a surfeit of the figures of his sexual quest but in a manner that robs him of its goal, of the comfort and forgetfulness it should provide. Rabbit reaches the second circle of his private Inferno: appetite becomes nausea, security gives way to panic, and the sexual sinner is condemned to the incessant running and buffeting of Dante's carnal damned.

Rabbit's immersion in sex is frightening and negatively instructive—instructive because his whole glandular existence is a contorted effort at discovering love. Rabbit's attempt to use everybody for his truncated kind of affection (mirrored in his obsession for all varieties of women) becomes an obscene travesty of the unselfish, genuine spirit of love. It is not just that *Eros* crowds out *Agape; Eros* itself is wronged (thus the significance of the humiliating fellatio scene)—and *Eros* in the name of total love revenges itself upon the culprit. Over a decade later, in *Rabbit Redux,* Updike would reveal the intensity of that revenge.

Chapter Five
Pigeon Feathers:
The Design of Design

> Claustrophobia attacks us even in air.
>
> —from "Earthworm"

The Reconstructive Memory

In *The Same Door,* the thematic stress is on the unexpected gifts of personal encounter; in *Pigeon Feathers and Other Stories* (1962) the accent shifts to the individual in greater spiritual isolation and in a struggle to come to terms with the universe itself, even though the context is the familiar round of ordinary events. In *The Same Door,* the narrative strategy is to produce the cumulative epiphany; in *Pigeon Feathers,* the evocative memory works more often to re-quicken a significant moment from the past that could lend meaning to the present. The farther Updike moves from his own shaping past, it seems, the tighter he holds its remnants.

These stories emphasize not only the spark of grace within the ordinary worldly happenings but the existence and awareness of design in all human events and conditions. All fiction consists of design, of course, but *Pigeon Feathers* ventures a double concentration upon it. Updike employs design to talk about design. The artistic and thematic matrices are virtually identical; the language and meaning of fictive metaphor become one. The paradigm of names in "Walter Briggs," the artists' models of "Still Life," the great rose window of "Wife-wooing," the patterns on the dead birds in "Pigeon Feathers," and similar elements in most of the other tales show that the architecture of the narrative composition and of the reality it evokes are essentially the same. Updike's artistry and his ontology in this collection strive to approximate and identify each other.

"The Persistence of Desire"

The second story of *Pigeon Feathers*, "The Persistence of Desire," treats not only the dynamics of vital memory but also a new encounter of the protagonist with the objects of his memory. Clyde Behn, happily married by his own confession and father of two children, returns to Olinger and chances on his lover of many years ago, also married now, in an eye-doctor's office. Their affair had ended painfully, one gathers, and both are upset by the sudden meeting; they are still attracted to each other and have survived in each other's thoughts. Alone with the girl in the reception room, Clyde asks to meet her again; and later, focusing fuzzily because of the medication in his eyes, he recklessly invades an examining room where she waits alone and pleads before her on his knees. When his treatment is finished, he leaves through the now-crowded waiting room; and from the blur of figures, the girl arises and puts a note in his shirt pocket, then goes out to her husband who waits in the car. Clyde can't read the note with his distorted pupils, but is made happy and excited by this admission of continued regard.

"The Persistence of Desire" is a curious modern fictive parallel to Wordsworth's famous "Tintern Abbey" poem—that inquiry into the interaction of passion, memory, and the resultant new reality. Like the Wordsworthian narrator, Clyde Behn views himself in a context of strange double identity—his past and present "I"— stimulated by the return to the childhood haunts and especially by the fateful meeting with his old love. He is able to gain a certain objectification of himself against the locale and desire of his past and thus truly to "see himself" briefly for perhaps the first time in his life. The symbolic quality of the action is important. Clyde travels from Massachusetts, his present home, back to Pennsylvania and back into his past. This last is emphasized in Clyde's recognition of how little things have changed. One reason for his return is eye trouble, but the vague and minor difficulty with his sight is as much metaphysical as physical (to call it "psychosomatic" would be just as valid); and Clyde's visit is intended to clarify his vision in both realms. Using a mild irony, Updike has Clyde obtain the greatest precision of inner sight while his eyes are literally blurred by the doctor's drops. In this awkward condition, he achieves a fleeting intimacy with the girl and soon after receives her promise-laden note.

Since Clyde cannot decipher the girl's message, he has not yet gained any decisive knowledge. But the confrontation with the object, or better said "the subject," of his memory makes him suddenly aware of his present spiritual desolation despite his comfortable domestic and vocational situation. When the girl asks him, "aren't you happy?" he replies, "I am, I am; but . . . happiness isn't everything." Clyde learns, simply, "the persistence of desire"— that the price of passion is its permanence and that love relationships, once established, can never be fully undone.

Janet also becomes for Clyde an orienting moment in the flux of life, and the early pages of the story prepare her role. The first sentence mentions the checkerboard pattern of the doctor's office floor, which renews Clyde's childhood feeling of intersection (the basis of an image Updike uses frequently in *Of the Farm*) that now reflects his confused sense of identity, a confusion deriving from the conflicting claims of past and present. When Clyde selects at random a magazine in the waiting room he reads that the cells of the human body completely replace themselves every seven years; and he also contrasts the ultramodern speedometer clock with the stopped grandfather clock in the same room. In this tension of mutability, then, the old girlfriend (who has changed so little) acts as his hold on time and helps him redefine his precarious identity. One of the duties of love is to provide a stable selfhood through the response of the other; it is not escape but fulfillment. Janet, however temporarily, does that for Clyde; and that is why he, in his alienation, so desperately wants to see her again.

During the examination, Dr. Pennypacker tells Clyde that he has a fungus on his eyelids and prescribes a cure. The mild disease reminds one of the Biblical scales upon the eyes, a stock metaphor for spiritual blindness. In the framework of the story, Janet provides a symbolic diagnosis and healing for Clyde's problem. Her presence first makes him aware of his "scales," his middle-class boredom; but it also offers a projected solution. If he cannot restore the past, he can at least come to knowledgeable, realistic terms with the present.

"Pigeon Feathers"

"Pigeon Feathers," the ninth story in the collection, was included among the O. Henry Prize Short Stories of 1962; and it exemplifies

Updike at his best. Its hero, fourteen-year-old David Kern, suffers through a terrifying religious crisis; the force of the tale is in rendering credible the experience of faith and doubt that takes place in an adolescent mind. The story has autobiographical contours: David has moved with his family from Olinger to the rural Firetown; and, like the Caldwell family in *The Centaur* and the Robinsons in *Of the Farm,* the Kerns have taken over the ancestral farm at the insistence of the mother and against the wishes of the school-teacher-father and son. Updike (in the foreward to *Olinger Stories*) recalls a similar move in his own youth, one from Shillington to Plowtown, that had had a profound effect on his maturation. The ten-mile displacement, he writes, "this strange distance, this less than total remove from my milieu, is for all I know the crucial detachment of my life."[1]

In any case, the resultant double perspective, the sense of existing in two places, precipitates for the hero of the story an alienation that finds expression in a religious dilemma. Already depressed by his new surroundings, David meets the devil in the pages of H. G. Wells's *The Outline of History;* and the boy travels through the doubt and despair that had afflicted the Victorians a century earlier. Wells shatters him with his arguments against the divinity of Jesus; and soon after, perched in blackness on the outhouse seat at night, David has a horrifying vision of death and of the dizzying infinity of the universe. No one helps him, and months go by while he suffers. One evening, at the instigation of the ancient grandmother, David is asked to kill the pigeons in the barn with the twenty-two caliber rifle he has received for his fifteenth birthday. He shoots six birds the next day while the rest escape; and he then goes to bury the little bodies. In examining the intricate formation of feathers and the colors on the dead pigeons, and in considering their beauty in spite of their worthlessness, he gains assurance that immortality must be in store for him.

The element of displacement is crucial to the story. The move from town to country makes David a self-styled geographical refugee; but, above all, it underscores his condition as a spiritual outsider. But that isolation changes when he learns that all men appear to be outsiders—that religion is an elaborate ruse designed not to help one face death honestly but to cushion its reality. In the town, furthermore, one is sufficiently occupied to avoid a contemplation of death; but, in the country, close to what should be the healing power of nature, one is drawn by the proximity of the soil to darker thoughts of death and decay. The arguments between David's parents about natural and organic farming amplify, for his distressed ears, his anxiety; for the strife about what kills the soil leads him to additional visions of the grave. In his hypertense condition, even the outhouse, resting above the pit of decomposing feces, triggers a horrid nightmare glimpse of a dying universe.

Personal participation in death restores—or first creates—David's faith. The killing of the pigeons is a catharsis, a cleansing involvement in violence and destruction that is a microform of the Classical tragic mode. But David, who feels like an avenger in the excitement of the shooting, also attains a measure of understanding about the meaning of death and of divinity in the scheme of being: "He had the sensation of a creator; . . . out of each of them he was making a full bird." The analogy, of course, is that man likewise is somehow fulfilled through death and that God in allowing death is not permitting a catastrophic absurdity but a good and necessary consummation. The horror of infinity changes to a trust in its intelligent perfection, unarticulated as its form may be. In the final words of the story, David is "robed in certainty: that the God who had lavished such craft upon these worthless birds would not destroy His whole creation by refusing to let David live forever.

The culminating action and the conclusion of the story sound suspiciously like a fictional updating of the Scholastic argument from design for God's existence, and one should not be inattentive to the possible irony in the whole performance. After all, the line of logic from a half-dozen dead pigeons to a boy's new assurance of personal immortality is broken by numerous forensic short circuits. But that philosophical argument is not the point of the story, nor should it be the center of criticism regarding the story. The point is that Updike, through symbolic action and analogy, has written a moving narrative that does not presume to convince one of the truth of religious faith but that does testify to an individual's achievement of it.

"Pigeon Feathers" employs a design and designs to attest to the fact of, or at least the faith in, cosmic design. Beyond that, the action represents an archetypal maturation ritual, a personal coming-of-age of a young man who is not satisfied by the formal ecclesiastical rites (catechism and confirmation) but who uses worldly implements (above all the gun) to fight through the trauma toward adulthood.

Beyond this ritual, the narrative is a concentrated history of modern man's struggle to assert himself in a lonely universe. The bleak generalities of an H. G. Wells, the neuroses of dispairing late Victorians, the conspiracy of silence among twentieth century Christians forced to compromise their dogmas—all these stagger the innocent generation and demand that it fashion its own unique bondage or freedom. The answers that its representatives find, those who are healthy enough, are molded from the stuff of daily trivia. If the path from six dead pigeons to a God who cares seems absurd, it is no more so than the tortuous directions mapped by wise men of the past few centuries.

"You'll Never Know, Dear, How Much I Love You"

The twelfth story, "You'll Never Know, Dear, How Much I Love You," is superficially like Joyce's famous "Araby" in the *Dubliners* collection. Updike's boy also hurries to a carnival; poor, charged with excitement and anticipation, full of the adolescent's romantic yearnings, he is eager to offer himself to the mysterious and glittering world; and he is disappointed by the world's rejection. Admittedly a lesser story than "Araby" because it lacks the symbolic density of that tale, Updike's story succeeds, nonetheless, on its own terms.

Ben is a ten-year-old who receives fifty cents from his parents to visit the traveling carnival that has just arrived in town that day. He races to the site at dusk, moves from booth to booth trying to absorb everything, buys a cotton candy, and then places all the remaining coins, one by one, on the board where the numbers wheel is whirling. He loses everything, his last forty cents, and turns to go; but the attendant calls him back and, with rough insulting kindness, returns thirty cents to him and tells him to leave. Ben departs embarrassed and disgraced, feeling cheated by this encounter with a misunderstanding adult world.

The fragile story depends upon the inversion of a metaphor for its effect. The world is represented as a gaudy woman, but here she does not seduce the innocent. Young Ben goes out gladly to be taken, but she will not have him and he is thrust back into his childishness. The stock vehicles of temptation are present (sex, gambling), but Ben is too young to be corrupted; he can only be thrust out of the way as an annoyance when he merely wants the exhilaration of participation. What is ultimately humiliating to him is that he is given the doubtful favor of the returned coins and thus singled out as unworthy of the world.

The title is part of the refrain from "You Are My Sunshine," the sadly sweet pop tune that every generation revives in its own beat. The girls dressed in white cowboy garb—cheap Americana—sing it at the carnival; and, filtered through Ben's tumescent young consciousness, it comes to represent his naïve longing for a falsely bright world and the transparent quality of the beckoning entertainment realm.

Updike connects the tale with "The Persistence of Desire" by noting that the "optically bothered Clyde Behn seems to me a late refraction of that child Ben who flees the carnival with 'tinted globes confusing his eyelashes.' " But Ben, as Updike also says, is "a pure Olinger child" who even in his unhappy adventure is being protected by the world from the world itself.[2] The alienation he feels is the result, paradoxically, of compassion and not the lack of it. Ben still roams inside Eden.

"A & P"

"A & P" has been anthologized in college and commercial collections. It is one of the brilliant pieces that redeem the few pages of inferior writing in the book. Sammy, the narrator, is a nineteen-year-old working as a checkout clerk in the A & P market on a Thursday afternoon. The scene is an unnamed Massachusetts town (Tarbox of *Couples?*) north of Boston and "five miles from a beach, with a big summer colony out on the Point."

Into the staid store in this staid place walk three girls barefoot and in swimming suits, probably the daughters of wealthy summer residents from the Point. Lengel, the store manager, a dour man who "teaches Sunday School and the rest," comes forward to chide them for what to him is their indecency. The girls are flustered, but they stand up to him, especially the cool, regal one in a tempting suit who, Sammy guesses, is used to snobbier markets than this one. Sammy quickly rings up the bill and gives the girls their purchase. As they leave, he tells Lengel, "I quit"; punctuates the manager's surprised protests by banging up a "No Sale" on the register; and walks out. Outside, the bathing-suit trio has already gone; and Sammy is left with a sharp, painful revelation of "how hard the world was going to be to me hereafter."

Updike has Sammy narrate the story in a breezy, late-teenage vernacular; the brashness of the language balances nicely the inherent sentimentality of the action. Sammy's references to one girl's breasts as "the two smoothest scoops of vanilla I had ever known" and to another girl as passable "raw material" cut the saccharine flavor of his impulsive and romantic gesture. Updike also alternates between the past and historical present tenses to provide a tight little dramatic episode that his fiction does not often exhibit. Since the tale builds upon an increasing tension of embarrassment, the play-by-play technique of the present tense description heightens the precise moments of strain and offers the reader, at the same time, a vicarious participation.

Sammy's reaction is the reflex of the still uncorrupted, of the youth still capable of the grand gesture because he has not learned the sad wisdom of compromise. But therein lie the pathos and the refreshing rashness of the story. Sammy's reckless vitality is echoed by the fancied percussion of the cash register: "Hello *(bing)* there, you *(gung)* hap-py *pee*-pul *(splat)*!" The undertone of sorrow resides in the depressing sight that awaits Sammy outside the supermarket: the girls for whom he has gallantly sacrificed his job have disappeared; in their place is a young married woman yelling at her spoiled children, a much commoner refrain to the heady tunes of wishful American romance.

"Lifeguard"

The speaker in this story is a youthful divinity student who spends his summers on an unnamed New England beach as a lifeguard. He self-consciously uses the props and duties of his summer vocation as a tangible metaphor of his future pastoral profession. The tower on which he perches is the pulpit; the Red Cross emblem on the back of his chair, the Christian symbol; the bathers and sunners his congregation (it *is* a Sunday morning); and he himself, the alert guardian of souls. His sermon-monologue turns on the unity of spirit and body, and he considers himself to be a person in whom the two are perfectly married. In reality he is quite puritanic, overly aware of the flesh, and attempts in a manner more Sophist than Protestant to justify his lust. "Every seduction is a conversion" emerges as the message of his discourse, but he is far more absorbed in a loving quasi-sublimation of his sexuality than in any serious hermeneutic; and, like the speakers in Browning's dramatic monologues, he reveals more of his own hidden psyche than of observed and interpreted truth.

"Lifeguard" has the traditional sermon format: an introduction, a statement of the text, exposition, bountiful illustrations, and concluding exhortation. But it is also a sermon parody and, withal, a confession—an exposé by one formally inside yet privately outside the edifice of theological endeavor. The irony of the story is that, despite the young student's insight, he does not see at all. He is surrounded by people to whom he is supposedly learning to minister, but he has no relationship with humanity. He is caught in an immense egotism that feeds on theology when theology ought instead to show him the way of humility.

Here again Updike has employed design to explicate design. The formal sermon structure is a vehicle, in this instance, that destroys the very substance of its text. The student preaches on the affinity of spirit and flesh, but his discourse is, in more ways than one, all flesh. It is a model of design, but it has no vitality. In a final irony, the young man disproves, by what he is, the very contention that he so skillfully argues. Spirit and flesh may very well be more intimately related than Pauline and Augustinian dualism have comprehended them to be; but, if they are, the way toward realizing that unity is through a passionate involvement—not a logical exercise—that the young man can elaborate upon but has never experienced.

The Jack and Clare Stories

Of the fourteen other stories in *Pigeon Feathers,* three are casually connected through the appearance of the same family. A young couple, Jack and Clare, living somewhere in the vicinity of Boston, are the personae in "Walter Briggs," "Should Wizard Hit Mommy?" and "The Crow in the Woods." In "Walter Briggs," Jack and family are returning home at night from Boston. To pass the time, husband and wife reminisce about their first months of married life together as employees at a Y.M.C.A. camp (Updike and his first wife did something of the same thing shortly after their marriage). In recalling the names of persons at the camp, they encounter the image of a fat bridge player whose last name eludes them. At home later and in bed beside his sleeping wife, Jack sifts through the camp memories again and finds the name. "Walter Briggs," he tells Clare, "knowing he wouldn't wake her."

The technical trick of the story is in constructing narration on the basis of a frustrating phenomenon that everyone has experienced—the memory block that eventually yields to probing and gives one some old bit of knowledge that the efforts at recall have magnified far out of proportion. In this story too the recovery of the name is not the important thing in itself; rather, the name is the cryptic key that opens the shared life of the past. And that, in turn, is significant not because the events were anything but commonplace but because they were shared. Irrelevant things assume meaning through the numinous energy of affection; and, in the extremely private code of this marital dialogue, to say "Walter Briggs" is to rediscover a forgotten pleasure of one's life—like finding an heirloom one had somehow misplaced. That Jack speaks to his slumbering wife makes no difference; he is simply affirming his joy about and satisfaction from their mutual past.

"Should Wizard Hit Mommy?" finds the same couple in less concord. A Freudian tale quite like "Incest" in *The Same Door* collection, in it the attraction between father and small daughter develops a subtle animosity between husband and wife, daughter and mother. Jack tells his daughter, now almost four, a spontaneous story about skunks in a futile attempt to make her take a Saturday afternoon nap. When he climaxes his narration with a dramatic description of Mommy Skunk's striking a cruel magician, the little girl is upset and insists on a retaliatory sequel: the wizard should hit Mommy back.

Updike uses the old frame story technique—the tale within a tale—in an atmosphere of innocence to produce a mild shock for the reader. Instead of the cozy association that the bedtime story usually prompts, a shadow of elemental violence and hatred darkens the scene, one made all the more unnerving since it is cast by a small child. Little Jo identifies Mommy Skunk with her own mother and demands punishment for her violation of a taboo—defying the preternatural. Her perverse behavior is obviously born out of fantasy and the unconscious, and therefore it is excusable but is, nonetheless, frightening. The daughter instinctively wishes the rival-mother dead, and the father succumbs as well by siding with the child against his wife—who is pregnant and therefore carrying a potential threat to his dominant maleness. Whether or not one accepts such transparent Freudian interpretation, the story succeeds in conveying the aura of primitive fear that invades the commonplace of a modern civilized household.

In "The Crow in the Woods," Jack arises on an early winter morning to tend to his baby daughter (the couple's only child in this story). Still blurry from an alcoholic party the night before and from lovemaking later, he nevertheless sees things with the hyperclarity of overwrought senses. His wife joins them and makes breakfast; with the food before him, Jack sees a nature epiphany through the window: a huge black bird lands in the snow-covered woods close by and sends flakes drifting down in beautiful confusion. He calls to his wife in an instant of joy, but she answers only, "Eat your egg." Cold sobriety destroys the ecstatic moment; the lovemaking communion of the night before dissolves in the practical necessities of daily living

Other Marriage Tales

"Wife-wooing" employs the rare second-person singular perspective; the speaker addresses his wife throughout the narration in the "you" form. Plot is almost wholly lacking; instead one finds descriptions of domestic action that carry archetypal and symbolic significance. A young couple sitting before their fireplace with their two small children, eating hamburgers and french fries purchased from a nearby drive-in, become the post-types of primitive humans who hunted and killed their sustenance and devoured it around the fire in the cave dwelling. Out of this parallel the speaker fashions the avatar of the elemental woman whom his wife represents. Whether she is in prehistory or sitting bare-thighed before a suburban hearth, she is fertility, domesticity, security. In the woman the man has his fulfillment, and to "woo" her is to court the elusive components of his own identity.

The Medieval image of the rose window, symbol of both purity and defloration, supports the religious nature of the man's total commitment to the marriage event. Through intercourse, through the rose window, the male sees into the design of himself and his world in a new sense. This Gothic pattern helps define also the male relationship to contemporary woman and clarifies the conclusion of the story. The wife, like the elemental woman and the Holy Virgin, has an earnest of grace for the man that he depends upon but that he may not take for granted. When, at the end, the wife comes to her husband in bed eager for sexual love, it is a gift that he must recognize and accept as such: it is as old as human history yet as new and unique as the individuality of experiencing can make it.

"Home" is a delightful and moving account of a young Pennsylvanian's return to his native area after a year in England. Robert (a mathematics teacher), his wife Joanne, and baby travel from the New York port, where their liner has docked, to the Pennsylvania small town with Robert's parents. The story is structured by the movement westward of car and passengers toward the old parental home. The land and the people seem alien to Robert and Joanne; they are undergoing culture shock. But the tension dissolves through an incident that Robert's irrepressibly curious schoolteacher-father precipitates. On the final stretch toward home, the father overtakes and startles a fat Pennsylvania Dutchman who is incautiously driving a large new car. When the Dutchman catches up to them, enraged and swearing, Robert's father stops his car; the Dutchman does likewise and walks back for an altercation. In the funny scene involving the Dutchman's redfaced obscenity and the father's dogged curiosity, Robert joins the argument in his own native Dutch accent (expertly reproduced by the author); and, through the unpleasantries, he finds a reentry, for his wife as well as himself, into the familiar past.

"The Astronomer" has as its protagonist the young man Walter who, in a condition of cosmic anxiety or of ontological *angst,* reads Kierkegaard as an antidote. He and his wife are visited in their Riverside Drive apartment by a Hungarian astronomer, an old friend from college days. The narrator fears the conversation, for the brilliant astronomer's cold acceptance of the Einsteinian universe and his familiarity with a mathematically plumbed infinity threaten the precarious scaffoldry of religious faith that Walter has erected. But later in the evening the guest confesses to a moment of terror in his life when he had been frightened by the American landscape while traveling through a barren stretch of New Mexico. That revelation heartens the young host; his friend also knows fear, is vulnerable and fallible; and, therefore, Walter's edifice of belief can logically stand.

Two deft tricks enhance this story. One is ironic reversal: Walter's terror springs from the mysteries of the heavens, but his friend who knows the secrets of space confesses to the fear of an earthly commonplace. The second device is a double unifying metaphor at the end of the story: after the astronomer's admission of fear, Walter sees the mess of coffee dregs, ashes, and wine glasses as a parallel to the "universal debris" that in his mind clutters outer space. His living room provides a microcosm of the universe that is comforting because it is familiar. But then this apartment hanging in darkness above the Hudson River seems to him a single inhabited star, and he is back again in the mild suffering of cosmic loneliness. Once more Updike employs the theme of natural design with his own esthetic patterns to stress human isolation.

The last of these marriage tales, "The Doctor's Wife," has for its setting a remote island in the Bahamas. Ralph and Eve, a young American couple, are vacationing there; and, in the particular incident that comprises the narrative, they submit to a malicious grilling by an English physician's bigoted wife regarding the possibility of Negro blood in Eve because of her dark tan. When Eve leaves to tend her children, Ralph is left alone with the Englishwoman. He overdefends his wife and thereby betrays her, for she is fiercely liberal and would just as soon be identified with a black heritage as not.

The predatory quality of the story is imaged mainly by the shark motif. The Englishwoman with her pointed face is sharklike, just as her conversation circles hungrily around the information she desires. But Ralph, corrupted by the woman's calculated hatred, also feels the lust to destroy. When he flees into the sea and hangs there, fearing the literal sharks and the cruel woman on land, he is enduring the punishment and the absolution for his cowardice.

Late Adolescence in Olinger

Two other Olinger tales in this collection could well be preliminary sketches for *The Centaur*. In "Flight," which concerns a love-hate relationship between an introspective teenage boy (an only child) and his histrionic mother, the title connotes the painful ambivalence of the boy's position. His life seems poised for "flight" in the sense of a brilliant career awaiting him, and his mother uses the metaphor of flying to encourage him. But the disappointment of her own failed vocational dreams causes her to place a pressure on her son that is often quite intolerable; as a result, the possibility of flight means also an escape from her neurotic presence. The double use of the term could be modeled after Joyce's bird imagery in *A Portrait of the Artist as a Young Man;* and, like Stephen Dedalus, Updike's Allen Dow turns to sexuality for inspiration and relief. He acquires a girlfriend while on a trip with the school debating team; Molly Bingaman, pretty but dull (like Penny in *The Centaur*), becomes a weapon for Allen to wield against his mother and also a source of security against his late-adolescent estrangement from himself.

Molly is ultimately unattainable for Allen; her earthiness and her higher social status in Olinger put her out of reach. She is part of the normal small-town milieu that Updike's semiautobiographical heroes can never quite inhabit—something like Thomas Mann's tormented esthetes—and Updike himself, in the foreword to *Olinger Stories,* remarks that Molly represents an enchantment of distance that plagues his sensitive young men. Allen gives up Molly at last to please his mother, but the price she pays is her son's liberation from her domination. He tells her, at least, that this battle is the last between them that she will win.

In "A Sense of Shelter," the counterpart story to "Flight," young William, the bright, stuttering Olinger High School senior, confesses love to his classmate, the beautiful Mary Landis. William is an outsider, while Mary is the classroom queen who blossoms too fast in the hothouse of adulation and starts to fade even before she finishes high school. Since Mary and William have known each other since childhood, the pathos of the story comes through the social and emotional distance that grows between them, even though they remain casually intimate. Mary has the greater, accelerated maturity; but William has the promising professional future ahead of him, and his impulsive proposal of marriage to her is both a gesture to the community and an attempt to take along something of his adolescence into adulthood. Mary refuses him, of course, and William is relieved. He has paid a ritual obeisance to the small-town code (to sow his wild oats and then settle down in an early local marriage) and been given his freedom. Now he can pursue, in his methodical way, the sober dream of an academic career.

But the melancholy fact is that William is not really free: he is only trading the "sense of shelter" that the Olinger schools and classmates have provided for a thoroughly planned, totally orthodox and secure professional career. The "Lavender Blue" lyrics that he croons to himself add an ironic gloss. He is not "king" nor is Mary his "queen"; they are both slaves of convention—and such is the gap between the American romantic vision and American reality.

New and Old Places, Fragments and Catch-Alls

"Still Life" stands by itself because of its unique setting. Leonard Hartz is a talented young American studying art under the "GI Bill" at the Constable School in England. He is attracted to an eighteen-year-old British student at the school, Robin Cox, who substitutes vivaciousness for artistic ability. "Still Life" aptly describes the nature of their relationship, for they never become more than cautious friends. Leonard is moved to jealousy at one point when an American acquaintance asks Robin to pose in the nude for him (she refuses), but even his jealousy leads nowhere. Their friendship seems metaphoric of stock British-American affinities: congenial but confused, sharing some common cultural traditions that invite familiarity but also disguise the essential differences not so easily overcome.

The next to the last story of the collection could have been more fortunately located in the "First Person Singular" section of *Assorted Prose.* Encumbered by the unwieldy title of "The Blessed Man of Boston, My Grandmother's Thimble, and Fanning Island," the story, one guesses, has only the thinnest veneer of invention over autobiography; indeed, it seems to serve as a catch-all for the reminiscences that Updike has not completely refined into fiction. The family memories and personal recollections are beautifully recorded; but, because the author has not provided the universality of true fiction, the artistic relevance is limited.

The final story, in contrast, is of the same nature as "The Blessed Man . . . ," but it succeeds precisely where that one fails. It has a similar exhaustive title—"Packed Dirt, Churchgoing, A Dying Cat, A Traded Car"—but a much greater internal unity and continuity. Above all, it does transform personal memory into something universally meaningful. If "The Blessed Man . . . " is a catch-all for the stories Updike would have liked to write and did not, "Packed Dirt . . . " draws together many of those he did create into a new composition and a new vision.

David Kern, the protagonist of "Pigeon Feathers," is the narrator of this story. He is now a mature family man, father of four children, living close to Boston. (In the course of this essay-story Updike returns also to Olinger, Alton, Greenwich Village, Manhattan's Upper West Side, Oxford, and the Caribbean Islands, collecting old motifs and images along the way.) Now a writer, David Kern still suffers from the cosmic vertigo that had frightened him as a fourteen-year-old boy. Diverted by lust, or driving to see his father hospitalized by a heart attack, or attending a cat struck by an automobile—his participation in the major and minor accidents of life reminds him both of the preciousness and brevity of his moment in time and space.

Young David in "Pigeon Feathers" finds solace and hope for immortality in a classic theological manner, by extending the evidence of design in nature to the universal design of divinity. The adult David no longer expresses his fears or faith so naïvely, but his approach to being and his defense against nihilism remain essentially the same. When he declares at the end of "Packed Dirt . . . " that "we in America need ceremonies," he is suggesting that the various rituals for approaches and departures, for being and death, impose at least a provisional order—an order that substitutes for the religiously based traditional order that is fading fast.

The Reconstructive Ritual

When the unexpected gift that characterizes *The Same Door* stories is no longer forthcoming to people, as is often the case in *Pigeon Feathers,* alienation is the result. It is alienation in many forms: isolation from the community, estrangement from those who used to be closest to one, and loneliness in the midst of the universe itself. But Updike's people seldom remain drifting in a spiritual vagrancy; for such drifting is a luxury that the residual work ethic, embodied in Updike's own artistic persistence, will not allow. His characters continue to go through the motions, and the repetition of the daily actions settles into new rituals that can generate, perhaps, new meaning. It is not that the unexpected gift no longer occasionally arrives; rather, it will not do for people to languish in hope for it. Grace still responds to the stimulus of works, and one must fashion his own design to recover the outlines of a master pattern.

Chapter Six
The Centaur:
Guilt through Redemption

Let us not mock God with metaphor,
analogy, sidestepping, transcendence,
making of the event a parable, a sign painted
in the faded credulity of earlier ages.
let us walk through the door.

—from "Seven Stanzas at Easter"

Myth and Story

The Centaur, published in 1963, is the most ambitious of Updike's works before *Couples.* Longer and more intricate than *Rabbit, Run,* this novel became a best seller and won the National Book Award for Fiction in 1964. While some reviewers greeted the book as the first evidence of Updike's willingness to confront the so-called larger-than-life issues, others called it a *roman manqué* at best and a "sell-out" to the popular fashions of fiction at worst. The aspect of the novel that bothered most critics was Updike's blend—or forced combination—of Classical myth and realistic narrative. Even a sympathetic commentator such as Arthur Mizener considered the Chiron-Prometheus material an unwise and artistically unrealized addition to the contemporary Olinger fiction.[1]

The novel begins with the attempt of George Caldwell, a middle-aged science teacher at Olinger High School, to interest an unruly class in evolutionary human history. Caldwell is also Chiron the centaur, part man and part stallion, and the mentor of the young Greek heroes. Caldwell is wounded in the ankle by a missile thrown by one of his students (the parallel mythic action is Chiron struck by a stray poisoned arrow shot by a battling centaur); he limps next door to Hummel's garage (Hephaestus's forge) to have the missile removed. Returning as Chiron, he relives a seductive encounter with Venus bathing in her forest pool (Vera Hummel the physical education teacher emerging from a locker-room shower). Back in the classroom, he strikes the obstreperous pupil Deifendorf (Hercules) with the arrow while Zimmerman the principal (Zeus) watches.

In the second chapter, the thirtyish Peter Caldwell recounts the experiences of the few winter days of early 1947, fourteen years earlier, that led to the "death" of George Caldwell, his teacher-father. Peter, now a "second-rate abstract expressionist" painter living in a Manhattan loft, narrates to his sleeping Negro mistress the initial events of those days: arising on a cold Monday morning to prepare for school, listening to the family conversation about his father's hypochondria, rushing late to school with his father, and picking up an obscene hitchhiker on the way. Following the brief interlude of chapter three (Chiron and his Olympian students), Peter resumes his reminiscence in chapter four. On that same Monday afternoon in the past, George Caldwell has been X-rayed for suspected stomach cancer; in the evening, the father and son plan to return home from a swimming meet in the nearby Alton Y.M.C.A., but, when the old family Buick does not start, they stay overnight in a cheap Alton hotel and walk to school in Olinger the next morning.

Chapter five presents, abruptly and without any explanation, George Caldwell's obituary, written in the style of a small-town newspaper by one of Caldwell's former pupils. Chapter six, a Surrealistic dream sequence, has Peter as Prometheus grieving over his father's death; but then he meets his father (still in the dream) and pleads with him to go on living. Chapter seven, which shifts to a third-person narration, depicts George Caldwell's conversation and actions with his fellow faculty members and Peter's fumbling pettings with Penny, his teenage girlfriend, at the evening basketball game. That night on the way home, the Buick stalls in a snowbank; and father and son are again marooned. Chapter eight resumes Peter's own narration. He and his father have stayed overnight at the Hummels'. By morning the area is snowed in and the schools are closed. In late afternoon, when the Buick is ready to go once more, the two Caldwells drive home, only to stall again on the long, snow-clogged dirt road that leads to their farm. They walk to the house. George tells his wife that the X-rays show him to be free of the feared cancer. Peter becomes sick from the exertion of the past days and stays in bed the next morning (Saturday) with a fever while his father leaves the house, one guesses to dig out the car. In chapter nine, Caldwell, now as Chiron, walks out to the black Buick, which he recognizes as the chariot of Zeus, and yields to death.

Surrealist and Cubist Analogues

An evaluation of the myth-realism blend depends on a right understanding of how it works. Updike is not writing allegory, for both dimensions of narrative in *The Centaur* are literally present: the modern fictive creation and the ancient legend that it approximates; thus there is nothing to allegorize. Nor is he simply composing, as Mizener has already correctly observed, updated versions of the Classical myths *à la* the method of John Erskine a few decades ago. His method and achievement can best be appreciated through analogies to Surrealist and Cubist painting. The intention and the effect of the double narrative in *The Centaur* are to expand literal reality through distortion—as in Surrealism (with its accompanying psychological expressive modes)—and through the simultaneous projection of many facets of a personality or action, as in Cubism. Since fiction, like all language, is temporally and spatially linear, one cannot, obviously, create the meaningful distortion and dislocation of reality and the simultaneous "thereness" of its aspects as the visual and plastic arts can. One uses, instead, the material of fiction to convert its necessary linearity into the illusion of what one would call, in literary terms, supra-realism or multi-realism.

Literary analogies to Surrealism appear, for example, at the beginning and end of chapter one, in the scene at Hummel's garage and then in the last few minutes of Caldwell's science-class lecture; in the dream sequence of chapter six; and in the concluding chapter in the description of Chiron's death. In all of these scenes the absence of a logical sequentiality, of cause and effect, renders the Surrealist impression. In the early scene of the first chapter, Hummel's garage (also Hephaestus's smithy) gains a Surrealist quality through the constant movement between myth and realistic narrative. The lame blacksmith uses an acetylene torch and a wire cutter to remove the arrow from Caldwell's ankle, and he is helped by a one-eyed boy who is also a Cyclops. The scene is precisely detailed yet impossible to believe—blacksmiths and garage mechanics are not surgeons—

until one realizes that the equine Chiron would indeed be tended by a smith, and that the action literally concerns Caldwell's car, which has an important part in the story otherwise. Helped by later comments in the novel, one can reconstruct the Surrealist scene: George Caldwell, struck in the ankle by a strange missile in the classroom, is Chiron the centaur wounded by a poisoned arrow; but Chiron's body also merges with Caldwell's car, and the operation in the garage is not the removal of a literal arrow—George retires to the garage to recover from a merely verbal shaft—but the repair of the Buick grille that Deifendorf, the obstreperous pupil, broke. The mingling of animal and mechanical qualities is a characteristic Surrealist device used effectively here mainly to destroy conventional concepts of time. To be forced to identify the ancient legendary centaur with a modern automobile shocks the intellect and imagination into an acceptance of atemporality that Updike needs for the success of his story.

Surrealism developed from the fascination with psychoanalysis in the first third of the twentieth century, and it is fitting, therefore, that the Freudian-tinted dream passage comprising chapter six should borrow the Surrealist style. The chapter begins with the teenaged Peter in a posture of suffering: "As I lay on my rock various persons visited me." The reference is obviously mythological—Prometheus chained to his mountain—but it assumes many other valid meanings. Following chapter five as it does (the obituary chapter), it seems to reveal Peter transfixed in grief over the death of his father. The town personae who emerge and fade, at any rate, are like the mourners at a funeral who come to offer condolences to the immediate bereaved.

But Peter lying on his rock can also be the boy in suspense, waiting to learn the fateful results of his father's X-ray tests. Or again, Peter's torture can be his awakening sexuality. His embarrassment over his biological changes, his misunderstood mixture of lust and curiosity figure in the anguish (insignificant to the adult but real to the awkward adolescent) represented by the Promethean punishment, particularly since the archetypal creativity of Prometheus, usually understood in its artistic aspects, can have sexual, progenitive connotations as well. And, finally, the torture of Prometheus has a literal parallel in the incessant itching of Peter's psoriasis—a modern, decidedly unromantic but nonetheless maddening variation of the legendary eagle that tears daily at Prometheus's liver.

One cannot classify these many uses of the myth as a complex symbolic device (instead of insisting on the Surrealist analogy) because they do not function in traditional literary-symbolic terms. All of these "meanings" of the Prometheus-Peter combination are manifestly present through the distortion that the dream context creates and are not the result of subtly placed hints that the reader must decode. As in nonliteral painting, one must grasp the *Gestalt* of the total scene in its equally significant multi-meanings and interrelations instead of trying to discover a cryptic key that logically explains the story. This absence of some dominant literal meaning in favor of the configurational construct provides the particularly powerful expression of reality that conventional symbolism cannot produce. One sacrifices a coherent story line for the impact of a total imaginative-emotional approach, but is a worthwhile trade.

One recognizes the quality of Updike's artistic risk in the final chapter, for in it he depends utterly upon the Surrealist method to carry the culminating sense of the story. Instead of presenting Caldwell's death in straightforward fashion and provoking a symbolic interpretation, Updike inverts the process. He shows only Chiron the centaur in the final scene and surrounds the circumstances of his death with a mythic opacity: "Chiron accepted death." Does that imply that Caldwell, his modern parallel, also dies? It is possible, as one reviewer maintained, that Chiron's death is symbolic of Caldwell's existential resignation—that he does not die physically, in love with death as he is, but chooses, for the sake of family and vocational duty, to return to the hell of daily teaching. The strategy of the Surrealist technique here is to give concluding emphasis to the combination of compassion and irony that pervades the novel. The compassion is bound up both in the myth and in the modern narrative. Chiron dies so that Prometheus may be expiated and liberated; Caldwell decides to go on living to serve his profession as teacher and fulfill his responsibility as family man, even though he is obsessed with death.

Although it is a bit confusing to speak of a myth behind the myth, an overriding archetypal pattern does determine the moral and social substance of *The Centaur,* just as it does in Updike's other novels. Whereas *The Poorhouse Fair* displayed the godless City of God and *Rabbit, Run* the quest for a non-existent Grail, *The Centaur* projects the paradoxical action of a redemption *into* guilt. This strange redemption utilizes the other analogy from the visual arts, the Cubist style. Wylie Sypher, who has examined the relationship of Cubism to fiction, says that the Cubist influence asserts itself in the twentieth century in the use of simultaneous perspective, in the strategy of "situating" the story between fact and fiction, in the dependence upon camouflage and counterfeit, and in the collage technique.[2] Without subscribing to a belief in Cubist attitudes and goals (it is, after all, no longer a vital style), Updike does work with these elements to a degree in his third novel. In *The Centaur*, the first and fourth Cubist influences, as Sypher describes them, are most obvious. The configurational structure of multi-meanings in the myth-realism blend, approached from the intrinsic and subjective view of Surrealism, becomes from the Cubist focus a *Gestalt* of simultaneous perspectives. Thus, when one asks what the formal point of view of *The Centaur* is, one discovers that it has none. It is mainly Peter's story; but Peter is, at the same time, a teenager and an adult; he reminisces lucidly but also recollects from the subconscious; he speaks in the first-person singular confessional and also with his father inhabits a scenic point of view—one done, moreover, in the historical present tense that makes those days in 1947 seem dramatically immediate. Even those chapters that exclude Peter as character have the sense of his presence, as if they were to be understood from the position of Peter the mature artist who is refashioning his father's past and thereby his own. In these ways, then, the simultaneous perspective of the Cubist style informs *The Centaur*.

Updike uses the collage technique even more obviously. The nine chapters of the novel with their various forms of narrative—myth-realism, confession, idyll, obituary, confession, dream, broad scene, confession, myth—compose a collage, while the seventh chapter (the broad scene) forms a smaller representative collage of its own. More difficult to describe, but significantly present, are the Cubist "situating" of narrative and the use of camouflage. Updike does not depend as necessarily as André Gide (whom Sypher discusses), for example, on transformed reportage or on history as the basis of his fiction, nor does he capitalize on the tensions between plot and autobiography as Gide does. Olinger is in a sense Shillington, of course; Peter "is" Updike himself as an adolescent with artistic aspirations; and George Caldwell "is" Updike's father, the Shillington high-school teacher. But Updike is not fictionalizing a personal emotional experience in *The Centaur:* his father had not yet died, and he himself has not evolved into a Bohemian artist seeking a rationale for his vocation but into a novelist who maintains a respectable middle-class status in spite of his ability to shock.

In his later short stories, especially in *The Music School* collection, Updike becomes increasingly involved in the Cubist *tableau-tableau,* the problem of self-conscious artistic creation; but, in *The Centaur,* he has not progressed to that degree of projected self-awareness as a novelist. Rather, he transfers the creative problem to Peter, and by this method Updike keeps himself behind the composition. Since Peter is an artist, it is natural that he translate his moral-vocational problems into artistic terms. His effort at a meaningful reconstruction of his and his father's past, therefore, approximates what Sypher calls a "facet of the double-consciousness of modern man, the *dédoublement* of existential experience.[3] The difference between Updike and Gide (Sypher's model) is that Gide takes this existential analysis upon himself directly as author-biographer, while Updike transfers it to his protagonist-narrator. But still more important is the fact that Updike's artistic and moral effort, like that of the Cubists, is first purposefully destructive in order to become creative. Both the Cubists and Updike fracture conventional reality as a prelude to a positive construction of a personal vision. At this point, then, one can begin to talk about the nature and purpose of Updike's compassionate-ironic redemptive myth-archetype in *The Centaur.*

Varieties of Time

The novel is saturated by concepts of time and by time consciousness, and the redemption archetype within its Surrealist and Cubist execution is involved in various manifestations of time: in *mythos* (the term to be used to distinguish myth per se from the myth-archetype), *historia* (in its double connotation of the historical past and of fictive narration), and memory (the epistemological vehicle used to mediate between *mythos* and *historia*). But these manifestations do not exhaust the categories of temporality in the story. Updike works with other distinctions of time that are difficult to describe because Western culture does not recognize the nuances, but one can identify them by borrowing ancient Greek terms (appropriately enough) and by demonstrating how they share in the construction of the narrative.

The sense of *aeon,* for example, is prevalent in the early part of the novel. Like the Latin *aeternitas,* it conveys the idea of an enormous length of time, even of immeasurable time. When Caldwell writes a fantastically large number on the board for the benefit of his class in the first chapter, the effect is to induce vertigo. So many zeroes produce the feeling of chaos and infinity; the immensity of time makes the mind reel and search for boundaries that it cannot find. This terrible limitlessness of time creates the infinite context of the novel. It is true that the stress upon *aeon* decreases in the later chapters, but the sense of its power lingers. In fact, the infinite past it represents is gradually transformed into a concern about an infinite future. Although Caldwell has the secular man's cynicism concerning a personal immortality, the mythic element deals directly with that concept. The myth assumes two kinds of immortality: Chiron, who possesses physical immortality, exchanges with the part-human Prometheus, so that the artificer may have eternal life on earth, while Chiron is rewarded with a heavenly immutability. Chiron, therefore, becomes the mythic representative of *aeon.*

Chronos is mechanical time—time passing methodically, sequentially, and measurably. In the first chapter, this time is demonstrated well not only by Caldwell's attempt to beat the bell but also by his wish to be saved by it; for this arbitrary time dictates one's days. Caldwell's creation clock in the initial chapter is a clever teaching device that is also a falsification; it encourages his students to confuse the simplicity of *chronos* with the subtlety of *aeon.* It allows them to control time in the modern empirical manner instead of being made wise by it. Yet the lives of the small-town Pennsylvanians are controlled by *chronos.* Pop Kramer, the grandfather who lives with the Caldwell family, is also old Kronos in the mythic parallel and stands for the domination of the generations by mechanical time. Updike often quotes the time of day throughout the narrative to show the modern obeisance to the artificially imposed minutes and hours of chronologizing. Caldwell is always racing the clock and usually losing; and, at the end of the novel, he as Chiron is even late for the final rendezvous with the death-chariot of Zeus.

Telos is a less spectacular but more crucial quality of time in the novel, for much of the novel's significance is in its teleological action. The concept of *telos* contains the two elements of integrity and consummation. It figures importantly first in Caldwell's lecture to his class: out of the chaos of the immense past, from the accidents of primitive matter and energy, come nonetheless the stubborn, instinctive, and vital gestures toward meaningful life. There *is* a natural movement toward meaning that old Caldwell believes in, and the question that *The Centaur* carries for Peter is whether he can locate a similar consummation and drive toward integrity in his father's suffering existence and in his own sojourn. Is there really a redemptive linearity in the successive preacher-teacher-artist vocations of the Caldwell generations, or is it the circular vanity of Ecclesiastes and Greek myth? Must the mature Peter Caldwell *create* a concrete justification for the life that his father freed him to?

Kairos, a final concept, is time measured not by duration but by experiential intensity. It is the relevant moment that redeems the dumb progression of *chronos* and that justifies the consummating tendency of *telos. Kairos* determines the narrative climaxes of *The Centaur,* for Caldwell's struggle, one guesses, is against the impulse to commit suicide. Especially after he learns he does not have the feared stomach cancer, he must rediscover the will to live—for he has already prepared himself to die. The decision to continue living for the sake of his family and his pupils is an agonizing *kairos* moment. Peter's own narration is directed by the *kairos* aspect of time; although he is passively reminiscent during the night of his narration, in bed with his sleeping mistress, the fact of the memory's action working upon him *now* is crucial. He is apparently at some point of personal reevaluation in his life that will lead to a decision. Updike leaves reader and protagonist alike in the suspense and tension of the *kairos* moment that will either force Peter to create his own meaning and identity or leave him in a spiritual paralysis still more crippling than the one that holds him.

The introduction of the young protagonist as involved narrator points to another time-related element. Memory itself in certain chapters of *The Centaur*—and perhaps in all of them, if one sees the whole novel as Peter's recollection—is the dominating fictive device. It is obviously not a category of time but a structure for encountering and ordering temporality. Peter's personal memory in the recollective chapters of *The Centaur* meets myth, a manifestation of man's collective memory (in the Jungian sense) in the other chapters, and deals with it in such a way that the personal memory assumes a surrogate-mythical function. If it is true, as Philip Rieff has declared in *The Triumph of the Therapeutic,* that fiction has supplanted the teaching function of myth, then one can see the new process in operation in this novel.[4] In it, personal memory, or fiction presenting the artistic illusion of personal memory, accomplishes the feat of uniting the subjective and objective aspects of experience that all good literature must somehow do. Myth, emerging from the past as stylized and crystallized memory, meets personal memory coming out of the present (the author's position) into the past (the achieved fiction). Where these two join is where the novel assumes its greatest vitality and most profound meaning, for here is where the subject and object concur in a unified, total artistic experience.

Mircea Eliade (in *Cosmos and History*) has argued that primitive man had a terror of history and protected himself from it by the insulating repetitive existence in terms of archetype, myth, and ritual, but that modern man has abandoned the sense of mythic relevance to trust in factuality instead.[5] Updike's fictive mode attempts, through the use of memory in close proximity to myth, to desacralize factuality for modern man—without denying history—and to place myth again in its necessary existential role. Through the same strategy, he empiricizes myth by forcing it under the scrutiny of personal memory. His fiction, therefore, fulfills in good part the sacred and secular functions that Eliade and Rieff demand of narrative prose.

Classical Myth and Christian Meaning

Updike uses Classical myth to shape a Christian-informed vision of life. Chiron the centaur as a dual being, part man and part horse, represents the disunity in unity of human nature; he is earthbound, yet possesses an intelligence that makes him vulnerable to longings for the infinite. But the centaurs were also partial divinities, inhabiting a vague superhuman position on the uncertain scale from Titans, gods, and demigods down to heroes and mortals. Chiron has immortality and is a mentor of the young heroes; thus he exists in this fashion also on the boundary between creatureliness and godliness. The duality of human nature is carried in the mythic aspect of the novel alone, then, and that in turn acts as the one pole of the myth-realism blend.

Since Chiron is also George Caldwell, he shows another facet of the tension between humanity and divinity that mankind endures. According to this combination, Chiron stands for the eternal and timeless realm to which men have always aspired; Caldwell represents the immanent, time-and-space-bound dilemma that limits men. Furthermore, apart from the mythic dimension altogether, Caldwell himself demonstrates the dual nature of his being. Described emphatically as a secularized Western man of the mid-twentieth century, he cannot be categorized in terms of the orthodox Christian *imago dei* versus Fallen Man. Instead, Caldwell is aligned to love on the one hand and to death on the other—these mark the extensions and limitations of his being. Behind the comic façade, Caldwell's teaching, his familial and social relationships, and his moral values are inspired by a profound compassion: that is his limitless, charismatic dimension. But, as scientist and as a physically ill man (or a hypochondriac), he is constantly faced with the imminence of death; and that is the dimension that always recalls him to his humanity.

Every person in *The Centaur* has his corresponding mythic identity or identities, and Peter Caldwell particularly reinforces the dualistic concept inherent in his father's characterization. Because Peter is also Prometheus (a primordial deity, neither god nor man, yet with traits of both), he is ideal for showing the flux of adolescence and the uncertainty of one's vocational choice. Peter, as the fifteen-year-old boy, still retains a degree of the divine innocence of childhood according, for instance, to the Wordsworthian paradigm, although he steadily succumbs to the corruption of the adult world. Or, like Prometheus in the Aeschylean drama (defying Zeus for the sake of mankind and strengthened in his rebellion by the foreknowledge that he and mankind will eventually mature to freedom), Peter is the pivotal figure in the struggle of the generations.

The use of myth can clarify the dilemma of creatureliness in relation to time, but it cannot halt time itself. Peter (in bed in his Manhattan artist's loft and reminiscing to his sleeping mistress) is caught up in his own attempt to stop time personally and artistically. The two efforts are often hard to distinguish from each other, yet here is another angle of the duality: two Peter Caldwells exist in the novel—the schoolboy and the adult painter; and the tension of the novel develops in large part from the effort to establish a continuity between them. If creatureliness is the result of a compromise between aspiration and reality, Peter as artist expresses the condition quite instructively. He has turned his back on the family professions of preacher and teacher in favor of the artist's freedom—has taken the unlimited risk that should provide total, personal meaning and fulfillment. But he has not discovered or created meaning and satisfaction. He is still young and not yet resigned to mediocrity, but he is already asking the agonizing question of the novel: what went wrong that prevented his self-fulfillment? *"Was it for this that my father gave up his life?"* Peter asks himself during a painful moment of his reappraisal. His effort to suspend those winter days of 1947 through memory, like his "second-rate abstract expressionist" paintings, is a move to create or re-create meaning from the elusive pieces of modern life where meaning is no longer inherent. Son of a scientist, grandson of a minister, and child of the enlightened, empirical generation, Peter in his private and professional desperation returns to mythicizing.

Yet the use of myth is not an escape device (employed to flee an unendurable present) nor a transparent attempt to apotheosize a shabby mundane existence. It is the beginning of a process that moves from theology to science to esthetics, and Peter the narrator defines his life exactly along these lines. The preacher-teacher-artist sequence that he speaks of and the final stage of which he represents exhibits not only a vocational progression or regression (he calls it "the classic degeneration") but also mythological and teleological correlatives. The preacher-teacher-artist professions are mythologized through Zeus, the divinity; Chiron, the mentor; and Prometheus, the culture-bringer. The direction is from the absolute authoritarianism of the supernatural to the independent rationalism of the empiricist to something not quite articulated. The novel as a whole describes an emergent pattern: man moves from a submissive worship of the divine creator to a scientific effort of scanning creation to the necessary assumption of the creator role himself.

The artist is also the one who suffers the anguish and responsibility of the creator role. The traditional God is no longer taken seriously. As the Protestant deity, he is dismissed with the spinster French teacher's banal *"Dieu est très fin,"* to which George Caldwell absently responds, "He's a wonderful old gentleman. I don't know where the hell we'd be without Him." But the successor to God, the modern scientist, is also not taken seriously. Chiron as the mythic counterpart enjoys a semi-respect as a sort of lackey to the gods, but Caldwell the science teacher, although he has personally endearing qualities, appears a cheerful fool to his pupils. Against this twofold absurdity, Peter as artist must fashion his own meaning and being. His composition with color, line, proportion, perspective

is a means of living metaphorically, of constructing a working model
for one's search after personal and ultimate meaning. In other words,
when theology and science lose their autonomy and inner structure,
art, which is always form, can offer substance. To this end Peter
Caldwell wishes to employ his art.

How then shall Peter Caldwell function in the fearful freedom of
his creator role? His answer is in work. Work involves suffering,
and therein another facet of creatureliness is exposed: man is the
one who works and suffers for the sake of meaning. In the Greek
and Hebrew-Christian myths, suffering has been related to meaning
through the motifs of original sin, vocation, and redemption. *Hubris,*
the desire to be equal with the gods, is punishable by the necessity
of labor (Adam, Sisyphus), suffering, and death. The effects of suffering and death can be relieved only by some expiatory action, but
labor becomes an end in itself and even lends a significance to the
twin curses of suffering and death.

In Updike's world, suffering and death are present; but original
sin as their cause and redemption as the cure are not important.
Instead, the gestures of a more elemental guilt and sacrifice inform
the structure and meaning of the novel; and both of these, in turn,
are balanced by the power of love and by the ordering force of
vocation. Guilt in George and Peter Caldwell and in their mythical
counterparts grows from the encounter with *Eros* that then becomes,
somehow, a conflict with divinity. Thus George Caldwell has with-
stood the charms of the naked "gym" teacher in the name of traditional morality—on the mythical level, Chiron is tempted to yield
to Venus's advances before the thunder of Zeus reminds him of his
place. Thus Peter's fumbling explorations with his girlfriend Penny
in the 1947 context are to be understood (the catalogue appended
to the novel instructs one) as the fateful opening of Pandora's box.
Although it is a poor pun, it is an apt symbol of Western attitudes
toward sin and sexuality, in which the loss of sexual innocence is
akin to the release of qualitative evil itself into the world.

Love, both sexual and familial, does impel guilt in *The Centaur,*
but it also leads still deeper into sacrifice; and, in the treatment of
this concept, the strategy of the novel structure, especially as seen
via the Surrealist-Cubist analogy, becomes quite transparent. The
theme of sacrifice appears early in the novel, as George Caldwell
explains to his science class that "while each cell is potentially
immortal. . . . The strain eventually wears it out and kills it. It

dies sacrificially, for the good of the whole." This statement expresses the way in which Caldwell sees his own role in the scheme of life.

The teleological aspect of Caldwell's final decision can now be observed in its personal-mythic context. What happens in the final pages of the novel in literal terms is never clear. Instead of depicting the action in a normal temporal-spatial manner and inviting mythic-symbolic interpretation, Updike presents the mythic dimension but asks the reader to fill in his conclusions about the realistic events. It is a curious post-Impressionistic tactic; in Impressionism one would be offered an emotional reaction to an event instead of a description of the event, but in these last pages of *The Centaur* one has, instead of the emotional response, the ultimate "meaning" of the event without a depiction of the event itself. Or more exactly, Updike uses the mythic action as a gloss upon the unwritten realistic narration. Chiron's identity becomes dominant in the concluding chapter. Chiron walks out to the stalled black Buick which he recognizes to be the chariot of Zeus; he pauses for a moment on the edge of a precipice (the abyss of time?)—and then? Updike writes only, after a brief recital in Greek of the Chiron-Prometheus story, that "Chiron accepted death."

The Creation of Personal Meaning

The reader is confronted with the same task that Peter faces: finding meaning in a situation in which sacrifice seems needful but doing so in a context where sacrifice no longer holds religious or cultural relevance. The archetypal model is present, but the contemporary substance is not. Chiron dies to liberate Prometheus from his agony; he is the expiation for Prometheus's theft of fire from the gods; but Prometheus also provides the welcome opportunity for Chiron to abandon a life he no longer wants. Demythologized, the ending of *The Centaur* suggests that scientific man dies in the context of the old order to make way for the new freedom of the imagination, destroying the limiting modern orthodoxies for the sake of a greater being. But how is Caldwell's sacrifice personally meaningful for Peter? This is the crux of the novel: the teacher has sacrificed himself somehow for the good of the artist; the intellect has prepared the way somehow for the integrating effort of the imagination. Yet the son, the artist, the guardian of the imagination, has not been able to profit from the sacrifice, nor will he ever be able to through passivity or grace alone. Something of ultimate worth has been offered him, but he must still create its value for himself and for his age.

Peter's meaning must be formed in the same anticipation in which his father acted, in a faith in the future which is faith because circumstances do not inspire hope. Prometheus means "fore-thought," and in the Aeschylean drama the suffering hero on his rock maintains a defiant faith by looking ahead to the prophesied release by his savior Hercules thirteen generations hence. In the novel, Peter returns fourteen years later for a brief visit to Alton and listens to a redemptive praise of his father by Deifendorf-Her-cules, the athlete of the old high school days who has become a teacher through Caldwell's influence.

Although Peter cannot vindicate his father's sacrifice through *works,* his creation of personal meaning must develop through *work* and not just through a reliance on the gracious memory of his father's love. Peter's meaning must grow out of the tension of faith and works, out of the tension of past and present, and out of the tension of temporal complexity that the novel depends upon. The force of love must be met by the power of vocation. This emphasis recalls the stress on craftsmanship in the fiction of Willa Cather, Sinclair Lewis, and John Dos Passos; and it has been largely overlooked in discussions of Updike. For Updike—perhaps even more than for Joyce, Proust, Mann, or Faulkner—the past, whether as *historia* or *mythos,* is a point of orientation that must be confirmed and fulfilled in vocation. His own meticulous artistry incarnates the will to create meaning out of one's profession from which an inherent meaning has departed. He believes in work as much as he believes in love, and his fiction is shaped by the desire that modern Americans not only give and find compassion but that they also ground that com-passion in tangible, ordered tasks.

The Centaur as a whole has a powerful teleological direction, energized by the stress upon maturity that the body of Updike's fiction illustrates. The main argument against understanding George Caldwell's death as literal suicide is that his mature option is to go on living and suffering. The central significance of Peter's lonely recollection *en deux* is that it is a belated act of maturation. Fourteen years earlier he was Peter-Priapus, a budding phallic god fearing and wondering at his awakening sexual self. Now almost thirty, he decides to conduct a crucial personal inventory as the first step toward true vocation. This, his moment of *kairos,* is the act whereby he begins to refashion himself and his future. Because it is a culminating moment as well, it is also *telos.* Peter now frees himself from the guilt of the past. He takes on the responsibility of faith in the future, faith in his art (hitherto "second-rate") as the vocation-risk that will form his meaning and that will redeem his creatureliness.

Chapter Seven

Of the Farm: The Failed Poet and the Urban Earth Mother

The landscape of love
can only be seen
through a slim windowpane
one's own breath fogs.

—"Erotic Epigrams, I"

Ellipsis in the Country

If fiction is in part the art of leaving things significantly unsaid, Updike succeeds admirably in his fourth novel, *Of the Farm*. Once more the book reviewers were willing to allow that the technique was perfectly controlled, but they argued again that the subject matter was neither significant nor especially interesting. A weekly news magazine, with typical clichéd hyperbole, likened the book to the composition of a painting on a pinhead; and a good critic, John Thompson, decided in *The New York Review of Books* that whatever truths the novel was masking were not worth uncovering.[1] Admittedly, Updike moves closer to the artistic-esoteric in *Of the Farm* than in his previous fiction, but the rewards are correspondingly greater for those who strive to appreciate the book's form. The best integrated of his first four novels, *Of the Farm* is a radically pared-down work that succeeds by virtue of its technical concentration and ellipsis.

The protagonist is Joey Robinson, a thirty-five-year-old Manhattan advertising consultant who has smothered poetic aspirations and who visits his widowed mother over a weekend on her eastern Pennsylvania farm. In his company are his recently acquired second wife Peggy and her precocious eleven-year-old son Richard. Joey is

78

a literary relative of Harry Angstrom and Peter Caldwell. Like the Caldwell family, the Robinsons moved from Olinger, at the insistence of the strong-willed mother, to a farm in the country against the wishes of the father (here again a high-school science teacher) and the son. Like Rabbit Angstrom, Joey is hypersensitive, unstable, and dominated by his mother; and he suffers the resultant sex-and-security complications with his women. The difference is that Joey, a Harvard graduate and a qualified success in his vocation, is respectable middle-class.

A main purpose of the visit is to give Joey's ailing mother and his new wife a chance to know each other better, but the weekend is not very successful. The women are alternately hostile and over-friendly; at times, they are defensive in their attitudes toward Joey; at other times, suspicious of his loyalties. Joey himself has to tangle not only with the sparring females but also with the ghosts of his past. The memories of his dead father, of his first wife Joan, and of their three children now living in Canada are revived by the old familiar surroundings and by photographs; and these memories release Joey's suppressed feelings of remorse and guilt.

Very little significant overt action occurs: Joey mows the overgrown field with the family tractor; he and his mother take a trip to the local supermarket; the two of them attend a Lutheran church service on Sunday morning. Instead of dynamic action, the novel is filled with conversation and description. The climax, if it can be called that, takes place on Sunday noon when old Mrs. Robinson, excited by the tensions of the visit, suffers a heart seizure on the way home from church. She is put to bed, the town doctor examines her briefly, and the son and family plan the return trip to New York that evening in spite of her illness.

The Crucial X and Vital Incongruity

A few years ago during a television interview, Updike remarked that he conceived the design of one of his novels as the figure of an "X." The concept fits this novel and reveals the visual bias of his creative technique—the surviving graphic orientation that, while certainly not antiintellectual, demands of the reader that he perceive *Gestalt* and not only verbalized ideas. The "X" serves as the model for metaphors of intersection and interaction, as the representative structure of characterization, as the unifying figure in the manipulation of time and space, and as both the integer and unknown quality of the story's problem.

The geometrically fashioned metaphors in *Of the Farm* seem whimsical at first, belabored Donne-like conceits; but they have a precise place in the book's scheme. Not only the "X," but squares, rhomboids, triangles, circles, curves, and angles frequently inform the imagery. Through the lines of the highway, the patterns of the fields and the farmhouse, and the contours of the women in his life, the protagonist is made to see and describe through a vocabulary of formal shapes and measurements. It is as if, against the loss of the old societal order, the author imposes a tentative artificial order of mathematical forms.

In the most general sense, the story is "X"-formed through its stress on intersection and interaction. The particular import of this emphasis may be a bit difficult to see since the energy of any piece of fiction depends upon interaction of people and events. The difference is that, while in most novels the interaction is a kind of anatomy that supports the thematic and cultural overlay (what humanist and social-oriented critics talk about), such interaction in *Of the Farm* is a simultaneous means and end. For example, the total act of the story is to depict literally the crux, the "X," of Joey's life. It is the intersection of his experience to date. The return to the old farm in these particular and peculiar circumstances brings together the two divergent lines of his existence: his childhood ideals, his first wife and three children, his stable sojourn versus the disillusionment of adulthood, the passion and vulgarity of the second marriage, and his essentially romantic new mode of life. These lines meet at the farm in the encounter with the mother (this meeting is the center of the "X"); then they cross and move off in two new directions. The farm, the mother, and the old life still hanging on must be sloughed off; and the passionate new life must be embraced with fuller commitment. The lengthening arms of the "X" now recede farther from each other, and Joey must choose and live conclusively with his choice.

Or, in another sense native to Updike's imagery and representative of the novel as a whole, the chiasmic pattern is elemental-sexual. The prone and outstretched female forms the "X," and to make love with her is to perform something "crucial" that touches the mysterious core of being. Hence Updike's concern with the convergence of the woman's thighs and with pudenda: here is the center of the "X" where decisive experience occurs. The woman as symbol of the mystery of being to be plumbed is a basic metaphor of the novel, and the "X" figure gives it an underlying stylized simplicity. In the Sunday morning church scene a depiction of the cross (an "X") precedes the sermon on woman's place in God's creation as both the security and secret of being, while the whole scene is itself another intersection, another blending of divergent strands in the book.

Recalling an ecstatic moment of the affair with Peggy before their marriage—a lover's morning in the city complete with music, fine weather, and the revealed flesh—Joey says, "I was transfixed. . . . I felt my heart pinned at the point where the snow and Bach and her bathing intersected." That passage is one of the epitomizing metaphors of the novel. The redemption of significant moments out of the plurality of experience provides the genuine, if precarious, spiritual foundation of Updike's fictive world. Yet the metaphor in this particular setting also introduces a crucial act, for this meeting is the last between Joey and Peggy unless he agrees to get a divorce. The need for decision creates meaning, and the sense of convergence that the "X"-shaped metaphor contains stresses the concentration of being into a decisive moment that determines the meaning. In other words, the technical shape of Updike's fiction creates the shape of its meaning.

If the geometric properties of the "X" form lead to such intricate analysis, the algebraic implications direct one toward more intellectualized possibilities. The "X" structure signifies an unknown quality and a functional interchangeability. Joey's weekend at the farm is an effort to uncover the secret of life's failures, much in the manner of Peter Caldwell's personal inventory in his artist's loft. The secret in *Of the Farm* is in the land, in Joey's past, his women, and his vocation—and all these subtly join during the two-day visit to elicit paradoxical understanding and to send him back to the city with a unique freedom. Ultimately, the unknown quality is Joey himself; and he gains identity only in relation to others. In this respect, the analogy of the "X" as an interchangeable symbol is helpful. Joey combined with his mother and later with Joan have produced only wrong solutions; but, with Peggy, his problems are being solved correctly. Even in love relationships, one remains inauthentic, unidentified, until one locates himself in the company

of the truly sympathetic lover. That Joey has done, and that is why
he needs Peggy so desperately.

The novel depends vitally on the "X" format but no less importantly on a fundamental incongruity that develops through setting,
character confrontations, and fictive mood and tone. The mere jux-
taposition of city and country supplies a basic disharmony of locales.
The Manhattanites on the Pennsylvania farm do not fit, and flashes
of description reveal their displacement, such as the glance at Peggy,
barefoot with painted red toenails, hoeing clumsily in the garden
soil, or Joey himself, now a smooth Madison Avenue "adman,"
mowing the shaggy rural field. The incongruity grows through the
depicted inability of the mother and the new daughter-in-law to
commune, although they can communicate, and through the pre-
cociousness of the eleven-year-old stepson Richard, who speaks like
a self-conscious college freshman and whose language jars against
the natural environment.

Strangest of all is the dissonant effect of the lush, evocative, lyrical
prose joined to the blunt discovery of normally private areas. Joey
can speak quite crudely to his wife and joke about her used Tampax
while he is rhapsodizing about her beauty and about the old charm
of the countryside. The gross comment performs the trick of height-
ened contrast, but the whole phenomenon illustrates Updike's artistic method in almost all of his fiction. The mundane, even the
hitherto unspeakable (if any of that remains in the post-censorship
era), are rendered selectively significant because of the author's per-
suasion that life, and therefore art, consist of the acknowledgment
and utilization of the trivial, a coming to terms with the daily little
things.

The Woman and the Land

Updike works in *Of the Farm* with artistic forms that threaten at
any moment to explode and disintegrate, but he also counteracts
that impulse with a pervasive trick of metaphor that reestablishes
unity. A "gimmick" exists in most Updike novels: the futurism of
The Poorhouse Fair, the present tense of *Rabbit, Run*, the myth-realism
combination of *The Centaur*. Although this device is less spectacular
in *Of the Farm*, it appears in the analogy of woman and land. The
analogy matures along the three closely related lines of sexuality,
fertility, and security. The locus of each pole of the analogy is

specific: the woman is always Peggy, and the land is always the old parental farm property, while the other women of the story are antagonistic contrasts to the image. Joan appears as a cold and distant female (she now lives in Canada), even though she has borne Joey three children; and old Mrs. Robinson, Joey's mother, has a brittle barrenness about her person, although she is most intimately connected with the farm. The parental farmland, in turn, has an exclusive connotation for Joey. In his mind it stands apart from the actual sameness of the surrounding fields and pastures and maintains itself against the steady invasion of new highways and creeping suburbia. Although Updike moves from one pole of the metaphor to another, the obvious interest centers upon Peggy: she is a city girl (although originally from Nebraska—farming country) whose physical and emotional nature invites the analogy of the land. She is big, broad, sensual, impulsive—and voluptuous, a word the Updike carefully avoids, describes her well.

The sexual chords of woman and land are sounded early and echo throughout the book. The intercourse image is dominant, and Joey is the husband in the double sense: he is the keeper of the woman and of the soil. He muses, "My wife is wide, wide-hipped and long-waisted, and surveyed from above, gives an impression of terrain, of a wealth whose ownership imposes upon my own body a sweet strain of extension; entered, she yields a variety of landscapes." In the scene described earlier, Joey mows the hourglass-shaped piece of grass "in one ecstatic straight thrust, up the middle"; and, during the same afternoon's work, "The tractor body was flecked with foam and I, rocked back and forth on the iron seat shaped like a woman's hips . . . excited by destruction, weightless, discovered in myself a swelling which I idly permitted to stand, thinking of Peggy."

The fertility imagery is connected with Peggy, with the land, and with blood and rain. Joey returns from the supermarket to see his wife, bikini-clad, hoeing the garden, and says, "We stopped the car beneath the pear tree whose surviving limbs disproportionately put forth the full tree's burden of fruit." By metaphoric association, the ripeness of the tree enhances the woman's fertility. Joey, in fact, in a moment of intense love for Peggy, thinks impulsively that he would like to make her pregnant. Later on, as he finishes mowing the hourglass plot of grass, the rain begins to fall; and Updike describes the scene again through sexual-fertile images that invite transposition: "And now the rain, having taken one last

breath, sighed and subsided into the earth, gently at first, sweetly
. . . then with such steady relaxed force, pattering on my hat,
soaking my thighs, that the closed flowers bobbed beneath the
drumming and the grass, whipped, gleamed."

The woman-land metaphor works to give Joey his needed comfort
and security against the pain of his lost children and first wife and
against the threat of the past that his mother and the farm somehow
darkly embody. He comes from tense dialogue with his mother and
from the fields to the seclusion of the bedroom and his wife. "You
never should have left your mother's womb," Peggy tells him in
bed, and he agrees. Like Rabbit Angstrom, who wants to "bury
himself" in his mistress, Joey uses his wife's body as psychological-
physical escape.

Anguish, Freedom, and Responsibility

The novel is also the dramatized moment of a philosophical tenet:
the concept of the paradox of existential freedom. Updike prefixes
the story with the familiar quotation from Sartre: "Consequently,
when, in all honesty, I've recognized that man is a being in whom
existence precedes essence, that he is a free being who, in various
circumstances, can want only his freedom, I have at the same time
recognized that I can want only the freedom of others." If *Rabbit,
Run* exudes a Kierkegaardian *angst,* the fear of nil beneath a surface
of senseless being, *Of the Farm* deals with anguish in its existential
setting as the intellectual-emotional result of the tension between
individual freedom and social responsibility.

Updike is not necessarily using the quotation from Sartre as a
text for his story; in fact, he neatly underscores the weakness of the
existence-before-essence stance when he has Joey cynically state that
"Truth is constantly being formed from the solidification of illusions." Nevertheless, Joey is caught in the existential predicament,
stretched taut amidst the many demands around him and pinned
precisely (to use Updike's own image) at the intersection of the
conflicts. He has made his choice, and perhaps it was the existential
one: to leave wife and children for the woman and for the liberation
he thought he desired. Now, at the farm, he is faced with another
decision, one more subtle but hardly less significant: he must decide
whether to sell the farm after his mother's death and thereby to free
himself still further from the burden of the past, to deny his essence

in favor of existence in another dimension. True, he never does make the decision unequivocally—he lets things ride instead—but, in leaving his mother and returning to the city, he decides in effect after all against the past and toward an undefined, or ill-defined, future.

Even if his decision were clearly rendered, the conflict of responsibility and freedom that causes anguish, and the other situations that aggravate it, would still remain. Joey still loves Joan, as he confesses to his mother, and he also suffers from the loss of his children; but, on the other hand, leaving them for Peggy has been his step to freedom. The paradox of existential freedom, then, is that one never becomes unconditionally free. One is always free only from and to something or someone; the condition that promotes anguish is the responsibility to past and future that remains.

Das ewig Weibliche

The godless City of God, the fruitless search for the Holy Grail, and the myth of heaven and earth seem to clarify well Updike's first three novels; but he is not as mythologically inclined in *Of the Farm*. What one does find is an ironic version of the myth of the eternal female, as it relates to the earth mother (who is also the archetypal terrible mother), the *femme fatale*, and the unattainable woman. All of these are contained in the Eve archetype (Eve is the focus of the Lutheran pastor's sermon), and all of them gain significance in their effect upon the male.

Joey absorbs himself in the feminine complex, much as Rabbit Angstrom did, by refusing to compete in the middle-class, adult world. A dangerous maneuver for Joey, it traps him in a disintegrating kind of union with the three women from which he must painfully extricate himself. His mother, curiously perhaps, has embodied all three of the archetypal forms: she has been the earth mother ("of the farm"), *femme fatale,* and unattainable woman for him. Her role as earth mother was artificial and grew from her insistence upon rural life, for she wanted the farm and forced country living upon her unwilling husband and son. It is an ironic situation, for the proximity to the soil produced no fertility. Since husband and son did not want to farm, the rural life has been a barren waste and a frustration. Mrs. Robinson was also the seductive female for her young son. One of Joey's vivid childhood recollections is of the desirable mother: "I seemed to be in bed, and a tall girl stood above me, and her hair came loose from her shoulder and fell forward filling the air with a swift liquid motion, and hung there, as a wing edged with light, and enclosed me in a tent as she bent lower to deliver her goodnight kiss." In that sense, she was already the unattainable woman for him; and that role is reinforced by her wish for his vocation, that he become a poet. Joey has failed in being one; he has failed to please her and feels rejected by her.

As a result, he has sought his special kind of mother-surrogate in Joan and has suffered the same kind of defeat. His first wife was also aloof but ambitious for him; she was another woman on a pedestal whom he could not reach. But, with Peggy, Joey has at last the chance for a true marriage. The situation is fundamentally ironic, and the price that he must pay is very high. The irony resides in the fact that Peggy, the *femme fatale,* the "vulgar woman" who has also slept around, is the only one who has the instincts and understanding of a good wife. The eternal female of myth *(das ewig Weibliche),* with her seductive, destructive propensities, is here the one who heals and fulfills.

In the light of this background, the weekend at the farm can be seen as a decisive struggle. On the surface, it provides opportunity for Peggy and Joey's mother to become acquainted. Beneath, it is a fight for Joey between the two women. Although it is unjust to cast old Mrs. Robinson as the conscious villainess, she does use all the weapons in her arsenal—memories, maternal respect, family pride, religion, age, illness—to get what she wants. She wants really only a vindication of her way and interpretation of life, but that is what Joey cannot allow her; for to do so would destroy his own future. The conflict is, in a sense, D. H. Lawrence's *Sons and Lovers* all over again; but Updike's protagonist finds the woman who can outcharm the mother. Peggy is the seductress who helps Joey free himself not only from the "terrible mother" who kills her children with over-possessiveness, but also from the unattainable female who generates guilt about sexuality and male identity. For Peggy is a genuine earth mother, not an artificial one; as seductress or *femme fatale,* she leads Joey to the death of his old self, it is true, but also into the first full and satisfying relationship of his life. "I'm the first woman he's ever met who was willing to let him be a man," Peggy tells the old woman in anger; and, while that cliché justifies the cruel divorce and remarriage, it is also true.

Peggy is also the archetypal Eve, and the young Lutheran pastor strengthens that identification through his sermon. One should not take the homily altogether seriously—Updike has a penchant for satirizing theologians and preachers—and this sexist Sunday morning discourse takes too many unwitting comic turns to be meant as genuine religious proclamation. The sermon, however, does neatly outline Joey's dilemma and his possible solution. Eve is the helpmeet, the creature who draws man away from his preoccupation with infinity and death and who incites him to an act of faith—his acknowledgment of his humanity by living with compassion and kindness. Peggy is and does these things for Joey. She could be called inferior to him, as the pastor insists that women must be (Joey's mother says that Peggy is stupid); but she is also his superior since she has come to terms with existence in a way that none of the others has by utilizing the power of her womanliness. If she is the secondary temptress (after Lilith?) who has destroyed, by passion, the innocence of Eden, she is also equipped and eager to support her man in the world that opens up beyond the flaming sword. The act of faith she leads him to commit is identical with the step toward freedom that secular man must take. Joey must cut himself off from the security of the past (the mother, the land), assume the anguish of responsibility, and immerse himself in creating new meaning out of personal relationships.

Continuity and Closure

Through this interpretation, the conclusion of the novel becomes clear. Joey, having made the decision against the mother, offers a final gesture of kindness. He has mowed the field (and thus symbolically put his past in order) and must return to the city, for there his future and freedom wait. But he leaves his slowly dying mother with the kindness of an illusion, with a compassionate lie. "When you sell my farm, don't sell it cheap. Get a good price," his mother tells him from her bed. The farm is important. It is the earnest of her life's meaning, the solid symbol of her identity in a world of absolutes fading fast. Joey writes, "I must answer in our old language, our only language, allusive and teasing, that with conspiratorial tact declared nothing and left the past apparently unrevised"—*apparently* unrevised, but everything has changed. Joey replies, in the last words of the book. "*Your* farm? . . . I've always thought of it as our farm." He willingly plays out the charade, not to deceive but to comfort, and that is an act of his new, complex responsibility.

Chapter Eight
The Music School: Strange Chords and Strained Cords

When you look   kool uoy nehW
into a mirror   rorrim a otni
it is not   ton si ti
yourself you see,   ees uoy flesruoy
but a kind   dnik a tub
of apish error   rorre hsipa fo
posed in fearful   lufraef ni desop
symmetry.   .yrtemmys

—"Mirror"

Reflections of Reality

Updike's third collection of short stories, *The Music School,* represents a continuation of his characteristic artistry but also a radical departure in theme and mood from his previous fiction. Published in 1966 and containing twenty stories orginally written for *The New Yorker* between 1962 and 1966, *The Music School* projects a brittleness and a neurotic insight into adult problems that the earlier collections only suggested. But Updike's personal vision has not moved off-center in any way; he has, in effect, done what the critics have been suggesting that he do: abandoned the boyhood context and moved on to the more painful and immediate actuality of urban and suburban sophistication. Olinger has yielded further to Manhattan and New England; and the high-school locale and young-marrieds milieu give way to the dissection of ailing and failed marriages among the worldly-wise. The characters have grown older and are now mostly in their thirties; they are professionally and economically successful but at some impasse in their personal and social lives. The adultery motif is stronger than any other throughout the book.

Many of these tales culminate not in the recognition of grace (as in *The Same Door*) nor of comforting design (as in *Pigeon Feathers*) but, instead, in a melancholy realization of failed or missed moments that could have changed one's life. A sense of "too late" and a corresponding mood of regret and sometimes remorse indwells *The Music School* stories. But the situations of loss neither rise to the nobility of tragedy nor sink into the paralysis of despair. Grief is something one learns to accommodate and assimilate, and the significant moment of many of the stories is the prosaic step of the protagonist toward learning to live with his loss. These are tales of adjustment and compromise; the artistic accomplishment is in making credible and absorbing the recovery of a personal equilibrium. Although the gift of grace is not emphasized, the fact that one *can* effect a recovery, that one can go on after all, is a gift in itself that the veteran of life accepts as such; therefore, in an important way, the people in *The Music School* move through alienation into a healing participation in things.

Updike depends in *The Music School* less crucially on the inherent qualities of memory and myth and much more on the evocative power of his own language. His metaphors become self-identical and self-contained, which is to say that, instead of reflecting some extrinsic reality, they project mainly themselves. The author's method is to create metaphors of metaphors—which does not mean that his fiction is twice removed from reality. Instead, a reciprocal cancellation process occurs whereby, as when one places two mirrors face to face, one achieves an illusion of infinity and therewith a model *for* infinity. This achievement is the reward for the artist's faith in pure form. When he pursues the potential of imaginative language into its deeper dimensions, he is blessed with a sudden reappearance of reality that the frontal assault would never compel.

The Maples' Marriage

Ten of the stories in *The Music School* have to do with marriage relationships (eleven, if one includes the premarital situation of "The Morning") that are clouded by approaching or realized divorces or affairs or both. Two tales, "Giving Blood" and "Twin Beds in Rome," return to Richard and Joan Maple of "Snowing in Greenwich Village." They have moved to New England, they now have four children, and their nine years of matrimony have nurtured mistrust and discord. In the first story, they are on their way to Boston to donate blood at a hospital for Joan's ailing aunt; and they fill the thiry-mile drive with accusations against each other. But, once in the hospital, the shared experience of giving blood draws them together and repairs the breach. Afterwards they eat lunch together like a pair of lovers at a roadside restaurant, but that mood is broken when Richard discovers he hasn't enough money to pay for the meal. The animosity returns, and they are estranged once more.

The return into the past is not just the nostalgic attempt to capture a childhood security, as the characters in the Olinger stories often strive to do. Instead, the relative vulnerability and innocence of the couple as they face a harmless but elemental operation reduces them to a momentary childhood that helps them see afresh themselves and their marriage. Updike emphasizes the childhood images: Richard sees the two of them as Hansel and Gretel; he fights the impulse to giggle; they recount their adolescent diseases; Joan's hair seems to Richard as if combed by her mother; Joan thinks the plastic sacks filled with their blood look like doll pillows. These thoughts constitute not only personal memory but a measure of collective memory also. "Mr. and Mrs. Maple were newly defined to themselves," Updike writes. The unique act of being bled, bringing them close to the mystery of their own bodies, renews the freshness and clarity and yet the mystery of all childhoods, of the preinitiation period of life. This return to the past is moral in that it gives the worldlywise Maples a sudden chance to see their contentious and bored adulthood through naïve eyes and effects their own condemnation of their present selves by their past ones.

The psychological deepening of the fictive moment into myth occurs through the sacrifice motif. Although the blood-giving is essentially an act of compassion (reluctant compassion on Richard's part), Updike weights the description with sacrificial images. Most directly, he refers to "the mystical union of the couple sacrificially bedded together." Blood and sacrifice have always been closely connected in human religiosity, and that combination, even in the secular setting, allows the story its mythic awareness. Yet, because it is a secular context, the myth becomes demythologized at once. Why are the Maples sacrificing and to whom? It is a sacrifice of themselves to each other. Since that is a possible interpretation of marriage in the western Christian tradition, the sacrifice does not seem all that momentous. And yet, in a society that has abandoned the transcendent realm, the organic quality of marriage—the mutual sacrifice resulting in a greater something, in a spiritual union— also fades; and remaining is a liaison of mutual destruction. The Maples' being bled simultaneously images the enervating effect they have on each other. The marriage effort has become the attempted sacrifice of the other to oneself, and thus the sacrificial subject and object have shifted. The underlying and perhaps even subliminal realization of this struggle for personal assertion shapes the psychological and mythical facets of the narrative moment.

Updike extends that moment into the future by projecting the motifs of childhood and sacrifice into a coherent pattern of judgment. Toward the end of the story, the Maples have eased, because of the hospital experience, into a lovers' mood at the restaurant; but Richard dispels it when, finding only a dollar in his wallet, he succumbs to a self-pitying rage at the frustrating ineffectiveness of his suburban existence that his near-empty billfold represents. The childish action ruins the precarious illusion of affection, but Joan does not respond in kind. "We'll both pay," she says quietly; and, although she refers to the restaurant bill, the meaning applies still better to their marriage. They *will* both pay, both sacrifice, if they stay together; and that payment is their self-inflicted condemnation. The Maples can look forward not to the gift of grace but only to their intrinsic judgment.

"Twin Beds in Rome," which continues the marital dilemma of the Maples, suggests another solution beyond the punishment of continuing in an unhappy union. Richard and Joan (no mention is made of their children) have traveled to Rome in an effort to give their faltering marriage a salutary change; but what happens there is not amorous adventure. On their first full day, they take a sightseeing walk; and, since Richard's shoes hurt him, he buys new ones. Then he has a stomach cramp so severe that they must return to the hotel, where he naps for an hour and recovers. Somehow the brief illness becomes the event that relaxes the tension of the marriage; although it does not reconcile them, it liberates them individually. They enjoy their newly felt personal freedom and their Roman vacation, and at the end Richard begins to fall in love with his wife again.

"Twin Beds in Rome" commences where "Giving Blood" concludes. One notices especially the progression of the judgment motif: the judgment has been made; the couple accepts it; and, in the act of acceptance, each suddenly finds a new freedom *from* the other. The act gives new import to the sacrifice theme. Now, it seems, when the Maples are ready to offer up the marriage itself, they locate a new value in the marriage union. What has been wrong, one sees in retrospect, is that the Maples, with typical modern introspection, objectified their marriage and transformed it into a thing with a problematic life of its own, instead of recalling that marriage is a most intimate meeting of persons designed to enhance and deepen love rather than destroy it. They have sought the solution to their dilemma in the mechanics of matrimony as an institution, rather than in a checking of their own failings as partners in the sacrament, but Updike finally has them see each other as vital metaphors of themselves instead of continuing the search for an illusory objective second image. This metaphor of metaphor in action leads the couple out of a marital dead end into personal freedom.

The title also hints at their progress: they have twin beds for the first time, here in the city of sensuality and passion, and forfeit the comforting habit of the double bed. Richard's illness, next, is the mild trauma that both signals and precipitates the liberation act. He is the weaker of the pair, and his hypersensitivity and grown-up childishness define their union; Joan indulges him and confirms her position of strength, while he employs her as the object of his tantrums and other irresponsibilities. Each needs the other to persist in his private neurosis, and the marriage is indeed based on a sickness.

Richard's psychosomatic stomach-ache becomes the fitting irritation that frees them. Like their marriage, the pain is a nagging and not quite definable one that exhausts Richard, just as the marital liaison saps both their energy. Just how the incident of the cramp releases the Maples to their individual freedom is unclear, and apparently the couple does not understand it either. But it does serve as the first event that takes their intent vision away from themselves and their entrapment; once they begin exploring Rome, they are drawn out of themselves, away from their preoccupation, and into a relatively healthy humor.

"The Music School"

A tentative approach to the inevitable sorrows and losses of daily life is expressed in an image from the title story of the collection, "The Music School," in which the hero sees and hears "hints of another world, a world where angels fumble, pause, and begin again." Updike's people are not angels, and the ideal that the concept of angels elicits is lost in the pedestrian detail of pragmatic striving and petty strife. Thus the "music school," where the young innocents play groping tunes on instruments they cannot handle, is not an image of divine harmony but a pathos-ridden paradigm of the exercises their elders practice in learning life's notes.

The music school is life. The thirtyish father, suspended in adultery and possible divorce, actually does participate through his daughter in her initiation into the musical mysteries; but the experience does not guide him toward any knowledge of universal design or metaphysical verities—only back in upon himself: "Vision, timidly, becomes percussion, percussion becomes music, music becomes emotion, emotion becomes—vision. Few of us have the heart to follow this circle to its end." The story itself progresses according to this pattern. In the first section, the protagonist describes a change in the Communion ritual as he had heard it described by a young priest the night before; that is the "vision." In the second section, he refers to a startling newspaper item: a casual acquaintance of his, a computer expert, has been mysteriously shot and killed; this is the "percussion" of life. In the third section, "percussion becomes music": he depicts the basement of the Baptist Church where his daughter and the other children practice their faltering lessons on the various instruments. That music leads to "emotion" in the fourth section, where the narrator relates the substance of the novel he never wrote about a computer programmer who dies, romantically, from the strain of an adulterous affair. This unlucky bloom of the narrator's imagination deeply affects him, and it prompts the renewed vision of the fifth section, one in which the themes of Eucharist, music, adultery, and suffering coalesce to form an original metaphor of the world as Host. Like the tough wafer of the revised Communion sacrament, the world "must be chewed" to insure one's active involvement; it dare no longer simply melt in the mouth as one passively absorbs it.

"The Music School" has no plot, no narrative continuity; it borrows the format of the informal essay but is fiction. How then are the motifs organized to produce an artistic integrity? For one, at the end of the tale, the narrator suggests that a "coda" is fitting to conclude the piece, hinting at a direct musical analogy. One can observe thematic variations, contrapuntal effects, and a polyphoniclike manipulation of motifs that strengthen the parallel to musical composition. The eating motif, for example, is mentioned in the initial section in the description of the Communion wafer; it is varied and continued in the second section: the computer expert is murdered while he sits at the breakfast table. In the third section it appears briefly in the self-denial of the daughter (she doesn't ask her father for candy), and in the final section it is developed through the narrator's memory of the Lutheran Eucharist celebration, a consubstantial eating of the body of Christ, the image of which is transferred at the end of the metaphor of the world that must be chewed to be fully experienced.

Or, again, the polyphonic use of themes is illustrated in the adultery trope. The celibacy of priests and the chastity of nuns in the initial section contrast with the brothel metaphor of the second. Within the context of childhood innocence in the third section, the narrator abruptly confesses his unfaithfulness; and, in the fourth, he imagines the hero of his unwritten novel to be dying of sexual guilt. In the last section, the reference to the role of persisting sexuality in failed marriages restates the trope in a discursive form. These themes are then mingled and merged, as in a musical composition, throughout the different sections. For example, the murdered computer expert becomes the passionate adulterous hero of the unwritten novel, and the reported detail of the programmer's death (he dies at the feet of his children) is transformed into the final image of the story, when the narrator's child comes to him from her lesson, and he writes, "her pleased smile, biting her lower lip, pierces my heart, and I die (I think I am dying) at her feet." Or the wafer that melts too soon serves as an analogy to explain why the narrator never wrote his novel: "the moment in my life it was meant to crystallize dissolved too quickly," just as it leads him to consider the necessity of harsh experiences (the tough wafer) for successfully encountering the unsentimental modern world.

A magnificent scene in the final section returns the reader to the guiding quotation and clarifies the overriding intention of the story. As the narrator sat, the previous night, with the priest and other friends, "a woman entered without knocking; she had come from the lawyers, and her eyes and hair were flung wide with suffering, as if she had come in out of a high wind. She saw our black-garbed guest, was amazed, ashamed perhaps, and took two backward steps. But then, in the hush, she regained her composure and sat down among us." She is like the music school angels who "fumble, pause, and begin again,"—and that describes also how Updike's painfully married people carry on in their dislocated society. They agonize, they are without direction, but they do not give up. They experiment and practice with the few given entities of their being, like the composer of music and like the "author" of the story himself; for they have, often, only the memory of grace (the recollection of the traditional Communion service), a precarious truce with the impersonal computer-culture about them, and the doubtful comfort of their continuing erotic vitality. But they maintain their courage and their wit; and, if they do not have the promise any longer of achieving finesse on life's instrument, they at least create a personal meaning in the act of trying.

"The Rescue"

In "The Rescue," the story immediately following "The Music School," Updike focuses on the disintegration of confidence in one's mate and the struggle to regain it through and in spite of the curse of self-consciousness. The setting is a new one for Updike (and one that he returns to later for a crucial sexual encounter of characters in *Couples*). Caroline Harris, a New England housewife, is with her son and husband at a New Hampshire ski resort. They are accompanied by Alice Smith, their divorcée neighbor, who, Caroline suspects, is sleeping with her husband. Riding up the ski lift with Alice, with the two males in the jolting chairs ahead of them, Caroline suffers the secret anger and jealousy of her unspoken accusation. She probes, therefore, for nuances of behavior that will betray Alice but finds nothing to confirm or assuage her fears. When the two Harris males ski away without waiting for the women, Caroline and Alice continue together down the "Greased Lightning" slope that frightens Caroline, a novice skier. Midway down the hill they come upon an accident: an older woman has hurt her leg in a fall and lies in the snow with her daughter kneeling at her side. Alice and Caroline remain with the woman while the daughter goes for help. In that span of time, while they are waiting for the rescue, Caroline watches her neighbor's fussy behavior during this mild emergency and decides that her husband could not, after all, "love anyone so finicking." When the rescue party arrives, she skies off smoothly, better than ever before, to her exonerated mate.

In reality, Caroline has solved nothing; she has not proved or disproved the existence of an affair. But she has convinced herself of her husband's innocence, at least for the time being; and her conviction is more important, for the time being, than the factual truth. It is more important, in Updike's context of fragile and broken marriages, because it takes a gesture of trust to create a truthful situation. One trusts, in other words, not because the partner is necessarily trustworthy but because such an attitude is the only one that allows for a sane and reasonably civilized relationship.

But even the impulse to trust cannot be generated in the extremely self-conscious atmosphere of modern marriage, and it is appropriate that Caroline Harris overcomes her suspicions and regains trust through a situation that demands forgetfulness of self. In the unself-consciousness that a moment of kindness and concern brings, she gains an assurance, illusory though it may be, that will help her to encounter her husband and marriage—at least to a degree—naturally again. She is one who, faltering toward divorce (skiing dangerously down the treacherous slope), finds the proper balance at the last moment. That she glides confidently and eagerly toward her husband, her skis feeling right for the first time, implies that she has also discovered a style of life before it is too late.

The title "The Rescue" carries an ambiguous but not an ironic connotation. The central physical action of the story, the rescue of the injured woman on the mountain side, parallels Caroline's own deliverance. It is revelation via metaphor; Caroline "did not as a rule like self-pitying women, but here in this one she seemed to confront a voluntary dramatization of her own inner sprain." In watching the other, she sees herself reflected; in helping her, she begins to heal herself. There is no implication that she mends her marital situation, for her doing so might be too much to expect in the pilgrims' progress toward divorce. But she does regain her sense of fidelity, the healthiest antidote she could possess against her husband's suspected or actual unfaithfulness.

"My Lover Has Dirty Fingernails"

"My Lover Has Dirty Fingernails" takes place in a psychoanalyst's office in a large city (New York?) and presents a feint-and-parry account of one session involving the doctor and his female patient. The story works consciously with the modern cliché of the emotional transference: the patient's falling in love with the analyst. The woman (married but unnamed in the story) is in the process of giving up her lover and is apparently visiting the psychiatrist to ease herself through the crisis. As the title and the dialogue during the session reveal, her problem is the need to fight off an acute fear of death, and her subconsciously dictated strategy is her involvement with an earthy man who is, for her, a counteraction to the sterile and mortality ridden city atmosphere.

But the emerging diagnosis is really only the superficial content of the tale; more important is the artistic handling of the super-aware excursion into the mind—one for which Updike uses a neat and simple device. He has the analyst distract the woman by objectifying the affair through the dissecting conversation and by shifting her attention subtly to himself. Most impressively, one experiences his success through the changes of perspective in the story. The woman's point of view appears throughout most of the narrative; but, toward the end, it gradually becomes the doctor's. In the final paragraph, the woman has left the office, and the doctor remains alone as the focus of interest.

The reader is left, nonetheless, at the end of the story with the feeling that the woman's "cure" may be worse than the neurosis. The doctor *is* winning, as he realizes; he remains coolly professional during his confrontation with his patient; but what he offers her, though it may be equilibrium, is made to seem less than the passion she is sacrificing. "At least I loved somebody who loved me, no matter how silly you make the reasons for it seem," she tells the analyst near the end of the hour. When one compares her sentiment to the final scene of the story—after the woman has gone, the psychiatrist "subsided into the tranquil surface of the furniture"—one finds that there may be, after all, a strange kind of affirmation in the chaotic lives of Updike's couples. They are still struggling with identity and love; they have not yet become part of the furniture; and, if their adulterous affairs are attempts to know others so that they will not know themselves too well, they escape thereby some of the dehumanization that threatens urban man. The psychoanalytically induced self-knowledge is not a final answer: it is only a diagnosis; and passion must find a new mode of expression that provides both self-forgetfulness and legitimate freedom.

Other Marriage Tales: Introspection, Passion, and Separation

The other six marriage stories compose variations on the same introspection-passion-separation theme. In "Avec la Bébé-sitter," an American family moves suddenly from Boston to the French Riviera to escape the husband's entanglement in an affair. On the sensual Mediterranean, where one would expect, perhaps, a seductive French governess who corrupts the marriage of innocent Americans, one finds instead a rather dowdy middle-aged widow who tries to help the family regain its composure. As baby sitter, she exposes the family's childishness: the husband and wife, instead of solving their marital problems, allow themselves to be taken care of—and this strange ménage is a symptom of a destructive liaison rather than a cure for it.

The epistolary "Four Sides of One Story," a quasi-modernization of the Tristan and Iseult legend, exists, like *The Centaur,* in a tension between the accepted unbelievability of folklore and the more insistent realism of modern fiction. But, where *The Centaur* takes advantage of the incongruity by making ancient myth and contemporary narrative elucidate each other, "Four Sides of One Story" offers no real justification for the baggage of the legend. Using it is merely a clever gimmick, although the story, as is always the case with Updike, contains moments of authentic feeling. The characterization is, however, too radically limited by what one knows of the folklore personae, and Updike does not manage to make his characters either figures of independent substance or complements to the legendary ones.

"The Stare" and "The Morning" present parallel narratives. In the first, the speaker returns to Manhattan to search for his former lover at their old haunts. He has ended the affair that had had both their households in turmoil; now, months later, he hopes to find her again. The story is built on the counteraction between repetitive image and sustained anticipation. His lover's curious stare, the most striking feature she possesses, is the image he needs to reencounter; and Updike always balances the man's recollection of that glance with his frustration at missing it now in his persistent New York search. Duped by some trait he had thought was hers alone, he follows look-alikes of his mistress; but he always comes close only to see not her stare but the unfamiliar face of an utter stranger. In this story the basic thematic sequence (introspection-passion-separation) is reversed and becomes separation-passion-introspection. The isolation from the lover induces new desire, but it leads not to fulfillment—only to pathetic self-confrontation.

"Love begins in earnest when we love what is limited," is the theme of "The Morning," and the text is given elaborate substance by an artistic concentration on color. Color not only forms moods here but also creates actual states of being in the sole "premarital" story of the collection. The protagonist (who reminds one of Dostoevski's Underground Man) is a young student—"of what, he had forgotten"—in the big city who has just been deserted by his lover, a nurse, because he will not marry her. The girl has left him, and he has only the sensuous-sensual memories; but she has left him so recently that memory is still part reflex, and he lives in half-anticipation of her return. The stages of his desire for her assume various colors: the white of her uniform connotes a professional purity that excites him; the blue, green, and brown of her off-duty clothes (some still in his closet) represent the normal world outside that she channeled to him; and the tan, blonde, and pink of her nakedness hold the remembered adventure and intimacy of their love.

Because the nurse is the center of his existence, her absence establishes the sense of the void which the reader feels along with the grieving student. The point of view never leaves the student's mind or the confines of the shabby apartment. This use of a restricted center of consciousness perspective reveals how utterly vacuous the student's daily life without his lover must be. The story reinforces its emotional effect through two expanded puns. The one is the concept of the nurse. "My nurse," the young man calls her; and, while he means it affectionately, it also hints at the psychological sickness he endures: he needs her as a substitute for the city outside. She has been the mediator and buffer between the world and him; and, in relating to her, he finds his surrogate and fulfillment for all responsibilities and desires. Because the girl is healthier than he is, she leaves him; and the consequence informs the story's title, "The Morning." The morning, that time of day when the nurse comes to him to minister to him, is now "the mourning"; for she has gone, and he is in fresh sorrow, still disbelieving his loss and only beginning to absorb its magnitude. Passion-separation-introspection is the sequence in this story, but their effect on the protagonist is nearly simultaneous.

The remaining marriage story, "Harv is Plowing Now," has a partial Olinger setting and units the now-dominant marital theme with the childhood reminiscence. The story moves through fictive personal recollection into universal history: the man who has grown up on the Pennsylvania farm and suffered through—still suffers— the effects of an affair sees his life stratified like the exposed layers of an archaeological find. At the bottom is the mythic substance of the collective unconscious, compressed in the childhood memory of Harv, the neighboring farmer, plowing his field in the recurrent spring ritual of fertility and rebirth. At the top are the myriad hours and days of mechanical time passing; and, in the middle, providing its own kind of existence, is the experience of the affair, past and yet present.

Updike makes the analogy with archaeological exploration (actually a multi-directed metaphor) work by playing with motif-phrases as in "The Music School." The great Noachic flood and the "inundation" of the love affair, the excavation of Ur and Harv's plowing, the digging at the desert find and the probing into the old affair on a bonfire-lit beach at night—these, grasped in configurational form, provide the sense of precariousness of one's sojourn in time and space but also one's fundamental security. Passion has failed, but the natural rites and one's personal survival are intact. The farmer plows, the archaeologist digs, the artist probes the memory—and all do so to effect some sort of resurrection. The artist recovers an incident from his personal past (an operation not nearly as trivial as it seems) and gives it a permanent place by locating it not in literal space-time but in metaphor.

History and fact, in other words, must deal with the finite and with the temporary, like the love affair that forms the content of the story; but the fictive transformation brings about something lasting. What matters to the self-conscious artist is not that the event literally took place but that he can use it as a device for structuring his universe. The experience of the affair may be like an artifact (as Updike renders it in this tale) to be carefully exhumed from the memory and the unconscious, but the story *about* the experience also possesses its archaeological parallel. Fiction is the artifact that remains fiction until somewhere and sometime the reader strikes the solid truth of metaphoric recognition and uncovers a relationship to himself that helps to order his being.

People from the Family Album

The other nine stories in *The Music School* collection fit no particular pattern. Taken together, they give one the sensation of paging through an old photo album—a pastime Updike is said to enjoy—and stopping here and there to study striking or eccentric characters. Three of the stories return, in degrees, to the old Olinger setting. "In Football Season," the first narrative of the book, has echoes of the high-school scenes in *The Centaur* and is a sharply evocative mood story. "The Family Meadow," in contrast, is mellow, like the fading pictures in the album. It describes a family reunion in a rural enclave of New Jersey (Olinger relatives are in attendance), and the mellowness grows against the awareness of accelerating change. Both the promise and the threat of the future pervade the reunion. The provocative teenaged Cousin Karin, half-Italian, in her tight, white Levis embodies the obliteration of the old family lines and the exciting new shapes that appear. The new houses of the building project on the fringes of the meadow, with their "bastard design," hold mainly the threat not of heterogeneity but of mass-produced uniformity like that depicted in *The Poorhouse Fair*.

The conflict in "The Family Meadow" is basically between nature and civilization; but, in the final story, "The Hermit," Updike purifies and climaxes that antagonism. Stanley, a middle-aged school janitor and part-time laborer for his contractor brother, chooses to withdraw from the village to live in the ruins of an old farmhouse surrounded by fields now reclaimed by the forest. His retreat into nature is also a mystical growth, but it seems to his convention-bound relatives and friends that he is degenerating from eccentricity into sheer craziness. A bit like Ike McCaslin in Faulkner's *The Bear*, Stanley must cast off the extraneous accumulations of society to experience nature totally—to become, as he feels it, "a thoroughly silver man." But his ritual purification is much more radical than Ike's: Stanley smashes his mirror, rejects visitors, stops reading, and bathes daily in his tiny, cold stream. His freedom at last undoes him when, returning naked from his bath one day, he surprises an eavesdropper, a young boy and potential disciple, and chases the terrified youngster through the woods to reassure him, not to assault or punish him. Three days later he is taken away forcibly as a menace to society, for his intent was never understood.

This ending may seem like a surprising last word from Updike, the advocate of enduring the middle-class life of quiet frustration, until one understands that eccentricity is a kind of vocation. It dawns on Stanley that to be a hermit is his calling; it is what he has been instinctively preparing himself for. Indeed, in *The Music School* other eccentrics figure in other tales; and the Indian (in the second story entitled "The Indian") provides a contrast to Stanley the hermit's egression. The Indian has moved out of nature into the New England town of Tarbox; he inhabits the village, jobless and yet proprietary, an enigmatic degeneration of his forebears but a silent judge of the moral heritage and present manners of the town. His vocation is his otherness.

The eccentric in "A Madman," the fourth story in *The Music School,* is Mr. Robinson, the self-appointed guide to a young American, who is newly arrived in Oxford to study English literature, and to his pregnant wife. Mr. Robinson, a humanist antique, is a walking and endlessly talking repository of poetry and impractical knowledge who attaches himself to the innocent Americans; rather than helping them find the flat they need, he conducts them (to their confusion and exasperation) through the cultural riches of the old university town. The tour is not just a matter of poor timing: the old man is obsolete even in Oxford, a slightly dotty relic of learning in a world that, perhaps to its misfortune, has passed him by.

"At a Bar in Charlotte Amalie" has an extensive catalogue of eccentrics. The Virgin Islands tourist setting allows for the gathering of strange characters in the bar. A scenic story with a deceptive forward movement, everything in it—language, gesture, description—is purposeful innuendo, to express the subtlety of sexual maneuvering among strangers. When at least two liaisons develop by the end, one recognizes that they have been in the making all along. The homosexual from Queens, although not quite the protagonist, is the focal point, the catalyst of the action, and the grotesque mediator between the straight world and a sub-world that exists as much in a collective unconscious as it does in the physical locale of the bar. This story uses the psychic stuff of Freud, Jung, and Sacher-Masoch; people wear their favorite aberrations like the latest fashion. That they are portrayed not as freaks but as credible personalities makes their behavior all the more disturbing. They are like Updike's quiet, middle-class neurotics suddenly put on Expressionistic display; their condition is rendered brutally public, so that they appear both pathetic and frightening.

"The Christian Roommates," Updike's only Harvard story to date, has Hub Palamountain, a young skeptic from Oregon, as its eccentric. He is the despair of Orson Ziegler, his proper South Dakota roommate, for Hub's unorthodox views and practices nearly unbalance Orson during their nerve-wracking freshman year in Cambridge. The irony of the tale is in the unusual opportunity that Hub presents to Orson: Hub could *be* his roommate's Harvard education, but Orson has already planned his life so meticulously and staidly that he never even sees the possibility; therefore, he receives only training and not a genuine education there. In this story the maverick has more humanity and compassion than the conventional pillar of the community. Hub is a wise fool, one who muddles through the irrationality of the age because he himself is comfortably balmy and not a neurotic struggling to locate some normalcy in himself or his surroundings.

It seems, at first, that "The Dark" concerns an insomniac fighting a case of nerves as he tries to find sleep. One then discovers that he is incurably ill (probably of lung cancer, for it is obliquely described) and that his sleeplessness, naturally enough, arises from a fear of death. The title refers to the agonizing loneliness of his present situation and also to the impending end of life, including his unanswered questions about immortality. His sleep at last is also a prefiguring of death: to "slip, blissfully, into oblivion" is an image for the nightly rest he seeks and for the death he anticipates.

Through the Mirror

Updike prefaces *The Music School* with lines from Wallace Stevens's poem, "To the One of Fictive Music." With an emphasis on the intricate interrelationships of nature, art, and love, the selection (like much of Stevens's verse) verbalizes a poetic entelechy. The subject-object dichotomy of one's creatureliness can be resolved in the act of love when that experience is articulated in a poetic celebration of it. In loving, one overcomes self-consciousness; but, in the poetic shaping of the experience, one gains a measure of esthetic distance without dissolving the experience itself. If it is true, as Sartre has said, that the ultimate evil lies in making abstractions out of concrete things, then Updike must be praised for trying the opposite. In naming and describing the adultery, the betrayal, the necessary separation, he tames the abstraction and makes it less terrible, makes it what it is in individual terms, and allows one to deal with it individually.

Updike's total vision seems less entelechial than Stevens's and more eschatological. One strives to see through the mirror to the Other. To say this is not just to substitute a theological concept for a philosophical one. The actualizing moment of entelechy is not the same as eschatological faith, and Updike's fiction drives distinctly toward the latter. Since this book is not the place to discuss Updike's theological vision, suffice it to say that he has one; and even in *The Music School,* when his people are touching uncertain chords, they are playing a composition that has already been written. A faith in divinity lingers even in the efforts of self-consciously secular man.

Chapter Nine
Couples: Tristan and Don Juan in Tarbox

> Their universe did not deserve their vows.
>
> —from "Room 28"

Sex and the "New Morality"

Couples seems to be Updike's answer to the critics who have frequently wondered publicly when he would write a "big" novel. In terms of concept and physical format, at least, it is an ambitious work (over 450 pages) that focuses on ten married pairs living in Tarbox, Massachusetts. Yet it was not, on the whole, received positively by the book reviewers. Its sexual attitudes and expressions were called sophomoric; its images overblown, its dialogue overwritten; its characters dull and virtually indistinguishable; its action erratic and unfulfilled.[1] Nevertheless, this novel was the third sensation that Updike created, after *Rabbit, Run* and *The Centaur.* The explicit yet poetically written sex scenes and the liberal use of formerly taboo language caused *Couples* to be treated as both a reflection and a generator of the postcensorship literary atmosphere. It remained on the best-seller lists for a good half-year following its early 1968 publication. As Updike himself laconically explained his purpose in a news magazine interview, "There's a lot of dry talk around about love and sex being somehow the new ground of our morality. . . . I thought I should describe the ground and ask, is it entirely to be wished for?"[2]

Updike's fictitious Tarbox is a small town in Plymouth County, Massachusetts, almost on the Atlantic Ocean and twenty-two miles southeast of Boston. Nine of the ten couples in the story already inhabit Tarbox at the start of the novel; they are middle-class to upper-middle-class members of the community; they are, on the average, in their mid-thirties; and most of them have children. Piet Hanema, who comes closest to being an individual protagonist, is a thirty-five-year-old building contractor of Dutch descent; he and his wife Angela have two small daughters. Piet is having an affair early in the novel with Georgene Thorne, whose husband Freddy is a dentist in Tarbox and who is also a kind of Lord of Misrule at parties. Piet's partner in the construction business is Matt Gallagher, a puritanical Catholic whose wife Terry has an affair with her pottery teacher, an older man who is not part of the group. Piet also sleeps eventually with Bea Guerin, whose husband Roger is independently wealthy and doesn't need to work. Two other sets of couples have interrelationships of various sorts. Of these, Frank and Janet Appleby and Harold and Marcia Smith (the other couples call the four the Applesmiths) trade spouses for a time, while the Jewish pair Ben and Irene Saltz and airline pilot Eddie Constantine and his wife Carol ("the Saltines"—Piet also sleeps with Carol) have a liaison that includes homosexual impulses. A bit on the fringes of this group are a ninth couple: the Korean nuclear physicist John Ong and his American wife Bernadette.

Into this group comes a tenth couple from Cambridge, research biologist Ken Whitman and his pregnant wife Foxy. The Whitmans hire Piet to renovate the house they have bought close to Tarbox Bay, and Piet's frequent presence at the house leads to an affair with Foxy. He sleeps with her during the months of her pregnancy (and gradually gives up Georgene) and continues to do so soon after the baby is born. Foxy becomes pregnant again, this time by Piet; and, when it becomes apparent that something must be done, they arrange through Freddy Thorne to visit a Boston abortionist. Freddy's price, before the abortion takes place, is a night with Angela Hanema. The abortion is successful, and no one is the wiser until some time later Georgene, in a fit of jealousy, tells Ken Whitman of the affair and the abortion. Ken and Foxy separate, and Foxy goes to the Virgin Islands. Angela and Piet also separate, and eventually both couples are divorced. Piet sells his share in the construction business to his partner, marries Foxy at last, and the two move to Lexington, where Piet becomes a building inspector.

Such a sketch by no means conveys the power of the novel or even the total scope of the action, merely its skeletal structure. For instance, the second chapter, "Applesmiths and Other Games," does not focus on Piet and Foxy at all but on the double affair among the Smiths and Applebys. Nor does this summary indicate the importance of the many parties among the couples, of the family scenes involving children, of the destruction of the Tarbox Congregational Church by fire, or of the fine stream-of-consciousness passages that fill in background action.

The Topography of Time

Although the architecture of temporality is not as immediately evident in *Couples* as in *The Centaur,* it is just as fundamental to the later novel. *Couples* is a static novel, yet Updike has aligned this narrative more directly to a historical epoch than any of his other fiction except *Rabbit Redux.* Much of the action occurs in 1963, during the final year of the John F. Kennedy presidency; and the action is, in fact, dramatically punctured by the news of his assassination. References are made also to Kennedy and the Cuban missile crisis, to Kennedy and the steel industry, to tensions between Arabs and Israelis, and to Charles De Gaulle, Marina Oswald, and Ho Chi Minh—all events and names that appear in texts about modern national and international history. But Updike provides in addition a sense of cyclical time by celebrating the passing and return of the seasons and by the pattern of Foxy's two pregnancies.

All these dimensions of time are put into a mythological focus at the end of the fourth chapter by the declaration of Freddy Thorne (who is in bed with Angela) that this is "one of those dark ages that visits mankind between millennia, between the death and rebirth of gods, when there is nothing to steer by but sex and stoicism and the stars." This statement carries some of the feeling of a third kind of time, a sort of suspension that pervades *Couples.* It is the feeling of traveling in a vast universe without actually moving anywhere, a universe in which history is being made that the individual inhabitants do not mold and that has no apparent meaning for them.

Couples has a number of narrative climaxes, but the action (as in *The Music School* stories), because of Updike's peculiar use of time, abandons the traditional crescendo pattern of fiction. That pattern demands linearity, a movement from one moment to another to create suspense, anticipation, and fulfillment. Linearity is basic to the Christian sense of time, while the traditional opposite of linearity is circularity, as in Stoicism and certain pessimistic Medieval doctrines and Eastern philosophies. All are imaged, for example, in fortune's wheel: life's significant events repeat themselves in cyclical fashion. *Couples* projects a time beyond the linear and cyclical. The counterpart to the void that one feels in the novel is simultaneousness, in which many things happen at once and everything is now. This simultaneousness that fills the book is, of course, a mood rather than a physical fact; but, since Updike's people (and the reader) feel it so intensely, it is as important as the physical fact. To produce such simultaneousness, Updike uses memory and association effectively. For instance, the squeaking noise that the children's pet hamster makes on his exercise wheel—*eek eeik*—reminds Piet of the native Dutch that his parents spoke; thereby, three generations are instantaneously joined. Dreams also (mostly Piet's) distort conventional time and create the illusion of omnipresence.

An atmosphere of fulfillment, of *telos,* that pervades the novel characterizes yet another kind of temporality. It is not apocalyptic, not the terrible exhilaration of an age ending in chaos (unlike the tone of many another contemporary novel), and not utopian, as if a new, perfect age were arriving. It is a distinct recognition of *having* arrived in "the post-pill paradise" and of discovering that this age is as frustrating and chaotic as any other. But the discovery is not all negative. For example, Freddy Thorne, charmed by vice, learns with some wonder that he and his friends are "all put here to *humanize* each other"; and this responsibility becomes a new challenge to the Tarbox mentality. The society that confronts itself in ripeness, in a full sensuality of experience, becomes jaded by mere sensation and seeks a deeper intrinsic meaning.

The Composite Protagonist

A certain sameness marks the Tarbox pairs: they are all in their thirties, they all endure the combined banes and blessings of suburbia, they share an intellectual depth that is a good degree greater than the storied adult-American television mentality and they are all affected by the hypersexuality of the group. They tend to sound alike in their conversations, and they are also described through an imagery that does not dramatically individualize them. Nevertheless, such characterization does not reveal poor craftsmanship; since the couples are presented as an intimate group, it is entirely credible to make them more homogeneous than the aggregate of personae in most other novels. One sees Updike's couples as strongly influenced by each other, but beyond this interaction, Updike seems more concerned about interrelationships than about individuals. *Couples* is a novel about group dynamics rather than about the fortunes of a hero. It is a configurative novel in which the parts of individual personalities are joined to form a composite personality.

It is quite ironic that the disorder of adultery should be expressed in such precise balances and nuances of sexual activity, but that is how the novel interprets life. Modes of behavior with the least societal approval evolve a very stringent sort of order. Thus Piet and Georgene as lovers, and later Piet and Foxy, develop rituals of courtesy in this most intimate of relationships; and such orderliness extends to broader group interactions. The spouse-swapping between the Smiths and Applebys proceeds, in spite of the underlying bitchery, with great tact; and the confrontation between the Hanemas and Whitmans, after the affair is exposed, is diplomatic and formally correct. More interesting still is the elaborate pattern of extramarital liaisons in *Couples:* Piet, married to Angela, sleeps with Georgene (who is married to Freddy) but leaves her for Foxy (married to Ken); Freddy, who arranges the abortion for Foxy, reveals the affair to jealous Georgene, who betrays Piet and Foxy to Ken and brings about two divorces. (In the meanwhile, Freddy has also slept with Angela as his price for arranging the abortion.) All of the arrangements are precariously exact, in other words; and if one part goes awry the whole design collapses. This pattern creates the remarkable suspense that fills a static novel; one awaits the false move that will initiate the fall.

Social sex assumes an esthetic integrity through the fullness of Updike's style. Rather negatively, on the other hand, he has illustrated a sociological verity that citizens of the late twentieth century are reluctantly accepting: that the accent on humans living together—on the corporate, organic aspect of life—is at least as important as the old mythically reinforced concept of unfettered individuality. The composite protagonist of *Couples* represents an awareness of the changing emphasis in societal forms and attempts to use the chemistry of group interaction more than individual behavior as a metaphor of human nature and society at large.

The truth is also that these people do not live well together, and one wonders why they continue to seek one another's company. One reason stressed by the dialogue and imagery is that they function, in this complex secular era, as a substitute church. The implication is not, however, that Updike is suggesting a return to the "real" church as a panacea for social and personal ills; he is obviously illustrating a belief that man without God needs some sort of surrogate, and, perhaps, that a destructive fellowship is better than none at all. However that may be, the novel frequently borrows the image of the church to clarify the characters' motives and actions. For example, Angela, when discussing with her husband the jaded condition of the group, cites Freddy's analysis: "He thinks we're a circle. A magic circle of heads to keep the night out. He told me he gets frightened if he doesn't see us over a weekend. He thinks we've made a church of each other."

More convincing than such overt declarations are the couples' actions that become substitute ritual and sacramental behavior. Some of these are conscious travesties, such as the morbid moment at the dinner party following President Kennedy's assassination, when Freddy, slicing ham, says, "Take, eat. . . . This is his body, given for thee." The scene would be blasphemous if a situation sensitive to blasphemy still existed; but, as it is used in the novel, the crude Eucharistic joke masks the need of the couples for fellowship and communion at a time of grief and despair. A dinner party on the night of Kennedy's death is not merely a thoughtless vulgarity but also the fumbling attempt of spiritually helpless people to ease their desolation. Food, drink, and sexual excitement are ingredients in the ritual that induces intimacy; and intimacy is necessary to counteract the personal dislocation caused by the shock of the assassination.

The conflagration of the church at the end of the novel must also be understood in the light of its ironic ritualistic import. Many reviews of *Couples* chided Updike for the blatant symbolism of the fire: the burning edifice signifying the end of the church as an institution, destroyed by the hot passion of sex. Such an interpretation is far too simplistic. The destruction of the church, itself a crucial ritual moment, is the one event in the novel that brings the townspeople together in an act of common interest; it is an ironic moment because they are united by destruction rather than by creation.[3]

Tristan and Don Juan

If Freddy Thorne is a perverse priest who guides his little congregation in the celebration of sensuality, he and his "church" are still not necessarily dedicated to evil. Rather, the ecclesiastical analogy seems to argue either that secular man needs to assert and reinforce his identity through sacred ceremony or that the believer must learn to accommodate the reality of the body in his faith. Updike explores both of these possibilities in *Couples* by offering suggestions of the Tristan and Don Juan legends. Updike had used the Tristan legend in a modern setting in "Four Sides of One Story" in *The Music School* collection. Before the appearance of that tale, he had exhibited his interest in the Tristan and Don Juan types through his *New Yorker* review of Denis de Rougemont's *Love in the Western World* and *Love Declared*.[4] In this review, he used the Swiss critic's works as a basis for declaring his own views about *Eros*, marriage, the death wish, and the search for meaning.

It is quite obvious that *Couples* builds thoroughly and extensively on Updike's continuing concern—although not always agreement—with de Rougemont's treatment of the passion myths. In his review, Updike asserts with de Rougemont that Tristan and Don Juan typify even in the twentieth century contrasting attitudes toward passion and marriage. In *Couples*, Piet is sometimes a Tristan, sometimes a Don Juan, and sometimes both at the same time; and the other characters supplement the mythic structure. This double archetypal pattern proceeds through three stages: first, the identification of the characters of the novel with their mythic types; second, the description of the meaning inherent in the narrative-myth combination; and third, the clarification of a new secular vision that the novel projects through the myth.

In the association of narrative and mythic characters, Angela plays the most apparent contrast to Piet as Tristan. She is both Iseult the Fair and Iseult of the White Hand; for her whiteness, her temperamental blend of passion and aloofness, and the otherworldly echo of her name all suggest her two roles. According to the legend, of course, Angela should be Piet's mistress instead of his wife; but Updike changes some angles of the tale. Foxy also has the roles of the two Iseults: she is described in terms of whiteness (her name is "Whitman"; her clothing and surroundings are often depicted through white imagery) and in terms of the combination of passion and unavailability.

In his Tristan role, Piet seeks the ideal woman who will assuage his fear of death and his longing for the infinite; as Don Juan, he attempts to conquer many women in order to outdo death in a frenzy of virility and to force the secret of infinity hidden in *Eros*. In Updike's review of the de Rougemont books, he states that 'Don Juan loves Woman under the guise of many women, exhaustingly'';[5] and Foxy writes a similar thought to Piet from her refuge in the Caribbean: "When you desire to be the world's husband, what right do I have to make you my own?" Piet does in fact sleep with three other wives, besides Angela and Foxy; and Angela's comment (to Freddy) that "Piet spends all his energy defying death" reveals the desperate impulse behind much of his lust. Other characters reinforce Piet's Don Juan status: Eddie Constantine with his many women in Puerto Rico is one; and Freddy Thorne, another, at least articulates a Don Juan philosophy even though he does not translate it into action. The interchangeability of persons slides easily into postures of promiscuity in the Don Juan framework; the couples as composite protagonist try to wrench a meaning out of life through indiscriminate sex.

These correspondences between personae in the novel and their archetypes have important ramifications. In his review of de Rougemont, Updike elaborates on some ancient Gnostic elements that the Swiss writer sees surviving in the Tristan legend and in the Courtly Love tradition: imagery of light and darkness, a double narcissism, the Maria Sophia concept, and the search for self-identity through passion. In *Couples,* these same elements appear with striking clarity. The light-dark imagery, signifying spiritual goodness versus carnal evil in the Gnostic and Manichean traditions, is used for somewhat different ends by Updike. His characters in passionate moments together are often immersed in bright light, but their moments of loneliness and fear of death are masked by darkness. All of Piet's women are variations of the Gnostic Maria Sophia, the Mother of Christ who merges with the eternal feminine and then, in the Medieval Courtly Love tradition (according to de Rougemont), becomes the subject of erotic reverence. Angela and Foxy seem to Piet to be filled with such ethereal wisdom; his relationship to them brings him close to this mysterious power that is a further defense against death.

The double narcissism that de Rougemont seeks to expose in Tristan and Iseult as the fallacious basis of love also affects Updike's characters. Piet is a modern Courtly Lover and a "secret dandy." The couples play at illicit sex because they have made the egotistical thrill of being desired a goal in itself and do not grasp the foundation of a sound marital union. For example, after the affair between Piet and Foxy is exposed and Piet is left alone, "what he felt, remembering Foxy, was a nostalgia for adultery itself—its adventure, the acrobatics its deceptions demand, the tension of its hidden strings, the new landscapes it makes us master."

Freddy Thorne best illustrates, however, the absurdity of narcissism in *Eros*. After he finally manages to bed down with Angela (his "ideal lover"), he becomes impotent and cannot perform; but when she falls asleep beside him, he masturbates. The unshared idea of passion is more exciting to him than a shared love relationship. Such narcissism leads in turn to the sensation of self-identity located in *Eros*. In the de Rougemont review, Updike describes it thus: "a man in love, confronting his beloved, seems to be in the presence of *his own spirit,* his self translated into another mode of being, a Form of Light greeting him at the gate of salvation."[6] Piet has this sensation with Georgene, Angela, Foxy, and Bea Guerin. He *needs* women in order to effect this mystical transformation into his true self, but it remains an essentially selfish act—as in fact many mystical efforts are.

The Don Juan model prompts similar interpretation. Updike works with concepts such as the attempted violation of life's secrets through passion, the obsession with quantity (the *number* of women seduced) instead of Tristan's economy (passionate concentration on one woman), the need for variety that degenerates into sadism to avoid boredom, and the inevitable change of the combination of *Eros* and goodness into that of *Eros* and evil. These concepts become clear in the third stage, the secular vision that *Couples* advances through the myths. Part of this vision is the realization of a vital connection between passion and death. Tristan seeks to avoid death by losing himself in the intense love of an idealized woman, while Don Juan tries to surpass death by the seduction of many women. However, Tristan's flight from authentic relationships exposes his secret death wish, and Don Juan's exhausting compulsion in itself is fatal. Although Piet is a more convincing Tristan than a Don Juan, he does embody both of these attitudes toward passion and death, and he also reveals in the process that *Couples* stresses death as much as sex. The novel is, if anything, death-obsessed; and the sexuality that the reviewers sensationalized becomes relevant only in conjunction with death. Scene after scene emphasizes the connection of sex and death, but it is most succinctly and vulgarly metaphorized by Freddy's comment that "death is being screwed by God. It'll be delicious."

A second part of the secular vision of *Couples,* one that follows the knowledge that participation in *Eros* only intensifies the awareness of death, is the intimation that substitutes for the Christian Incarnation persist even where the Incarnation itself is ignored. According to the traditional doctrine of the church, a basic relationship exists between love and death; God's love was demonstrated in the Incarnation of Christ, and through his sacrificial death the curse of death upon man was removed. This was *Agape*-love, a self-giving power quite different from the narcissistic passion called *Eros.* Updike remarks, summarizing de Rougemont, that "Gnosticism is an attempt to make the 'transition from Eros to the Spirit' without passing through the paradox of the Incarnation," and he may purposely be sending his Tarbox characters along the same path.[7] Since most of his people do not accept the old Christian Incarnation way but persist in a Gnostic-tinged effort toward reconciliation, they need a surrogate for the Incarnation—and they find it, of course, in sex. Toward the end of the novel, following a lyrical-philosophical description of oral sex shared by Piet and Foxy (who have now separated from their spouses), Updike writes: "Thus on the Sunday morning, beneath the hanging clangor of bells." In this passage, the physical union instead of the spiritual service on a Sunday morning, the "eating" of each other instead of the Communion wafer, and the substitution of the lovers' bodies for the body of Christ prompt the recognition that at least two of the Tarbox group are attempting an erotic embody-ment with religious overtones that is intended as a substitute for the old incarnational theology.

A third part of the secular vision is a demythologizing process that destroys the power of the Tristan and Don Juan complexes to create a new kind of love that is more mature, permanent, and realistic. It is imaged in the marathon three-day love-making between Piet and Foxy. During that weekend they travel *through* passion and emerge purged, one feels, on the far side of promiscuity and selfish love. But the question is, what do they become? Updike implies at the close of his de Rougemont review that a myth is no longer necessary to express the contemporary situation: "Might it not simply be that sex has become involved in the Promethean protest forced upon Man by his paradoxical position in the Universe as a self-conscious animal? Our fundamental anxiety is that we do not exist—or will cease to exist. Only in being loved do we find external corroboration of the supremely high valuation each ego secretly assigns itself. This exalted arena, then, is above all others the one where men and women will insist upon their freedom to choose—to choose that other being in whose existence their own existence is confirmed and amplified."[8]

One might ask whether it is indeed true that myths are no longer necessary, whether modern man's problems of loving are not caused in part by the absence of *viable* myths of love—which is to say deeply felt beliefs about love and models for authentic loving. In any case, contemporary civilization has no archetype for persons who assert their identity by choosing to share themselves with other persons (Christ is not that archetype, for he lacks the sexual dimension); therefore, a novel such as *Couples* fills an important cultural role. It suggests some possibilities for filling the void left by demythologizing and secularization—or, at the very least, it shows convincingly that the void must be filled.

Chapter Ten
Bech: A Book:
The Protestant as Jew

See, now, the libidinous flare,
spinning on its stick in vain resistance
to the upright ego and mortality's gravity:
behold, above, the sudden bloom,
turquoise, each tip a comet,
of pride—followed, after an empty bang,
by an ebbing amber galaxy, despair.

—from "Fireworks"

The Altered Ego

Bech: A Book, published in 1970, is a collection of seven stories
with the same protagonist: the middle-aged Jewish novelist Henry
Bech. The collection is sufficiently unified that one can read it as
a loosely organized novel, with the stories representing a succession
of chapters treating various episodes in the hero's life. The suggestion
of a casual novel format is strengthened by a consistency of characters
and actions, and by a similarity of mood and imagery in all of the
tales. The details of the individual stories complement each other,
and although one finds no progression of narrative as such throughout the book, the seven stories do give a fairly thorough portrait of
the main character. The book also utilizes a secondary fiction, that
Bech is an actual historical person, a contemporary author whom
Updike knows and is writing about. Thus Bech's own foreword,
giving his skeptical blessing to the venture, introduces the book.
Two appendices also appear: the first contains excerpts from Bech's
"unpublished Russian journal"; the second, a bibliography of works
by and about Bech, includes titles of bogus essays in real journals

by critics such as Alfred Kazin and Leslie Fiedler.. The device does not harm the effectiveness of the primary fiction—the seven stories about Bech—but, in fact, provides the pleasant impression of an inside joke that the reader soon comprehends.

As in Updike's other novels, he gives himself a handicap in *Bech: A Book* and then strives to overcome it. In *The Poorhouse Fair*, it was the challenge to a young author to write empathetically about the aged; in *Couples*, to make obscene language and a confusing aggregate of people function artfully. In *Bech: A Book*, Updike the Protestant enters the preserve of the modern Jewish novelists. Not only does he choose to describe the innermost life of a Jew—an attempt rarely made by gentile authors—but he also selects a Jewish writer as hero, one whose personality, presumably, would be even more complex than that of a nonartist. Updike's characterization for the most part succeeds, both because he universalizes Bech's Jewishness into postures of authentic modern humanity in the manner of Saul Bellow's and Philip Roth's best writing and because he is careful to underplay the use of dialect and of the archetypal Jewish family and the Old World allusions that are the stock in trade of Bernard Malamud. Bech is an intellectual Jew (although not a Jewish intellectual), much more like Bellow's Moses Herzog than Malamud's Morris Bober.

It is tempting to project Bech as Updike's alter ego since certain superficial parallels exist, but the essential similarities are lacking. Updike, like Bech, has traveled to eastern Europe on an officially sponsored cultural exchange tour; and, like Bech, he is in constant danger of losing his status as an independent artist and of submitting instead to cultural objectification, to the process whereby a contemporary artist becomes a static showpiece of the society he has sought to unsettle. But Bech is a "blocked" novelist, and Updike is not. After Bech has enjoyed some solid successes, enough and of such quality to make him a "major" writer in Updike's invented world, he has hit a sterile period—perhaps he has even written himself out. The single most consistent theme throughout the seven stories is Bech's frustrating inability to produce. It is a problem that Updike does not share; and if Bech is in any significant way his alter ego, it must be only in the sense of incarnating the fear of impotence that any artist has.

Bech: A Book is different from Updike's previous fiction in the scope and nature of its humor. Hitherto, Updike had largely limited his use of humor to his poetry and to the satire collected in *Assorted Prose* and had reserved for his fiction a certain wit often more cynical than comic. *Bech* is sometimes quite funny, as if, in temporarily adopting a Jewish hero, Updike had also accepted the imperative of Jewish humor. Humor appears in the dialogue of *Couples*, it is true, but there its effect is radically weakened by the overriding awareness of guilt and death. *Bech: A Book* emits an attitude of liberation, as if its author had learned to endure some of life's enigmas and to smile at them.

The Seven Stories

The first story, "Rich in Russia," is presented nominally as a lecture to a class of students regarding Bech's 1964 trip to the Soviet Union, where he is celebrated as an author of stature and given over fifteen hundred dollars' worth of rubles for Russian translations of his works. He tries hard to spend the rubles (apparently, he can't take the money out of the country); but he finds little to buy until, on the last day of his visit, he goes with Kate his translator to a Moscow shop and spends almost the whole sum for furs. As he hurries to catch his plane a short time later, his suitcase opens, and he drops furs, toys, and books on the runway. He and Kate, who is crying, gather them again; and he departs.

The story turns on irony. Bech is indeed "rich in Russia," but he can't take the riches with him except in the form of exotic gifts. More than that, his richness is really personified in Kate, his loyal and emotional translator. When he kisses her at the airport, "he realized, horrified, that he should have slept with her." He has taken her and her dedication for granted; therefore, he has missed, more than a sexual encounter, the chance to know a valuable person well.

"Bech in Rumania," the second story, continues the novelist's cultural exchange tour of Eastern Europe. The counterpart to Kate in this tale is Petrescu, the translator who accompanies Bech on a trip to meet the head of the Rumanian Writers' Union. While on a sightseeing tour, Bech goes to a Bucharest performance of Eugene O'Neill's *Desire Under the Elms* and to a nightclub with another author ("the hottest Red writer this side of Solzhenitsyn") and his wife. Bech's conversations with Petrescu, combined with the running descriptions of life in modern Rumania as Bech sees it, comprise the essential story. The primary impression that results is the difficulty of communicating between two cultures. Bech and Petrescu like and respect each other, but a genuine friendship is thwarted by the lack of time and by the official busyness of the visit. The American Embassy people in Bucharest are enthusiastic bumblers, and the Rumanian leaders are rigid bureaucrats. The absence of rapport is epitomized by Bech's chauffeur, a taciturn Rumanian whose violent driving and constant hornblowing upset his passenger. The chauffeur seems to comprehend no English, yet he indicates at the end that he has indeed understood but has not tried to communicate. While on the plane leaving the country, Bech answers the unfamiliar words of a seatmate with *"Pardon, je ne comprends pas. Je suis Américain."* The statement fits his whole experience in the country, where "he realized that for four days he had been afraid." Bech thinks of himself "as a sort of low-flying U-2," as he tells an American from the Embassy, but his reconnaissance is not very effective on any level.

"The Bulgarian Poetess," winner of the First O. Henry Prize for 1966, is the first of Updike's stories to result from his 1964–1965 trip to Eastern Europe. In this tale, Bech arrives in Sofia, Bulgaria, for his last visit before returning to New York. Here he finds, unexpectedly, the "central woman"—the ideal he has always sought—in the person of a young poetess who arrives late to his reception. Although she is just as intensely attracted to him, they have only three brief meetings. At the last one, they exchange inscribed books (her poems and his novel) and separate, probably forever.

The success of the story depends not so much on the East-West romance theme as it does on the varied, repetitive use of mirror imagery that sustains the emotionality. How the mirror device works is described by Bech as he discusses the structure of his one good novel: "a counter-melody of imagery, interlocking images which had risen to the top and drowned his story." In Updike's story, the image of ghosts from Hawthorne's tale "Roger Malvin's Burial," the "shadow world" of the American embassies, the reflection from the polished table, the mirrors of the Moscow and Sofia ballets, and the Communists "behind the mirror" merge to suggest the enigmatic identity of the participants in the context of international tension. Bech's self-consciousness is dissolved in the encounter with

Vera Glavanakova, the Bulgarian poetess; but his new sense of being remains intact only through the necessary separation from her.

"Bech Takes Pot Luck," the fourth story, reminds one a good deal of Saul Bellow's fiction and specifically of his protagonist Moses Herzog's strained living. Returned to the United States, Bech spends August on a Massachusetts island with his mistress, her sister, and the sister's children; but his vacation is interrupted by the appearance of one of his former students, named Wendell, from a Columbia University writing course. Bech and his mistress are not getting on well together, and the sister is suffering through a divorce. The young student enters the chaotic household and, through his ability to amuse the children and his general adeptness at beachfront living, provides some order and relief. When Norma, Bech's mistress, learns that the young man has L.S.D. at his apartment, she wants to try it, but he suggests that they smoke marijuana first "as a dry run." That evening, Bech, Norma, Beatrice the sister, and Wendell smoke the "grass." Nothing happens to Norma, but Bech becomes ill and vomits. Norma and Wendell drive away (to get rid of the L.S.D., it turns out, because Wendell feels guilty about Bech's nausea); and, in the interim, Bech and Beatrice establish a beginning intimacy. That night he sneaks away from Norma's bed to sleep with her sister, and "by fall the word went out on the literary circuit that Bech had shifted mistresses again."

The thrust of the story becomes clear through a consideration of the title's pun. The "pot luck" refers both to the drug and the sisters. Since Bech doesn't know how it will affect him, smoking "pot" becomes a matter of "pot luck." Furthermore, because of the marijuana, Norma and Wendell leave for a time, making it possible for Bech and Beatrice, both intoxicated, to set the stage for their affair; in that sense, pot luck is also at work. Pot luck also means taking whatever is offered, just as Bech accepts Beatrice's implicit offer of herself. However, the story does not capitalize on the drug vogue in order to achieve sensation but to integrate the theme. Certain traits of the characters are magnified, as if by the marijuana's influence, so that Updike can fit Norma's shrill greediness, Bech's aggressiveness, Beatrice's submission, and Wendell's naïveté into a pattern of contrived accident that marks another stage of the hero's restless career.

In "Bech Panics," Updike uses the framing device of a slide lecture (a narrator showing slides of Bech) to tell the story of Bech's per-

formance as a lecturer at a Virginia girls' school. Now separated
from Norma and involved with Bea, her sister, Bech is bothered
by the two roles his new mistress plays as lover to him and as mother
to her three young children; uncomfortable alone and with Bea, he
alternates between his Riverside Drive apartment and her upstate
New York home. From this ambivalence he flees in March to Virginia; but the abrupt transition to the rural college and pristine-
looking girls, instead of relaxing him, instills a basic dread and an
awareness of death that daze him. He undergoes an accelerated crisis
of self-doubt, prays against his will, and then fulfills his duties as
guest speaker. On the second evening, a young Jewish professor
suggests that he sleep with her; the slide-lecturer-as-narrator offers
two versions of Bech's response. First, he says, Bech rejected her
invitation and wept in front of the surprised woman. But then he
says it is possible that Bech accepted the offer and sought to cure
his spiritual sickness with her body. The next day Bech returns to
New York and his uncomprehending mistress.

"Bech Panics" is, in terms of moral import, the profoundest story
of the collection. Bech's temporary displacement, his retreat to the
Virginia countryside, somehow makes him aware of the futility of
language and reinforces his self-doubt; for his profession is that of
language-craftsman. His fruitless argument with a black girl at the
college, his artificial performance for the students, and the college
poetry contest he is asked to judge emphasize the failure of language
as a redemptive instrument. When alone in the woods between
assignments, he prays a wordless prayer, however, and finds a measure of relief. As an ironic finale, Bech is taken to the airport by
"a homely, tall, long-toothed woman" whose seductive drawl on
the telephone had originally overcome his reluctance to travel to
the campus. Words are deceptive, and the writer has to learn to
accommodate deception without despair.

The story has a brutal and primitive undertone that contrasts
with the genteel surface rhythms. Even the demure girls threaten
Bech with a collective primal and smothering fertility, and his
lovemaking with the young professor (if it indeed occurred) is described in grotesque anatomical terms. Bech panics because he has
been shocked by rural nature out of the somnolent urban habits he
has formed. He has nurtured his artist's impotence as a comfortable
excuse to avoid facing squarely the dread of being, much as some
neurotics love their illness; but his malingering is exposed by his

new knowledge of the real problem—the need to locate meaning in an infinitely complex universe.

In "Bech Swings?," the novelist, now through with Bea, arrives in London to promote an English anthology of his writings. At a party he meets Merissa, a young and wealthy divorcée who takes him home with her. Without discovering much more about her or her background, he accompanies her in the ensuing evenings to a number of London's "mod" clubs, while on two day-time occasions he submits to an interview by a persistent and overly serious young American. Upon leaving London and flying back to New York, he reads a silly and pretentious *Observer* review by the American; but in a London tabloid he finds the column "Merissa's Week" (she is the daughter of the paper's owner) in which Merissa flatters him breezily as a man of the world.

The story begins with "Bech arrived in London with the daffodils," and Wordsworth's "I Wandered Lonely as a Cloud" becomes a central image. Bech is a lonely wanderer, and many things in springtime England remind him, in a melancholy way, of the season's gaiety celebrated in the Romantic's poem. Wordsworth's famous definition of poetic composition also figures in the tale. "The spontaneous overflow of powerful feelings . . . from emotion recollected in tranquillity" does not work for Bech as a depiction of artistic creation or of lovemaking because, as Merissa reminds him in his impotence, he does not act "in tranquillity." Instead of developing a reflective creativity, Bech is becoming neurotically self-conscious. The narrator and Bech occasionally fuse, as particular descriptions by the narrator lodge in Bech's mind and become part of his compulsive phrasing. He articulates events while he experiences them, and he is so absorbed in introspective observation that he has little time for qualitative living. When Merissa in her gossip column reveals a perspective of him that he hadn't expected, he is charmed; but his pleasure is marred by the knowledge that he has once again played a role with her and has not revealed his authentic self. "He had become a character by Henry Bech" is the final sentence; the delusion of self-consciousness grows, and the shift from private novelist to celebrity seems complete.

The question mark of the title is important. Bech "swings" dubiously, not sure if he is enjoying or despairing. He is too self-aware for uninhibited participation, and the title carries the tone of proper incredulity even as it declares Bech's own intent.

"Bech Enters Heaven," the weakest story of the collection, is nonetheless an admirable display of wit. The story centers on two parallel episodes. In the first, when Bech is a precocious thirteen-year-old, he is taken from school by his mother one day to the northern end of Manhattan to attend a ceremony honoring literary luminaries. Young Bech is impressed. Years later, as a middle-aged novelist, he receives an invitation to attend a similar ceremony at which he himself is to be one of those honored. This gathering turns out to be a modern literary pantheon, a writers' heaven, into which Bech is formally admitted.

The tale is a parody both of Jewish-mother-and-son fiction and of the rituals by which America elevates and thereby ruins its artists. Mrs. Bech is ambitious for her son, and their visit to the ceremony is a crucial event that helps to formulate his vocational direction. The dialogue between the mother and boy does not ring quite true but sounds, understandably enough, like a gentile's imitation of Jewish-American diction and syntax. But artificiality does not seriously harm the story. If anything, it increases the hollowness of literary fame that Bech gains years later and the meaninglessness of the rites whereby such writers receive a sterile immortality. The final sentences are, "He had made it, he was here, in Heaven. Now what?" Even the ultimate achievement is cursed by boredom, and ennui pervades the pantheon.

The Success of Failure

Bech is another in Updike's long line of protagonists who are complex failures. Conner in *The Poorhouse Fair* is a bureaucratic success but a human failure; Harry Angstrom (before his *Rabbit Redux* maturation) is a sexual success but a total failure otherwise; George Caldwell is a social failure but a compassionate man; Joey Robinson is a failure as son, husband, and father; and the couples of Tarbox are all failures in love and friendship. Henry Bech is a social and cultural success; but, according to his own secret knowledge, he is a vocational failure—a bit of a "schlemiel," something of a *poseur,* a talented man who, spoiled by the selfish praise of a voracious society, has never fulfilled his promise. But one perceives more solid humanity in Bech than in all of Updike's previous heroes except George Caldwell. Bech is believable, likeable, and trustworthy. One senses in Updike's portrayal of him a new artistic toughness that will come to mark the author's style in his prime.

Chapter Eleven
Rabbit Redux: The Space Beyond Myth

Kierkegaard smolders,/ But Eliot's ashes are dead.

—from "Thoughts While Driving Home"

Alternatives to Mythic Fiction

In *Couples* Updike uses myth to destroy itself, and through that novel he not only demythologizes *Eros* but also shows the possibility of demythologizing fiction itself. But how does an author write mythless fiction? Updike tests some possibilities in *Bech: A Book.* There he works with current events, with fantasy as history, with a configuration of images, and with certain narrator tricks. The emphasis on contemporary world events and moods, already heavy in *Couples,* comes to the fore in the stories of Bech in Eastern Europe (in Bech's impressions of Russia, Bulgaria, Rumania) and in "Bech Takes Pot Luck" (through his participation in the emergent drug culture of the 1960s). The experiment with fantasy as history (Updike attempts the opposite, history as fantasy, in his long poem "Midpoint") introduces Bech as a real person rather than as a fictional figure, although Updike obviously does not expect anyone to accept Bech's actual existence. The orchestration of images replacing a dominant narrative line, a strategy Updike applies skillfully in "The Music School" story, dictates the structure of "The Bulgarian Poetess." The narrative-rhetorical tricks operate in "Bech Panics" (an unidentified narrator relates the story in the framework of a slide lecture) and in "Bech Swings?" (Bech's musings merge with the narrator's imagery). Significantly, the only story relying on myth, "Bech Enters Heaven," is the single inferior tale in the collection.

In *Rabbit Redux* (the title means "Rabbit led back") Updike settles on two of the alternatives to a fiction supported by myth: on the stress on contemporary world events and on the orchestration of images.[1] He abandons the fantasy-as-history playfulness entirely and limits the narrative-rhetorical tricks to one innovation: the "reproduction" of news stories in rough form as they appear on Rabbit's typesetting machine. The two alternatives that he does develop basically contradict each other as modes of structuring a novel. The accent on current events presupposes a marked historical continuity in the book, but the emphasis on image constellations suggests an ahistorical approach. Updike not only reconciles these divergent tendencies; he makes them reinforce each other to provide a unique fictive integrity that replaces a reliance on myth.

A conventional story line does inhabit *Rabbit Redux*. The time is late July through October 1969, ten years after the events of *Rabbit, Run*. Harry Angstrom (no one has called him Rabbit for years, although Updike still does) is now thirty-six, a typesetter; he has grown politically conservative and is reunited with his wife Janice. They live with their only child, the thirteen-year-old Nelson, in Penn Villas, the new housing development on the outskirts of Brewer, Pennsylvania. In the first chapter, entitled "Pop/Mom/Moon," Harry learns that Janice is having an affair with Stavros, a salesman of Greek descent who works with her at her father's automobile sales lot. During a summer weekend Rabbit and Janice have a confrontation regarding her affair, after which she leaves him and Nelson to move in with Stavros. On that Sunday afternoon Harry (with Nelson) visits his parents in neighboring Mount Judge to celebrate his mother's birthday. Old Mrs. Angstrom, now sixty-five, is slowly dying of Parkinson's Disease. That night the four of them sit in the sickroom and watch the television coverage of the first manned moon landing.

In the second chapter, called "Jill," when Rabbit visits a local black bar at the invitation of a Negro co-worker, he is maneuvered into taking home with him the eighteen-year-old runaway rich girl Jill, whose white presence in the black community is dangerous and awkward. Jill, a naïve radical idealist, becomes Harry's lover but also acts as a combined older sister and substitute mother for Nelson. Janice remains with Stavros even though he asks Harry to take her back. Harry's dying mother, who has always hated Janice, fights the possibility of a new reconciliation.

In the third chapter, "Skeeter," Harry arrives home from work one day to find that Jill has taken in a young Negro, a Vietnam veteran called Skeeter who has jumped bail following a drugs-dealing charge and who proclaims himself to be the black Jesus. He becomes a contentious member of the strange household, makes love to Jill, supplies her with increasingly stronger drugs, and seeks to give Harry an education in black history, radical politics, and in anti-Establishment life style. Rabbit gradually succumbs. He smokes marijuana nightly with Jill and Skeeter and also absorbs (with Nelson sitting in) their arguments about the immorality of the Vietnam war and about the exploitative and repressive nature of modern American society. One night they are spied on from outside as Jill and Skeeter are sexually involved. Rabbit has already been warned by two neighbors to disperse his shocking ménage or suffer the consequences. On a Saturday night soon after, while he and Nelson are visiting the divorcée Peggy Fosnacht and her son, Rabbit receives a call from Skeeter urging him to come home. They return to find the house in flames. Jill, probably in a doped sleep, dies in the fire in spite of Nelson's frantic pleas to save her. Early the next morning Harry finds Skeeter and drives him out of town to aid his escape from the searching police.

In the final chapter, "Mim," Harry and Nelson have moved in with Harry's parents in Mount Judge. Harry loses his job with the declining Verity Press. When his sister Mim, now a high-priced call girl on the West Coast, comes east for a visit, she in her tough way reorganizes the lives of her relatives. She not only encourages Rabbit toward a reunion with Janice but also expedites it by sleeping with Stavros. After Janice has helped Stavros through a terrifying heart seizure one night, she, in a spirit of confused self-sacrifice (she fears that their affair will kill him), decides to leave him at last. She and Rabbit meet at their gutted Penn Villas house, drive to a motel, and, without making love, sleep together.

The Orchestration of Tropes

Such a narrative summation reads like a caricature because the story line of *Rabbit Redux* is mainly a vehicle of orientation in a work of fiction that succeeds by other means. The novel is crucially aligned to historical world events. Some are specifically datable, such as the first manned moon flight and landing, the race riots in

York and Reading (Pennsylvania), and the Chappaquiddick drowning of Mary Jo Kopechne with its repercussions on Senator Edward Kennedy's political career. Others are continuous: the Vietnam war, the increasing drugs traffic, the growing polarization of segments of American society, and the deterioration of the cities. All of these merge with the orchestration of images to give the book its substance.

The trope of space and space-exploration images is dominant. It is displayed literally in the fragments of recorded conversation from American astronauts and Russian cosmonauts during space flights and dockings that prefix each of the four sections; in the depiction of the televised moon landing that Rabbit and his relatives watch; and in the account of Rabbit, Janice, and Nelson in a movie theater viewing Stanley Kubrick's *2001: A Space Odyssey*. These references act as the context for metaphoric uses of space. The maneuvers of space docking provide the background for images of security and physical contact. The spectral figures of the astronauts on the moon set the tone for the strong ghost imagery, which stands for the insubstantial quality of American life and for the haunting memory of better times. The phenomenon of floating free in space becomes the basis for images of Janice's liberation from Rabbit, of sexual excitement, or of drug-inspired sensations. The spaciousness of space offers an ironic counterpart to the images of density in the black ghettos and in American cities generally.

The space-docking maneuver underlies many scenes. For example, Harry is thinking of his mother while riding home from work: "Rabbit's mind, as the bus dips into its bag of gears and surges and shudders, noses closer into the image of her." At the critical moment, when Jill and Skeeter—her head between his thighs—are spied through a window, they seem to Rabbit "an interlocked machine." The final scenes of the book, ones in which Harry and Janice cautiously reconcile and sleep together in the Safe Haven Motel, are done in forthright space coupling imagery: "he and she seem to be slowly revolving, afraid of jarring one another away"; and, "In a space of silence, he can't gauge how much, he feels them drift along sideways deeper into being married."

The apparitionlike figures of the astronauts on the moon, as transmitted by television, are the natural models for ghost metaphors and sensations. Janice sees Rabbit as "a ghost, white, soft." Jill, wan and "transparent," seems ghostly to Rabbit and appears as a ghost in his bedroom some weeks after her death. Old Mrs. Ang-

strom is a "shade" and an "apparition"; Rabbit calls Skeeter a "spook."
Rabbit dreams of a spectral white city; his mother dreams of him
and Mim as ghosts. The condition of floating free is reworked
metaphorically as Janice masturbates and thinks of herself as "Floating now like a ballerina among the sparse planets of her life"; and
as Rabbit, coming home with Jill after smoking marijuana ("This
smoky creature at his side has halved his weight"), "floats up the
steps to the porchlet." The ironic opposite of immense space is the
cramped space of Mount Judge and Brewer and the lack of physical
and spiritual room that Skeeter as black man feels.

A second trope, almost as pervasive as the space trope, deals in
a great variety of underwater imagery. Its historical bases are the
United States-Russian agreement to ban atomic weapons from the
ocean floor and the drowning of Mary Jo Kopechne. Its fictive
orientation is Janice's drowning of the baby Becky in *Rabbit, Run.*
Employed metaphorically, it serves many dimensions of the novel.
Old Mrs. Angstrom has nightmares of drowning; Skeeter has Nelson
read an "underwater" passage from William Lloyd Garrison *("let the
Republic sink beneath the waves of oblivion . . . ");* Jill, indulging in
oral sex, is "like a little girl bobbing for apples"; when Harry
supports the sickened Nelson during the fire in which Jill burns,
"He is holding him up from drowning. If Harry were to let go, he
would drown too."

Other tropes contribute to the fundamental organization of the
novel. The persistent black-white trope, based on contemporary race
relations, incarnates more specifically the relation between Rabbit
and Skeeter and between Skeeter and Jill; it also underscores the
oversimplifications of Rabbit's thinking, in which things are "black
and white" with no shades of gray; and it stresses the urgent tan-
gibility of America's problems versus its transparent solutions. The
winged-figure trope, which harks back to Janice's feeling that a
third person is in the room when Becky drowns, is prominent.
When Rabbit talks to Janice by telephone, he "sees her wings hover,
her song suspended: imagines himself soaring, rootless, free." Rabbit masturbates lying on his stomach because he feels God is over
him, "spreading His feathered wings as above a crib." When Stavros
has his seizure, Janice again feels "a third person in the room"; and
when Harry and Janice are in bed in the motel, "All sorts of winged
presences exert themselves in the air above their covers." The mirror
trope, which continues to fascinate Updike, provides images of

attempts at reciprocal understanding. Harry sees himself reflected by Peggy Fosnacht; Jill explains God, spirit, and matter to Nelson through mirror analogies; Harry observes obliquely (through mirrors) what he fears to see directly: his house afire and Skeeter. Effective are also the Jesus trope (Harry's last minutes with Skeeter are filled with Jesus symbolism); the basketball trope (Harry explains the Vietnam war as "a kind of head fake. To keep the other guy off balance"); and the Peter Rabbit trope (Rabbit sneezes at critical moments, like Peter Rabbit in Mr. MacGregor's garden).

The tropes function not only individually to provide an imagistic consistency and continuity throughout the novel; they also merge, blending in and out of each other, to produce a sense of interconnectedness and interchangeability that gives the book its integrity and vast allusiveness. Moreover, the "big" subjects of war, sex, violence, space exploration, drugs, America's polarization and loss of self-confidence are related better than ever to the Middle-American milieu in Updike's writing through the orchestration of tropes. For example, early in the novel, Janice and Rabbit make love in the light of the television screen, "by the bluish flicker of module models pantomiming flight, of riot troops standing before smashed supermarkets, of a rowboat landing in Florida having crossed the Atlantic, of situation comedies and western melodramas, of great gray momentary faces unstable as quicksilver." But this scene also mingles images of ghosts, mirrors, black and white, Peter Rabbit, and space exploration. The realistic background and the network of tropes merge, then, in a description in which Janice's body becomes simultaneously the newly discovered moonscape and a Vietnam battlefield. In mid-novel, when Rabbit, Jill, Skeeter, and Nelson engage in an acute political-cultural discussion about race relations and America's future, Updike creates a mélange of space, underwater, black-white, Jesus, mirrors, and winged-figures tropes. In the concluding motel scene the tropes and images of space coupling, floating in space, ghosts, winged figures, Peter Rabbit, and black-white interact.

The immensely intricate interplay of tropes produces an effect like that of a long and complex poem, and yet the novel's traditional domain of fictive historicity is not lost. It is caught up and transformed by the imagistic effort, while the story line itself, although outdone by the tropes' effects, is still sufficiently assertive to prevent the novel from becoming a pseudopoem. *Rabbit Redux* is not grounded in history and reinforced by fictive imagery; it is based on the imagery and is reinforced by history.

Hence the novel, for all of its absorption in contemporary problems, does not become social propaganda but diffuses its concern through esthetic channels. The sense of the disintegrating quality of American life in the 1960s is transmitted not only by the image clusters (ghosts, drowning, the emptiness of space, the tension of black and white) but also by references to nostalgia and by expressions of banality. Updike has always excelled at evoking nostalgia. In *Rabbit Redux* he recalls the Lone Ranger, Big Little Books, old pop tunes, children's games on summer evenings, and the vital centers of small towns before the shopping malls destroyed them; the recollection, however, is not intended to create the pleasant ache for lost good times but to shape a framework for comprehending the drastic nature of modern America's deterioration. The present contrasts with the "decades when Americans moved within the American dream, laughing at it, starving on it, but living it, humming it, the national anthem everywhere. . . . Rabbit had come in on the end of it, as the world shrank like an apple going bad and America was no longer the wisest hick town within a boat ride of Europe."

This novel lacks the liberal-redemptive presence of a Reverend Eccles who, a key figure in *Rabbit, Run,* is not even alluded to here. Instead, Updike prefigures the second section with the inane remark of a space hero—Neil Armstrong saying, "It's different but it's very pretty out here"—and intensifies the climate of banality with details of MacDonald's hamburger stands, shoddy motels, and neon-ornamented bars. The magnificence of outer space is tempered by the tawdriness of Middle America; the potential tragedy of the characters' lives is undone by their vulgarities.

Instructive Motion

Above all, *Rabbit Redux* is effectively vulgar and sometimes even efficiently perverse; a decade earlier it would have been considered obscene. Its attentiveness to the sounds, tastes, and smells of sexual union along with the usual visual-tactile description; its matter-of-fact treatment of promiscuity; and its use of a sexual-profane language publicly taboo a generation ago render it offensive by traditional standards, but its "obscenity" is precisely directed.

Copulation, its variations, and its vocabulary are an expression of outraged sensibility, an indulgence in the very irresponsibility that provokes outrage, and a refuge from the exhausting personal-social reality that condones both the outrage and its causes. Little lyric sex animates the book, much less than appears in *Couples;* the sexual exercises in *Rabbit Redux* usually have an ulterior purpose. Skeeter exerts a revenge on Jill's body for what he perceives as the white man's humiliation of his race; Jill makes love to Rabbit in lieu of paying rent, as a protest against her parents' wealthy-wasteful existence, and also as a sensual catharsis that provides temporary relief from her teenaged intellectual and emotional confusion; Rabbit copulates with Jill as a substitute for his wife and with Peggy Fosnacht (on the night of the fire) as a social obligation. Janice appropriates her lover's body to celebrate and assert her discovery of feminine identity; and, Mim, who has made sex a profession and a life style, not only sells her body but also derives her pragmatic values from her call girl experiences.

The novel does not exploit sex for its sensation value; there is still less ground for that charge against *Rabbit Redux* than against *Couples.* Instead, nostalgia, banality, vulgarity, and obscenity combine to establish the atmosphere of national deterioration; but they are also a cause of the deterioration. Updike's America is now afflicted by a longing for the security of the romanticized past that seems in contradiction to the adventurous, futuristic spirit imperative to the space-age mentality; the country is cursed by a poverty of the imagination and by a vulgarity of taste that betray its former high-minded hopes and intentions; it is pervaded by an obscenity that dehumanizes relationships on every level and that exposes the great cost of technological triumph. In this sad situation the personal and political positions of Left, Right, and Center are all equally ineffective, yet it is instructive to follow Rabbit's journey toward increasing political awareness, for it is not wasted motion.

In *Rabbit Redux* Harry Angstrom undergoes a quest, a seduction, a conversion, and an education. This sequel to *Rabbit, Run* is also a quest novel, but it has neither the mythic dimension of the quest that the earlier book had nor the willing participation of the protagonist in the quest. Rabbit at twenty-six, ten years younger, saw himself gladly as a spiritual searcher, even though he was too naïve to understand himself as representative of the American effort of the 1950s to escape a paralyzing ennui. In that novel his self-image of the searcher is also a convenient disguise for the immaturity and lust that really direct his behavior. Now, approaching middle age, he has become sedentary and is a reluctant quester. The threat of change has already turned him reactionary, and he resists the rapid and perplexing transformations in American society. In *Rabbit, Run* he is the restless quester among those who wish him to remain constant; in *Rabbit Redux* he is the stubborn conservative among those who urge change. In the early novel, ironically, for all of his struggle to change, he cannot; in the sequel, ironically, for all of his struggle to remain the same, he changes.

Rabbit's seduction-and-conversion experiences recall a text of the theology student's sermon in the short story "Lifeguard": "Every seduction is a conversion." Updike introduces the third section of the novel with the words of a "Background Voice Aboard Soyuz 5": "We've been raped, we've been raped!" and indeed, this part of *Rabbit Redux* plays with ravishment. Jill is "raped" by Skeeter (she takes pleasure in the game of violation) while Rabbit reads them, at Skeeter's request, a brutal passage from *The Life and Times of Frederick Douglass* about black slave-woman and white-master relations. Later that night Skeeter masturbates while Harry finishes the passage, and Harry almost yields to the lure of homosexuality. But the crux of his seduction and conversion is not sexual; the sexuality, along with the marijuana and the evening readings and talks, is mainly an instrument that gradually draws Rabbit away from his defense of America's moral superiority and toward a negative-critical view of his country's history and present state. In the process, his privacy and his house are violated and his son exposed to corrupting influence, but Harry is also to blame, since he does not resist these infringements. Tricked into taking Jill and Skeeter into his household, he accepts them with a good-natured hospitality mixed with curiosity and fear. His seduction is by them, and his conversation is more a personal response to them than a change of mind or heart.

Of what, then, does Harry's education consist? His lessons are political and sociological, corrected by decisive personal experience. Rabbit's drift to the left is characterized by acts of radical apolitical behavior—giving refuge to a runaway rich girl and a bail jumper, as well as smoking illegal narcotics—and not at all by political activity. In fact, returned to his parents' home after Jill's death, he again defends the necessity of the Vietnam war to his sister. But he does learn. He learns, a bit, to reflect and to react less on visceral reflex. He learns the advantages of enduring in a marriage, of accepting the subtly deepening and unifying dimensions of its daily routine rather than expecting the excitement of a lover. He learns to forgive, and to function while suffering. In sum, he acquires, no doubt belatedly, a fair degree of maturity and emerges not as the despicable fugitive of the *Rabbit, Run* conclusion but as a man who has asserted himself in the midst of overwhelming personal weaknesses and social confusion and gained a measure of dignity thereby.

The "redux" of the novel's title has connotations of recovery from illness that come to apply spiritually to Harry. He has been a ghost, a Peter Rabbit, a mirror image, an underwater struggler, a space drifter, and a victim of a demonic Jesus; but he survives all these to choose, beyond them, a new start with his partner in guilt, shame, and promise. Although he has been sent on a quest against his will, he performs, if not gracefully, at least with a humanity that has an aura of grace. Thus, whereas *Rabbit, Run* stops with the quest dissolved into physical panic ("he runs. Ah: runs. Runs"), the end of *Rabbit Redux* is a resolution of quietness and equanimity: "He. She. Sleeps. O.K.?"

The Social Impact of Fictive Risks

Few novelists would dare to conclude a long and serious novel with "O.K." Fewer still could make that slangy word carry the accumulated weight of emotional meaning that Updike gives it. The ending of *Rabbit Redux* reminds one of Updike's fondness for gimmickry and of his ability to convert the gimmick into fine art. Updike has erected almost flagrantly difficult obstacles for himself in this novel and has overcome them, not merely for the sake of meeting the challenge (although one guesses that this aspect fascinates him), but to create the superior literature resulting from the imaginative realignments that his risks generate.

Updike writes *Rabbit Redux* in the historical present, as he did *Rabbit, Run,* and the effects of that technique reinforce the continuation of the earlier novel's action. The composition of a sequel, however, is a strategy associated nowadays with inferior fiction. Not only must Updike offset the negative overtones of sequel fiction; he must also develop an unpromising protagonist, for Harry Angstrom at the close of *Rabbit, Run* looks like dead-end material. Updike makes the momentum of the earlier novel work for him. The small-city atmosphere of Brewer is perfect for framing the urban, racial, and moral crises of the new book. Rabbit's own evolution from an irresponsible and romantic drifter to lower-middle-class conservative and patriot is entirely credible. His characterization in *Rabbit Redux* is a brilliant coup on Updike's part that makes a familiar figure reusable and, like the locale, dramatizes the varieties of crisis.

A sequel, carefully handled, is an ideal vehicle for stressing both continuity and change. *Rabbit Redux* not only conveys both but also shows how they relate. The absence of deep beliefs, of strong traditions, or of a sustaining vision accompanies and sharpens the tangible problems of America, increases its self-doubt, and causes antagonism among its citizens. In such situations some fall back on the superficial creeds of national infallibility and messianic mission, reasserting the old values with vehemence, while others assume a supercritical posture and belittle the old values and their modern consequences. One seeks security either in continuity or in change. *Rabbit, Run* was successful in the early 1960s, among other reasons, because it showed Rabbit as a sad caricature of the American dreamer. Between that novel and its sequel the very dream has disintegrated; America has become a caricature of its old self. Rabbit, now caught in the tension between continuity and change, between a stubborn worship of the dream and a firsthand experience of its dissolution, is not the substance of the caricature in *Rabbit Redux* but the one who absorbs and reflects it. In this capacity he is just as apt an agent for registering the mood of the late 1960s and beyond as he was for the decade of *Rabbit, Run.*

The schizoid and paranoid symptoms of the polarized nation that Harry exhibits are magnified in Skeeter, whose characterization is the second gimmick-risk in *Rabbit Redux.* The depiction of an amoral, crazy Negro offered in the context of the volatile contemporary racial situation is the most audacious yet of Updike's experiments with borrowed voices. Judged by normal, logical standards, Skeeter is scarcely a believable character. His experiential, emotional, and prophetic capacities are too rich for a single person and tempt one to regard him as a type rather than as an individual. As Vietnam war veteran turned antiwar, drugs dealer, self-proclaimed revolutionary, and black messiah, he is an incarnation of the fearful shapes that have transformed the American dream into a nightmare. Because Skeeter is too powerful a creation for the otherwise realistic cast of the novel, his portrayal threatens to unbalance the whole artistic effort. But one must grant his viability as a credible individual and not only as a type when one recognizes that he is as he is for sound psychological and social reasons. His schizophrenia is manifested in his fragmented personality, in his manic but futile attempts to integrate his real and ideal identities as traumatized war veteran, minor criminal, seducer and lover, racial avenger and redeemer. He lives his paranoia in fear of white persecution and in the delusion of grandeur as self-styled savior.

Because both of Skeeter's illnesses have social dimensions and explicit social causes, one cannot dismiss them as merely personal psychoses. The schizophrenic strain is national, perhaps global, and is particularly virulent in Skeeter because he has been subjected to it in so many roles: as black man in a white society, as soldier in a controversial war, and as a sensitive person in a callous world. His paranoiac fears have some basis in fact: he is indeed sought after by the police, the object of a plot to trap him and others. Skeeter is unbelievable when judged against the old patterns of reality, but he is an embodiment of newer forms of it. He may appear to be an exaggeration, but the new patterns often partake of excess, and, seen in those terms, Skeeter is both a fitting example of the modern hyperexperience and a conceivable product of it.

A third gimmick is the interpolation of special typeset paragraphs in the narrative. The paragraphs are typographically distinct from the rest of the novel; done in the "blacker" and denser newspaper style, they include mistakes of individual letters, words, and lines as well as their corrections. Updike integrates this anomalous aspect into the remainder of the book by linking it to Harry's job as a typesetter. The passages that Harry composes in type for *The Brewer Vat* relate to the dominant tropes of the book, to its plot, and to Harry's interior monologue as he works. Beyond that unifying function, the typeset paragraphs show Harry's transitional cognitive process and the mutability of language itself. Harry, a professional typesetter and an avid newspaper reader, is a Gutenberg man; he is at home with the linear thought and with the sequential action to which the printed page has accustomed him. As a conservative, he thinks not only within the framework of the old content of Western society but also, naturally enough, in terms of its patterns. But, influenced by television, he has started to change even before his seduction and responds to the increasing vocality of the electronic age, to its multi-sensuous impressions, to its illusions of simultaneous activity, to the tendency of its inhabitants to suspend final judgments. Janice says of him, "He put his life into rules he feels melting away now. I mean, I know he thinks he's missing something, he's always reading the paper and watching the news." He handles his typesetter like a computer and foreshadows thereby the fate of his nearly obsolete machine and of his job.

Matured Fiction

Rabbit Redux, as one reviewer commented, is the work of "an awesomely accomplished writer," but Updike's brilliance is almost the book's undoing.[2] Its near flawlessness tends to alienate. Harry's fight with Janice, his fist fight with Skeeter, and the fire that kills Jill, for instance, are scenes of intended emotional intensity so perfectly rendered that they nearly become esthetic curiosities: the reader stops to admire and analyze them but does not yield to unselfconscious involvement in the fictive illusion. Yet one must recall that this is fiction beyond myth that demands a different quality of response: it asks one to maintain a double vision—to keep in mind even during the imagination's exercises that the fictive illusion *is* an illusion, although a necessary one. This illusion models possibilities of existence in order to help one avoid and select. This balancing between reality and illusion can too easily slip into a schizophrenia of the sort that Updike portrays in *Rabbit Redux,* but it need not. Updike's venture beyond myth is not a denial of the imagination but an indication of increased reliance on it. *Rabbit Redux* not only confirms the maturation of Updike as artist but also contributes to the maturation of fiction itself.

Chapter Twelve
More Fiction of the Seventies: The Exertions of Eros

This churning is our journey.

—from "Tossing and Turning"

The Texts of Sex

During the dozen years following the publication of *Rabbit Redux,* Updike continued his prolific writer's way. From 1972 through 1983 he published four novels, four short story collections, a book-length play, a collection of poems, and two collections of nonfiction prose. Considering the fact that this period included some of the most tumultous years of his life, during which he suffered through a divorce and then remarried, one is amazed anew at the sustained pace and consistently high quality of his writing. Indeed, of all these works (taking each of the collections as a whole), only two could be considered—judged against the high standards of Updike's art—as inferior: the play *Buchanan Dying* and the novel *Marry Me.*

Buchanan Dying (1974), which Updike himself labelled a "closet drama," is a tedious historical play on the life and last hours of James Buchanan, fifteenth president of the United States and the only one from Updike's native state of Pennsylvania. Updike reports in his afterword that he first attempted to turn the material of his Buchanan research into a historical novel, the fourth one of a "tetrology, of which the first novel would be set in the future, the second in the present, the third in the remembered past, and the fourth in the historical past."[1] The first three were realized in *The Poorhouse Fair, Rabbit, Run,* and *The Centaur* respectively, but the fourth refused to take shape as a novel, so Updike recast it as a play to be read. He would have done better to abandon it. Although it is not the "full-scale literary disaster" that one usually sympathetic reviewer called it, in its stilted and pretentious diction it comes close.[2] The nearly eighty-page afterword, which presents and comments on Updike's research for the play, is far more interesting and adeptly composed than the dramatic part of the text of twice that length, demonstrating once more that Updike is an essayist of the first rank; but at the same time he joins the company of major American novelists such as Henry James and Saul Bellow who were failures as dramatists.[3]

But even *Buchanan Dying*, pedantic as it is, pays considerable attention to what has clearly become Updike's dominant theme: the relationship between the sexes. To say this is not to report a discovery. Updike has been identified at least since the late sixties as *the* American novelist of modern middle-class sexual behavior. His pursuit of that subject has become relentless, however, to the point that all of his fiction since *Couples* (and including it, of course) has been permeated by themes and images of sexuality.[4] Hence it is appropriate and instructive to organize these chapters on Updike's fiction since 1971 according to literary categories that provide entry to the interpretation of the sexual dimension. Such interpretation, in turn, will serve as a perspective for viewing the totality of Updike's fictive world.

In the present chapter I will begin with readings of representative stories from the *Museums and Women* collection, which collection is, of the eight texts, the one least controlled by, and focused on, the thematics of sexuality—although it is certainly strongly marked by that concern. After that I will turn to the last three novels of the decade and interpret each in terms of sexuality combined with some other emphasized aspect. I will treat the triangle of sex, religion, and language in *A Month of Sundays;* the stress on (and the stresses of) sex and family or sex and domesticity in *Marry Me;* and the combination of sex and politics in *The Coup*. In chapter thirteen I will address the short-story collections *Problems* and *Too Far to Go,* and explicate examples that convey the central theme of both: the dissolution of a marriage and the varieties of attendant suffering. Finally, in chapter fourteen I will look at Updike's two major fictional works of the eighties to date, examining the sex and economics liaison in *Rabbit Is Rich* and the sex and success emphasis in *Beck Is*

Back, and will conclude with a brief comment on Updike's place in American letters.

A word of explanation is, however, in order. In a 1968 interview Updike said, "The author's deepest pride, as I have experienced it, is not in his incidental wisdom but in his ability to keep an organized mass of images moving forward, to feel life engendering itself under his hands. But no doubt fiction is also a mode of spying; we read it as we look in windows or listen to gossip, to learn what other people *do*."[5] Without slighting Updike's—to my mind—more-than-incidental wisdom, I intend to pay closest attention to his "organized mass of images" and treat these as they convey, transposed, what the artist sees from looking in other people's windows.

Museums and Women: Liminal States

The title story (originally published in 1969) of this 1972 collection is crafted as a meditative reminiscence by the narrator-protagonist William Young (manifestly an Updike alter ego) on six significant women in his life and their connection to museums he and they have visited. The recounting of his relationships to these six merges with the imagery of four terms he finds evoked by the two key title words—museums and women—conjoined (and which also echo in his name): radiance, antiquity, mystery, and duty. The story proceeds as a developing interplay of this imagery and of the characterizations of the six women in William's life. For example, William's mother, obviously the first woman in his consciousness and the one who takes him to the local provincial museum, "like the museum" is for her adolescent son "an unsearchable mixture of knowledge and ignorance . . . a mystery so deep it never formed into a question," while the woman—the sixth one of the story— who becomes his lover shares with him in a New York gallery (probably the Cooper-Hewitt) "a translucent interval" and represents to him, along with the museum, "the limits of unsearchability"— radiance and mystery paired.

Yet the orchestration of images based on the quartet of concepts, and of the depiction of the six women interacting with the narrator in museums, disguises a persistent plot line that surfaces toward the end of the story with clarity and power. The narrator's progression, in his relationship with women, has been from mother love, to adolescent infatuation (with the freckled popular girl in his school), to courtship and marriage, to esthetic reflection (on the eighteenth-century figurine of the sleeping girl), to casual erotic friendship, to an extramarital attachment. The common denominator in these is the inaccessibility, one way or another, of all of the women, and William's experience with them has centered on his desire both to know them intimately and to preserve their ineffability. His response to them has been like his passion for museums, where "we seek the untouched, the never-before-discovered, and it is their final unsearchability that leads us to hope, and return." One is not surprised, then, to learn that William has had a serious affair with the sixth woman of the story but has chosen what he perceives as duty over mystery and remains with his wife; this situation, described in the final section, constitutes the main conflict of the story's plot.

A seventh female enters the story at midpoint and reappears toward the close to help resolve via imagery what is left unresolved in the literal action: the headless marble Attic sphinx in the Boston museum, the focal point of William's college-days visit there with the girl (at this time marked by "something mute and remote") he will marry, is glimpsed again years later when William meets his lover, their affair over, in that same gallery. The sphinx combines the four qualities of radiance, antiquity, mystery, and duty that inform William's striving with women. Headless, she suggests the absence of vision that typifies William's erotic sojourn; interacting with the delicate figurine of the slumbering girl, she spells the blend of fascination, danger and premonition that William feels in his dealings with women; and finally, she contrasts in her classic and "pagan" way with the Judeo-Christian imagery that begins and ends the narrative: the imagery of a lost Eden, its portal watched by the archangel rather than a woman with a lion's body. William's mother, the first woman who guides him through the "paradisiacal grounds" redolent of Adam's articulating presence, is replaced by William's wife, who seems to him initially to be "someone guarding the gates"; and in the story's final paragraph, William leaving the museum and his abandoned lover there looks back at the building ("the motionless uniformed guard like a wittily disguised archangel") and feels the loss of innocent wonder and the first hints of jadedness from a surfeit of experiencing. Unsearchability can lead to ennui. The narrator expects "to enter more and more museums, and to be a little less enchanted by each new entrance," and that muted anticipation clearly applies to his future with women as well.

The staging of a mood of world weariness at the end of "Museums and Women" is self-conscious design on Updike's part. It recalls the epigram from Ecclesiastes 3:11–13—the biblical text famous for its evocation of "vanity"—that prefaces the collection, and it anticipates other biblical elements that mark stories such as this one. "I Will Not Let Thee Go Except Thou Bless Me," the fifth story of the collection, are also the words spoken by Jacob in Genesis 32:26 to the angel with whom he has struggled throughout the night. That account, erotic in itself, is employed here in quasi-allegorical fashion to deepen a modern tale of desire and departure. The main components of the Genesis account concern Jacob (destined to become an Israelite patriarch) on the way to his brother Esau's land, wrestling an angel of Yahweh. Because of Jacob's formidable strength the angel cannot prevail until he dislocates Jacob's thigh with a divine touch, but even then Jacob holds him in his grip until he is blessed by the angel and christened with the new name of "Israel."

The Jacob figure in Updike's story is Tom Brideson, a computer software expert about to be transferred to Texas with his wife Lou (one of Jacob's wives is Leah) and their children. The Brideson's attend a predeparture party on the eve of their journey, and there Tom encounters Maggie, his former lover. With her white dress and great white sleeves, she suggests an angel, and her struggles to escape Tom's grasp as they dance are the equivalent of Jacob's contest with the angel. Tom, ironically, does not get the "blessing" from her that he wants—some assurance that she still loves him. Instead, she tells him that he is "nothing," pronouncing his loss of identity instead of a new identity of the sort that Jacob/Israel receives.

But toward its conclusion the story leaves the Genesis model and takes an instructive turn. On the way home Lou reports that Maggie has kissed her "warmly" as she left whereas she was aloof to Tom. The story ends with:

> He must not appear too interested, or seem to gloat. "Well," Tom said, "she may have been drunk."
> "Or else very tired," said Lou, "like the rest of us."

What Tom takes as evidence of Maggie's continued affection for him, bestowed on his wife as surrogate, could just as well be a kiss of good riddance or an impulsive gesture of sympathy for his wife. Weariness at the end of this tale is female exasperation at the male's persistent obliviousness to the emotional distress he causes, a masculine failing that attends many of the dissolving relationships inhabiting Updike's fiction.

A more immediately lethal sexual triangle is handled in the brief story "The Orphaned Swimming Pool," barely six pages long. It begins with an elaborate simile that is expanded into an illustrative narration in the paragraphs that follow: "Marriages, like chemical unions, release upon dissolution packets of the energy locked up in their bonding." The imagery also reminds one of atomic fission and could be a punning comment on the breakdown of the "nuclear" family. At any rate, here a swimming pool becomes the literal focus of a divorce in progress, of its aftermath, and of the instability of neighborhood ties in seemingly solid suburbia. The two-year-old pool, at first the locus of the Turners' uxorial pleasures, through Updike's adoption of a scenic point of view mirrors their separation in the neglect it suffers; then as both Ted and Linda Turner vanish during this late-sixties summer, the neighbors take over the pool, and its use extends to strangers exhaustively accounted for in a comic catalogue of over thirty assorted types. This busy traffic represents the energy let free by one couple's separation. The bizarre listing is matched by the spectacle of Tom and a woman trapped inside the house, by the hordes of pool users, during a clandestine visit, so that "the root of the divorce" is spotted as the lovers flee that evening.

When Linda returns home in the fall, divorced, she sees in the pool images of her broken marriage: "The nylon divider had parted, and its two halves floated independently." Above all, "Linda saw that the pool in truth had no bottom, it held bottomless loss, it was one huge blue tear." This could be the tear of weeping or the tear of rending; both ways it signifies the grief over the end of love. Further, the ex-wife's vision of the pool as bottomless likens it to the classical abyss, symbol of humankind's worst fears. This symbolic weight is too much for such an innocuous object as a suburban swimming pool, but it works as a conveyor of the sense of disproportion and unreality that accompanies the breakdown of deep attachments.

In "The Orphaned Swimming Pool" a suburban community attends a long ritual of separation; in "I Am Dying, Egypt, Dying" an international fellowship of travellers imitates a lengthy rite of passage. The thirty-three page tale is one of Updike's longest, comprehensive enough to contain the complexity of interaction between Clem, a wealthy young American from Buffalo, and more than twenty other characters accompanying him on a luxury boat trip down the Nile in 1967 during the Israel-Egypt conflict. One could profitably engage the old "Ship of Fools" motif to interpret this story, for the motley group floating down the river, dressed in often outlandish costumes and indulging in antic behavior, reminds one of the mad passengers of the *stultifera navis* set adrift on European rivers during the Renaissance and constituting a popular theme of iconography. Stock elements of the Ship of Fools symbolism included a wine glass and a naked woman, and Updike reproduces these in scenes of heavy drinking and of the bikini-clad Swedish girl who desires Clem. Yet Clem himself is too sober to fit such a designation, and his neutral demeanor reminds one far more of Robert Musil's "man without qualities"—an apt *typos* for expressing the superficiality and overadaptability supposed to characterize *homo technicus*.

The words comprising the story's title are uttered twice by the dying Antony to Cleopatra toward the close of Act IV of the Shakespearean drama, and it is sharply ironic that the passionate Roman should be made to serve as a forebear of the bland American. Clem is dying in Egypt only in the sense that he seeks to avoid, in his placid but consuming egotism, all experience that could arouse and unsettle him, and thus the voyage, although it has the trappings of a ritual journey, is for him not a passage that leads to a new stage of being. His *stasis* is stressed, and is carried by two tropes that permeate the narrative. The first (actually two tropes that interact) is the language of mirrors counterposed to that of scratching, and the other is the figuration of parentheses. Clem, of course, is the polished entity who reflects others, without an identity of his own, and the one who resists being scratched—touched in any significant way—by others. And he is the one who exists in parentheses: in a world, and with a provisionary status, that separates him from other people. But the parentheses also mean his "in between state" (a favorite Updike concept), or as the anthropologist Victor W. Turner puts it, his "liminal period" in the rite of passage, the period of transition during which nothing decisive happens.[6] Clem's problem is that he cannot escape this nowhere condition, cannot grow, and condemns himself to an impoverished emotional life.

This story can be read just as profitably as a lightly disguised criticism of United States foreign policy. Viewed from this angle, Clem stands for the rich, blasé, desirable, and enviable America which assumes itself to be at the center of the world's interest, which exerts its great influence globally with an amiable, unwitting destructiveness, and manages always to insulate itself from the worst of human suffering. America's liminal period presents a terrible burden to the rest of humanity, for other nations are spellbound by the wasteful self-absorption of this amorphous giant.

Like "The Orphaned Swimming Pool," "Egypt" concludes with an evocation of the void: "Gazing into the abyss of the trip that was over, [Clem] . . . saw that he had been happy." The "abyss" of the voyage must refer to its emptiness; if Clem has found pleasure in this vacuity, he may be even further removed from participation in erotic existence than he was at the start. His ritual passage seems to be a regression.

It would be misleading to imply that all of the other *Museums and Women* tales deal with the disintegration of love relationships. "I am Dying, Egypt, Dying," possibly the most impressive narrative in the collection, is in fact about the inability to enter into, rather than sustain, such a relationship. Nevertheless it is not incorrect to view this collection as evidence of Updike's deepening concern, if not to say outright obsession, in the early seventies with deteriorating marital, domestic, and broader social-erotic affections. Four other stories from among the fourteen (including the four just analyzed) comprising the first and major part of *Museums and Women* develop facets of the subject. "The Day of the Dying Rabbit" depicts discord within a family on holiday, with marriage problems threatening in the background; "The Witness" shows a middle-aged man's embarrassing attempt to use an affair as an antidote for a bad marriage; in "Solitaire" a husband plays the card game alone while his guilty imagination pits wife against mistress; and "When Everyone Was Pregnant" is a nostalgic trip back to the fifties from the narrator's seventies perspective, evoking young marriages and interlocking domestic lives, and with the predictable theme of infidelity running throughout.

Of the ten stories, some of them experimental, in the middle section called "Other Modes," only one deals with sexuality: the

whimsical "During the Jurassic," in which the familiar Updike
triangle of desire is acted out at a party attended by lustful dinosaurs.
The five stories comprising the final section on "The Maples" are
indeed on the subject, describing the continuing decline of Richard
and Joan Maple's conjugal fortunes; these stories reappear later in
Too Far to Go (in which context I will treat them), where in the
company of the other Maple tales they make up the chronicle of
that couple's marriage and its demise. It is portentous that the
Maple tales conclude *Museums and Women*, for virtually all of Updike's fiction written since then stresses the pleasures and agonies
of those who love neither wisely nor well. It is, however, short-
sighted to conclude, from reading the *Museums and Women* stories,
as Donald J. Greiner does, that "marriage is a relic."[7] The marriage
bonds are indeed vulnerable to the extreme, but as one learns by
the end of *Too Far to Go,* they are also as resilient as anything that
exists.

A Month of Sundays: The Language of the Libido

Updike's seventh novel, as resolutely sexual as *Couples* and *Rabbit
Redux,* both lightens and complicates the dramatization of lovers'
(including married pairs') liaisons in his earlier fiction by adding
the ingredient of humor—an element largely missing heretofore,
except in *Bech: A Book.* The title suggests the improbability of the
novel's plot: what happens here should not occur in "a month of
Sundays," but Updike's preacher-narrator in his enforced recuper-
ative retreat describes the events of his frenetic life (anything but
pastoral), that have "found him in a desert place," a southwestern
rest home for erring clergy—and does it in a comic mode that makes
this a realistically funny book. The humor inhabits the Reverend
Marshfield's language itself; his daily quota of confessional prose,
composed in his room and commenting on his present condition as
well as his past, is full of puns, "Freudian" slips and typographical
errors, and other instances of word play that indicate his near-
compulsive wit, his salaciousness, and his precarious proximity to
an emotional breakdown. It is, in fact, a performance much like
those of Peter De Vries's punning, sex-and-religion plagued protagonists in novels such as *The Mackerel Plaza* and *Forever Panting.*

The first paragraph of *A Month of Sundays* advertises the book's
mood and obsessions: "Forgive me," Marshfield commences, "my

denomination and my town: I am a Christian minister, and an American. I write these pages at some point in the time of Richard Nixon's unravelling. Though the yielding is mine, the temptation belongs to others: my keepers have set before me a sheaf of blank sheets—a month's worth, in their estimation. Sullying these is to be my sole therapy." The "point in . . . time" (a wicked echoing of a Nixon cliché) is 1973, and Nixon's "unravelling" about a year before his resignation from the presidency to avoid impeachment suggests the collapse of the web of lies that held together his government but also the disintegration of Marshfield's personality and vocation under sexual and religious pressures. The sheets to be sullied are a masturbator's linens as well as stationery, and this pun sets up the Freudian-defined tension of pen/penis, between writing and masturbation, the resolution of which is intended as Marshfield's sole/soul therapy.

In keeping with the comic mode's liveliness, Updike's busy novel displays a confusion of things happening that needs to be orchestrated by the reader. Marshfield's accounts of his tense marriage to Jane, the no-nonsense daughter of his mentor (an ethics professor), of his affair with Alicia—his organist—and his dalliances with other wives of his congregation, and of the visits he dreads to his senile father mix with the rest-home writing he undertakes, above all the four sermons he composes there (one for each Sunday), with his description of his rounds of golf, poker, and drinking amidst his convalescing colleagues, and with his running report of his efforts to seduce Ms. Prynne, the spa's manager. In all of these Marshfield's state of mind, and of body, is crucial and determines the plot development. The narrative of *A Month of Sundays* can be read most instructively against the traditional plot of bad fortune and recovery—a version of the hero myth in which the nadir of the protagonist's journey, his descent to the underworld, his time of total alienation and isolation, leads predictably to the happy reversal of fortunes, to recuperation and reintegration into society. In Marshfield's case, however, the positive transformation is never fully accomplished and is possibly hardly achieved at all.

The central action of the novel, obscured by many distractions, is Marshfield's "therapy." It consists of his writing "ad libidum" his daily allotment of confessional discourse that is intended to guide him toward self-knowledge, we assume, and return him to emotional and societal equilibrium. Much of Marshfield's composition comprising the novel's text is aligned to psychoanalytical, religious-confessional, and storyteller's assumptions: he relates what strike him as significant elements of his past in order to understand his present; by discovering older influences and assessing past behavior he may hope to identify the reasons for his present dilemma and gain the insight necessary to will change. But guilt, consisting of a sense of culpability for misbehavior, also pervades his personality. To assuage it he gives it a specific religious coloration: guilt results from the betrayal of orthodox Christian beliefs, he implies, and then asserts his own conservative faithfulness against the damaging, enervating liberal Christianity that surrounds him. It is, of course, ironic that Marshfield the conservative clergyman should need to find his "cure" in the flabby psychological self-help atmosphere of the sanitarium rather than, say, the pastoral-care context of his own profession.

Finally, Marshfield is a preacher who learns through his enforced writing the attractions of raconteurship, an interpreter of sacred texts and proclaimer of a religious message who discovers storytelling, and his recounting of his life in anecdotal form becomes a pleasure for him. In his autotherapeutic role, then, he is seeking to overcome his "distraction" (the term his church gingerly gives to his overwrought condition), the confusions of mind that have caused his destructive actions, and to get himself recentered as minister, husband, father, and friend. In his role as spiritual leader he is attempting to articulate his own creed, to find a faith that will help him to function in what he perceives to be a religious atmosphere that begs the real issues of belief. And as a narrator, he simply wishes to tell a good story.

It becomes quickly clear that in all of these efforts, themselves interrelated, the matters of sex, religion, and language are intricately and perhaps hopelessly intertwined.[8] Marshfield's "distraction" seems to be basically a familiar sexual problem: he has a strong libidinal appetite; he is immature in his sexual development and outlook (although forty-one years old) and is aroused by the traditionally forbidden—naked bodies, sexual intercourse and its variations, genitalia, and obscene language—as is evidenced by his voyeurism (he watches his associate pastor and organist make love), by his obsessive masturbation, and fascination with sexual terminology; he is undisciplined and irresponsible in his intersexual relations—a seducer, a womanizer, and an adulterer; he is on certain occasions impotent.

But the fact that he is this way and the fact that he, his wife, and his congregation know that he is this way do not help him toward recovery. He and they see his condition described but not diagnosed. Some knowledge of why he is thus inspires a first step toward recovery, such as it is: his sexual immaturity is at least in part the result of religious frustration. His adolescence in a parsonage as the son of an overwhelming liberal Protestant minister-father, his marriage to a reasonably well-adjusted woman who does not share his penchant for erotic excitement, his restless quest for certainty on elusive doctrinal matters have conspired to produce in him a bafflement that needs the relief of something like sexual excess. That excess is indulged in through his lively and sometimes funny affair with his organist and through his seduction, under the guise of spiritual and marital (!) counselling, of a number of women in his church.

The behavior pattern is common enough, and the psychological explanation of it is standard. Marshfield himself provides it; the reader does not need to superimpose it. Things become truly interesting when one adds, to sex and religion, language as the third component. Updike has long been intrigued by the implications of this threesome. One recalls the thesis of the theology student's mock sermon in the early short story "Lifeguard": "Every seduction is a conversion," or Piet Hanema's meditation on oral-genital sex and religious meaning in *Couples* that Marshfield enlarges on in *A Month of Sundays*. In this novel language is still more intensely implicated in the problem, its analysis, and its attempted solution. Language contributes to the problem in that Marshfield uses his glibness to satisfy—and justify—his libidinous appetite. By sophistry he talks his way to sexual conquest of women in his congregation, and by self-deceptive argument he rationalizes the seductions. Beyond that, writing for Marshfield is an erotic solitary pleasure not unlike masturbation, something not in any sense evil but gratuitous, that can be indulged in to avoid facing issues of identity and responsibility. Language serves as an obvious overt aspect of Marshfield's self-diagnosis in that he literally describes, largely by narrating crucial incidents of his past, and glosses the personal history that has made him a sexual vagrant. Apart from that, the Freudian slips, puns, and typos that he makes and nurtures indicate his overattention to the sexual aspects that unbalances his personality. His interpretations, in footnotes, of each such mutant term constitute a self-conscious effort to address and redress his condition (the typos and analyses of them comprise the "gimmick" of this novel, not unlike the typeset headlines in *Rabbit Redux* and later in *Rabbit Is Rich*).

Language functions above all in the novel as the basis of Marshfield's endeavor to heal himself. The daily writing assignment imposed upon him is itself intended as curative, although Marshfield merely plays with much of it and uses it to evade honest self-confrontation. But the four sermons that he prepares for his four Sundays at the rest home are the best indication of how language is employed toward emotional and spiritual healing. The sermons, in themselves brilliant if often perverse homiletical exercises, serve as a gauge of Marshfield's gradually improving state of mind. They shift from a hysterical defense of adultery (the first) to a petulant treatise on miracles (the second) to a self-indulgent but fairly credible meditation on healing through isolation (the third) to a finally preachable fourth one on immortality, the resurrection of the body, and a Pascalian species of belief. By the fourth Sunday, in other words, Marshfield has written himself through to a new control over himself and to what looks like a resolution of his personal crisis of religious faith.[9]

The evolution, then, comprises in good part the plot of the novel: the narrator finds his way through conflict to a certain kind of new self-coherence and identity, and he does so both by describing "plots" of his past life that he has unravelled and by engaging in an imaginative-discursive art, sermon writing, to establish and confirm the new sense of self. That is not, however, the whole story. All the while another plot is unfolding, consisting of Marshfield's attempt to seduce Ms. Prynne, the large and imposing manager of the sanitarium. Although this action emerges as a counter-plot to the rest of the narrative, it also takes advantage of the sex-religion-language triangle. Marshfield finds Ms. Prynne distinctly undesirable at first (she reminds him of a turtle), but the longer he is without women the more attractive she seems, and eventually, as the one who reads his daily production, she becomes the focus of his sexual attention. He speaks seldom to her but communicates passionately through his confessional pages. As his time at the rest home draws short he courts her with increasing fervor—and vulgarity—and in ways that parody eschatological expectation. This seduction at the end becomes the occasion for outrageous theological analogies: "with the same unkillable intuition that leads me to laud the utterly *absconditus Deus,* I feel that there is a place in you for me," Marshfield writes to her, and two days later on the eve of his departure: "Even so, come," echoing the *Maranatha* of I Corinthians 16:22 and the conclusion (22:20, "Come, Lord Jesus!") in the Book of Revelation. Comparing the aloof Ms. Prynne to the absent God and then beseeching her gracious presence, in the manner of the early Christian church pleading for Christ's return, for sexual union is scandalous and perversely funny. That she does actually appear and make love to him at the last minute is an apt finish to his correspondence (critic George Hunt thinks it is a "somewhat silly sexual climax"[10]) but an unsettling omen for his future. Marshfield has experienced grace in the Lutheran sense (at least he claims that he has) and generosity in the sexual sense, but one does not expect him therefore to change his ways. We are left with the impression that he will return sooner or later to his destructive patterns, and that nothing really has been resolved except the crisis that brought him to the Southwest in the first place.

If basic things are left inconclusive, it may be because the novel also acts, and can be read, as an allegory of two situations that likewise remain unresolved. One is the relationship of contemporary Americans to sex and religion; the other is the relationship of the present-day literary artist to his/her audience. In the first of these, Updike has Marshfield stand for the citizens of Middle America, wishing to be steadfast in their faith and resolute in their sexuality, but afflicted with a lifelong immaturity that renders them prone to confusions of spirit and flesh—often to overvaluations of either one at the expense of the other—compounded by an inability even to articulate the dilemma. In the second, Marshfield composing under duress for Ms. Prynne, his "Ideal Reader," is a figure of the Western novelist writing confessionally, self-indulgently, yet under the compulsion to satisfy the ineluctable standards of a not very responsive readership. It is a relationship doomed to fail, except at the rare moments when language transcends lack, and author and reader together witness how the miracle of humans offering themselves and accepting each other redeems lifetimes of alienation. Updike dramatizes such a moment at the end of *A Month of Sundays,* and the novel itself inspires a similar experience for the sympathetic reader.

Marry Me: The Failure of Romance

Even the best novelists parody themselves, inadvertently, at least once in their careers (Hemingway did it in *Across the River and into the Trees,* Faulkner in *A Fable*), and Updike succumbed to self-parody in *Marry Me.* Published in 1976 and written (like *A Month of Sundays*) while Updike lived alone in Boston prior to his second marriage, *Marry Me* is set in 1962 in a New England town named Greenwood, one year before the Tarbox events of *Couples.* The novel is a simplified version of *Couples* that focuses on a single affair and its effects on two families, rather than on the interlocking erotic maneuvers of the earlier book. Yet it gains nothing through this reduced scope.

Four aspects of the story that might work otherwise to help generate the usual high quality of Updike's narrative prose conspire here to produce a poor imitation. First, whereas Updike's male protagonists are often unlikeable and occasionally despicable but usually plausible, this one is neither likeable nor credible. Second, the formal structuring of the text, in other instances an important device for plot reinforcement, works in *Marry Me* as artificial and strained. Third, Updike's generic identification of the book as a "romance," which should lead to a deciphering of its mysteries, mainly confuses and obscures. Fourth, the stress of the action on sex and domesticity is only partially successful in evoking a believable sense of the pain that children and spouse suffer in a family fractured by infidelity.

Jerry Conant, the thirty-year-old main character, belongs to the lineage of Updike's weak men, represented by Harry Angstrom of *Rabbit, Run,* Jerry Robinson from *Of the Farm,* and Richard Maple from the Maples short stories. They are, in our current vernacular, "wimps": indecisive, overly sensitive, self-indulgent types who depend on and exploit stronger persons—here stronger women—for their emotional equilibrium. Updike's writing displays a curious tolerance for such men; a surprising amount of his fiction is devoted to describing the agonies they endure as a result of their tender sensibilities. Jerry Conant reminds one much of Jerry Robinson: both are young Manhattan professionals burdened with vulnerable natures (and the attendant allergies) who think a great deal about religion and death in connection with sex, and both use and are used by the women close to them. But whereas Jerry Robinson has made a crucial decision and is learning to live with its consequences (he has divorced his first wife and is adjusting to his second), Jerry Conant stays racked by indecision: whether to wed Sally, his married lover, or to remain with his wife and their children. The material in both books tends toward sentimentality, but where Updike transcends it in *Of the Farm* through a taut, finely balanced narrative structure and convincing dialogue, he lets bathos dominate in *Marry Me.* A main reason it does is that Jerry, by himself and with Sally, appears congenitally silly. One could argue that adults in the throes of infatuation are, in fact, that way and that Updike has caught the tone of such characteristic conversation and behavior, if it were not that the writing itself, like the situations it describes, is excessive. Updike could bring off the conclusion of *Rabbit Redux* with "O.K.?" but the risk fails in *Marry Me.* Even sympathetic readers can absorb only a limited amount of dialogue on the order of:

Whenever a distance between them seemed about to grow, she would call, "Hey?"
 "Hi," he'd answer gravely.
 "Hi," she answered back.

Such scenes remind one how close Updike, who regularly spins fine fiction out of ordinary stuff, often is to self-parody, and how easy is the slide into it.

In *Of the Farm* Updike checks the impulse toward the maudlin through the discipline of the novella's chiasmic form as well as through a certain cthonic rootedness of setting and action; in *Couples* through a fairly precise orchestration of the ten pairs' interactions. He attempts, unsuccessfully, a similar control in *Marry Me* through fashioning symmetries of structure and plot. The paired long middle chapters are intended to balance each other: "The Reacting of Ruth" is followed by "The Reacting of Richard," both focusing, more or less, on the responses of the lovers' mates to the affair. The final chapter, "Wyoming," consists of three journeys: one taken by Jerry, Sally, and her children; one by Jerry, Ruth, their children; and one by Jerry alone. The three obviously invite comparison. The plot contrasts two couples, each with three children, and the central action of the liaison between Jerry and Sally is complemented by the brief affair that Richard and Joan had. These symmetries and others do not, however, constitute anything more than a gratuitous pattern—or to put it in formalist terms, the balances and counterpoints do not cohere to produce a meaningful configuration that would lend the superficial story some substance.

Updike has not given a descriptive label to any other of his novels, and it is not clear why he should have chosen to call *Marry Me* a romance. Since he has supplied it with that name, however, one checks to see if it offers some clue toward a clearer understanding of the author's strategy—and is disappointed to learn that it does not. *Marry Me* is manifestly not a romance in the traditional literary generic sense; it is not a Medieval tale, such as those comprising the material of the Arthurian romances, reflecting the heroic and chivalrous temper attached to the feudal era. Nor can it be read instructively as a modern ironic version of such a tale, although one recalls that Updike has exercised such a tactic ("Four Sides of One Story," on the Tristan-Iseult material), and recognizes in Jerry the same transparent courtly love gestures that characterize Piet Hanema in *Couples*. What the Medieval romance and Updike's novel have mainly in common is the fascination with adultery and a lyric celebration of it—but that surely does not legitimize *Marry Me* as a romance.

It is also not a romance according to a second, less constrained definition of the genre as a companion form to the novel, a fanciful or exotic narrative of love. It is indeed overdone, but the excess is in the presentation of the characters' behavior against a realistic, "novelistic" background of ordinary life, unlike the thoroughgoing extravagance of all dimensions of authentic romance. One suspects, then, that "romance" here means merely a story of lovers playing out their illusions and infatuations, depicted relatively uncritically (and in a less sexually explicit idiom) by an indulgent author. It signals Updike's attitude toward his characters, in other words, as a tolerance that he is otherwise, as a rule, not ready to grant. But since that attitude covers a lapse of artistic discipline and results in a banality of plot and characterization, romance understood thus is more excuse than explanation.

Marry Me, in Updike's nod to experimental fiction, has three, possibly four endings, and all of them, as befits the romance effort, are "happy." All of them involve an exotic journey, an escape to some desirable distant spot, yet all of this passionate travel is collapsed into Jerry's worn metaphor, close to the end, of the lovers' passage in his imagined conversation with an absent Sally:

> *"There was a place I went to with you."*
> *"Any woman in bed will take you there."*

That sentiment and its (in)articulation convey the inferiority of a writing performance that is not redeemed by a fashionably oblique conclusion.

Marry Me works best where the adornments of romance are overcome by the concentration on the tensions of sex and family. Updike often pays slight attention to the children of his couples in conflict, although one knows from his earlier fiction that he can in fact portray children compellingly. It is strange, therefore, that in *Couples, A Month of Sundays,* and some of the Maple stories the adolescents are hardly more than part of the furniture, and stranger still that the domestic scenes of *Marry Me* are the most convincing aspects of the narrative. The scene in the "Reacting of Ruth" section, for example, where Jerry's wife strikes him in the children's stunned presence at the Sunday dinner table is a powerfully described moment of family anguish and crisis, incited by sexual turmoil, that could take its place among passages of Updike's finer writing from all of his fiction. It is also an instance of how Updike exploits skillfully the sense of a family as burden and restriction and as the tenaciously central aspect of the illicit lovers' lives that generates both guilt and the longing for freedom. Imagery of weight and binding connotes the severity of domestic responsibility in *Marry Me:* children must be carried and held on to, and they are prominently and even relentlessly present in the narrative's various endings. The mature reminder of this immature account is that passion, as the extravagant focus on the loved one, cannot for long avoid the demands of other loved ones; that the ensuing conflicts infect desire with guilt and sooner or later force decisions that leave someone the loser. A root meaning of passion, one recalls, is "suffering."

Early on, Jerry says to Sally on the beach, "The fucking sun won't stand still," marking his frustration with their domestic dilemma by the obscene addition to a phrase inspired by Andrew Marvell's "To His Coy Mistress" poem. Neither will the families go away. If Updike had developed the sentiments of the situation rather than its sentimentality, and if he had attended still more resolutely to the lovers and their children rather than their childishness, he might have produced a better novel and perhaps even a worthy "romance."

The Coup: America as Africa

If it took a failure like *Marry Me* to inspire Updike's next novel, it may have been worth the fiasco, for *The Coup,* published in 1978, is regarded by some as among the best long fictional works he has composed thus far.[11] That is not excessive praise; *The Coup* is a startling recovery from the mawkishness of *Marry Me,* an abrupt change of pace from the stress on white, American middle-class marital mores to an account of sexual and revolutionary politics of another continent and color. It is as if, having for once botched the self-assigned artistic challenge (the "gimmick" of *Marry Me* would be the attempt to write a contemporary romance of quality and depth), Updike sets himself another, harder one and meets it brilliantly.

The Coup is the most complex and densely packed novel that Updike has written: a blend of fiction and history, of the comic and tragic; a fairly ostentatious display of esoteric knowledge mixed with invention; a stunning example of sheer linguistic virtuosity; and a return to the mythic that Updike had largely abandoned by the era of *Rabbit Redux* but now revived and tempered by a crucial irony as well as by satire and even farce. Absolutely central, however, is the character portrayal of the protagonist, who is sometimes first person and sometimes third person narrator of the memoirs that comprise the text: Colonel Hakim Félix Ellelloû, forty-year-old Moslem-Marxist ex-president of the sub-Saharan, west African country of Kush. Ellelloû is the apotheosis of Skeeter, the black radical of *Rabbit Redux*, a gifted, sensitive, immensely complicated military man who is driven by rage, ambition, and patriotic devotion to take part in a 1968 revolution in his country that gets rid of the old king, his mentor, and eventually leaves Ellelloû in control. He and his country seem in many ways identical and inseparable, yet the novel unfolds as the inexorable and highly ironic dissolution of the ties between them as Ellelloû wanders incognito and increasingly alienated through the land, is sent from power by another coup, and is finally exiled to France.

The Coup was inspired at least in part by a three-week tour that Updike took in 1973 (also the time of the novel's action), as Fulbright lecturer across Africa, an itinerary that led him through Ghana and Nigeria, east to Tanzania and Kenya, and finally to Ethiopia. Kush seems to be most like the real west African nation of Chad—although Ellelloû himself has resemblances to Haile Selassie, who was still monarch of Ethiopia when Updike visited there—and some of the key incidents of the narration are based on fact, such as the catastrophic drought which in 1973 has already ravaged Kush for five years and which in actuality killed thousands of sub-Saharans during that time. An Afrophile of sorts, Updike has clearly done his homework on that continent, for the novel bristles with knowledgeable description and references.[12] Such thorough preparation helps to justify Updike's temerity in assuming a persona so different from his own: speaking as and through a black Francophone African ruler is considerably more audacious than Updike's prior greatest risk: taking on the role of Henry Bech, the contemporary American Jewish novelist.

Nevertheless, Updike's characterization of Colonel Ellelloû is basically a tour de force rather than an insider's portrayal of a person from a radically different culture. It could hardly be otherwise: three decades in that environment might give a writer the requisite insights and intuitions to write intimately about its otherness; three weeks would not suffice for even the most ingenious novelist-biographer. The evidence for this view is that Ellelloû is easily comprehensible to American—and, one would think—other Western, "First World" readers as well. He exists in what is for foreigners (namely Western readers) an exotic setting, his habits are strange, his fortunes and actions to our lights often bizarre; yet he is withal a cunningly designed version of the wonted Updike "hero," and we gain through his portrayal little sense of "the African mind." We would probably learn more of Africa, in fact, if Updike had fashioned an American protagonist to experience one or more of those cultures, for that character would have provided us with a familiar point of view and offered the necessary elements for comparison—would have forced the author to present the foreign experience comparatively.

The main value of the Ellelloû depiction is the refracted perspective on American society it intends. That Ellelloû should be the foreign interpreter of America is ironic, for he is no Alexis de Toqueville. He hates America passionately, even though (or because) one of his four wives is an American he met in the 1950s while an exchange student at the fictitious McCarthy College in "Franchise, Wisconsin," but also because of his first-hand experience of American excess and of American racist attitudes, and above all because of his Marxist and Moslem convictions. Seen through Ellelloû's eyes, the United States in a vulgar land of profligacy, greed, and utter corruption that attempts to exploit the rest of the world, and it serves as his principle negative model: he wants to make Kush precisely what America is not, and to keep it uncontaminated by America's "obscenity and glut."

This effort, and its failure, inform two of the very forceful passages in *The Coup,* scenes that are a blend of grim humor and social criticism. In the earlier of these, in which an American foreign aid official is immolated standing atop a mountain of processed food shipped to the border of Kush by the United States for the starving inhabitants, Ellelloû's decision to martyr the American is a protest against the arrogant and condescending "help" from a superpower that does not bother to consider the possible damage its naïve and self-serving relief policies might cause. The other, scene, toward the end, describes Ellelloû's shocked discovery of the fully Americanized industrial town, named for him, at an oil drilling site in the remote center of Kush. Ellelloû's abortive attempt to lead the townspeople to destroy this desecration of their landscape and culture, this perverse technological oasis so improbable as to seem unreal, is the start of his downfall. Ellelloû's inability to prove his identity, and his isolation in the town allows his disloyal protégés back in the capital to prepare his demise. He is at last overcome by the very capitalistic technology and spirit from which he had hoped to save his people.

Such ironic and social-critical characterization and plotting are rendered artistically illuminating and given depth through certain image patterns and pervasive mythic motifs. For example, the imagery of emptiness and of nothingness is used to represent simultaneously the near-hopeless barrenness of Kush and the spiritual desolation of both the United States and the Soviet Union, the two technological forces conspiring to exert the greater influence in Africa. Quotations from the Kòran ("Does there not pass over man a space of time when his life is a blank?"), depictions of the parched countryside and the constant craving for water, and confessions and accusations of a vacuity of soul shape the wasteland atmosphere that, although its locale here is the African desert, is made to stand for the disease of Western consumerist society as surely as, say, the industrial pollution and urban blight of eastern Pennsylvania that frame the Rabbit novels. Not incidentally, one of Updike's most perceptive critics, Joyce Markle, argues that *The Coup* is Updike's

Nabokovian book, that its consistencies are so many and blatant as to reveal that it is "Ellelloû's fantasy as *Lolita* is Humbert Humbert's or *Pale Fire* is Kinbote's," and that the shadowy, unreliable narrator might even not be African at all.[13] Although this view may take the speculation on Ellelloû's identity too far, it is true that at least some of the narrator's memoirs are sheer fabrication and that a nothingness, therefore, is at the heart of the novel's telling.

Reference to a wasteland leads one to think of myth (and of Medieval romance), for the archetype of the Fisher King in his blighted landscape constitutes an overt mythic element of the novel. Ellelloû sees himself as that now ineffectual fertility king, complete with wound (his sore mouth, his crippling hatred), languishing in his arid land and awaiting renewal. Yet as Markle points out, "he is also Oedipus and when he is banished, fertility returns and the desert gets its rain."[14] Further, Ellelloû enacts the mythic role of the king, or god, who travels disguised and unrecognized among his subjects, and who like Ulysses returning home at last, dressed as a begger, discloses himself to those who have usurped his power. Unlike the Homeric epic, however, *The Coup* at this point turns comic once again as Ellelloû (rather than slaughtering the upstarts, Odysseus-style) calmly participates in the discussion regarding his fate. Just as important is the variation on the dying king myth crafted throughout the novel. Ellelloû takes part in toppling the old king and eventually orchestrates his public beheading, but here all similarity to Frazer's *Golden Bough* version of the myth ends, for the severed head ends up (in a description fully as surreal as those treated earlier) as an electronic oracle, wired Disneyland style by the Russians in a cave across the Kush border to utter propaganda against Ellelloû and the West. Ellelloû himself does not, of course, face execution as the deposed ruler but retires to comfortable exile in France to write his memoirs.

In every case, then, a serious employment of myth is somehow short-circuited by a subtly humorous or farcical twist. Markle thinks that *The Coup* is "a fable about the end of fables."[15] One could say just as well that it involves a renewed engagement of myth to show the impotence of myth. Or, in the language of a current critical approach, myth is appropriated by Updike to "deconstruct" itself, and in doing so to demonstrate how fiction on revolution, its style adroitly handled, can also comment on a revolution of fiction. For like *A Month of Sundays* most spectacularly among Updike's novels,

and like most of our best fiction, *The Coup* is about writing im-
aginatively (a basic meaning of fiction has to do with making,
fabricating) in order to create a tentative meaning for those conditions in which the tradition has lost its authority.

At the same time, *The Coup* is also emphatically about sexuality
and politics, and that combination is elucidated through the often
funny and sometimes poignant narration of Ellelloû's fortunes with
his mistress and four wives. This account is not unlike the "Museums
and Women" narrator's recollection and metaphoric ordering of his
relations with the women who influenced him, with the difference
that Ellelloû's mates threaten to overwhelm him by their immediacy.
Yet in this surfeit of the feminine, Updike explores the ramifications
of a Western male fantasy—another way in which the novel is more
about America than Africa: what if one—the male—could legiti-
mately, with social approval, have a number of women and assign
them roles and tasks at will? Ellelloû has among his wives a mother
figure (with whom he practices a proper Oedipal relationship), an
exotic (for his tastes) American blend of virgin and bitch, a practical
spouse, and a young seductive playmate. In his mistress and protégé
Katunda he also encounters the lower caste Pygmalion who becomes
his nemesis, for she is one of those who, caught in a lust for power,
plans his political demise and uses him for her own career.

All of these together, including Katunda before her betrayal,
obviously do not provide Ellelloû with any sort of balanced or
satisfying domestic, sexual, or social life. One is warned, in case it
is necessary, through this wealth and confusion of female types, that
the male fantasy, if it could be fulfilled in the West, would be more
of a nightmare than a dream. More than that, the arrangement
suggests that sex and politics linked make for—simply—sexual
politics, which means that collaboration between the sexes in matters
of civil governance, social justice, etc., cannot occur effectively
without full equality and respect granted to women and men by
each other.

Chapter Thirteen
Problems and *Too Far to Go:*
Love above the Void

> The tide sighs and rises in my sleep.
> The flame is furious in its cell below.
>
> —from "Phenomena"

Problems: Multiple Choice

Updike begins the prefatory author's note to this collection, published in 1979, with the words, "Seven years since my last short story collection? There must have been problems." Those problems are indirectly identified a few sentences later by Updike describing the years of the stories' composition, 1971–1978, as a "curve of sad time"—the time during which he separated from and then divorced his first wife. Thus many (but by no means all) of the twenty-three stories concern couples in various stages of separation or in the aftermath of a divorce, often with children figuring prominently in the action.

One not on that subject is "The Gun Shop," a grandfather-father-son story that reminds one a good deal of *The Centaur,* although here, in the familiar Pennsylvania context, it is the aging grandfather who is effusive and touching rather than the father (like George Caldwell in that novel). At the risk of typing the tale too neatly, one can accurately label it a Freudian-oriented story of subtle competition between the generations. "Hit me again and I'll kill you," the unruly fourteen-year-old son tells his father Ben, the protagonist, who has disciplined him, and Ben's final words of the story, expressing pride at his son's marksmanship, are "You're killing me!" In between, during the visit to the gun repair shop which takes up most of the story, the discussion of weaponry and war, while the

161

crusty old gunsmith works, initiates the spoiled boy into respect for craftsmanship and death. The boy outshooting the father at the end enacts a ritual of the succession of generations, and Ben's relief is for the evidence that his son shows, even in "his murderous concentration," of incipient readiness for a harsh world.

Problems is dedicated to Updike's four children, and five more stories in the collection deal primarily with a middle-aged male protagonist's often painful relationships with his offspring: "Nevada," "Son," "Daughter, Last Glimpses Of," "Separating," and "Guilt-Gems." "Nevada," the only one of these I shall discuss, connects a father caring for his two daughters to the familiar theme of sexuality. Fred Culp (less culpable than many of Updike's males), bringing the children from Reno back home to Denver while his recently divorced ex-wife goes on a honeymoon with her new husband, takes on a welter of formidable tasks: absorbing the loss of the wife he still loves, softening his oldest daughter's resentment over her mother's breakup of the family, preparing her for her sexual maturation (she is sixteen), and caring discreetly for his own sexual desires. Culp, playing the ubiquitous slot machines en route for his younger daughter's entertainment, and with little success, is the forlorn ex-husband, stoically muddling through a bad time, hoping for some measure of luck that will help him toward recovery.

"Transaction," although it dramatizes a night shared by the protagonist "Ed" (he never reveals his true name) and Ann, a prostitute, is in a sense also a father-daughter story, for Ed is forty and Ann twenty-two, and he feels a paternal affection of sorts for the tough girl. But that is not the emphasis of the story. Ed has never been with a prostitute before, and the experience now, in a hotel in an unfamiliar city, both excites and intimidates him. For a time, though, the intimidation prevails and makes him unable to perform—which impotence becomes the story's "problem." When he does manage at last, and the "transaction" is completed—sex for money—Ed discovers that the girl has left him with more than that exchange: "What she had given him, delicately, was death. She had made sex finite." An astronomer, Ed now sees "through it, into the spaces between the stars." It is the Christmas season, and the two have made love on the bed close to where Ed has stacked the presents bought for his family. Ann's gift to him, the reader is invited to see, is what results from the transaction: she demystifies sex for him and makes him wiser if, perhaps, less happy. Yet the girl herself remains mysterious, a night person evoking a combination of innocence and corruption, of delight and death like William Blake's cryptic verses in Ed's book of poems.

"Problems," the title story, is a slight, witty piece presenting the divorced or separated protagonist's woes with his (ex-)spouse, family, mistress/new wife, and guilt as six mathematical puzzles to be solved. It is a negligible tale that would not, one suspects, have found a publisher (it appeared first in *The New Yorker*) without Updike's reputation to lend it weight. "Domestic Life in America," the story immediately following it in the collection, is a traditional and more substantial version of the same situation and even continues, at a few points, the geometry motif. In it Fraser visits both his estranged wife and family and his lover and family during the Christmas season and becomes involved—or embroiled—half-insider and half-outsider, in the daily lives of both. He is clearly most comfortable with his own family, and indeed, since they seem on the whole more attractive than his lover and her children, one wonders why he has left. Fraser himself seems to wonder the same thing, yet he is not, apparently, reconsidering his decision. The title keys the story toward a social-critical reading: families in various stages of dissolution and strained by anger, grief, and guilt carry on. The implication is that this is standard domestic life in America—and perhaps it is.

Two related stories on the subject of lovers and their families that do little credit to *Problems* are "Love Song, for a Moog Synthesizer" and "The Fairy Godfathers." The lovers in the throes of separation from spouses and children are Tod and Pumpkin—whose names suggest their intellectual level and the tone of the stories. Both narratives come close to the self-parody of *Marry Me*. The characters' self-indulgent behavior and their saccharin dialogue ("Oh, Pumpkin, how long can this go on?") in the service of yet two more plots of marital and extramarital distress accrue to induce a sense of excess, of the author belaboring a theme and a mode of expressing it beyond the bounds of interest and value. " 'Oh, Pumpkin,' Tod would say. 'Nobody likes us'." It is easy to see why.

A far better story that varies the theme is "The Faint," featuring Freddy Python, middle-aged Boston real estate developer and man-about-town who, following a typical evening out, folds constrictorlike "his mind around the evening's seized pleasures." His victim at the moment is the lovely Corinna, yet he does not wish to absorb but to be rid of her, for her torpid and disorganized style (and it is a style) has come to bore and irritate him. The narrative's irony is that, through a display of weakness, she traps him and, in a sudden reversal of the snake imagery, soon after he "felt himself engorged by pride" in her, "he was lost in her. . . . He was inside her." On a rare evening out, namely, attending with Freddy a one-woman play on Emily Dickinson, Corinna faints during the intermission (conveniently), and, lying unconscious, captivates him with her mysterious, enveloping beauty. He is mesmerized, and one is not surprised to learn that they marry.

Part of the pleasure of this text comes from tracing other aspects of the snake imagery and discovering how Corinna almost from the start is described through reptile metaphors, although one has been led by Freddy's last name to see him as the snake. Corinna "rotate[s] languidly through her two rooms"; "her tongue was darting about like a rabbit in the headlights"; unconscious, she has an "utterly limp and ponderous body"; as a child she would rip her party dresses "right down the middle" like a snake shedding its skin; and her faint, she claims, was caused by a dress ("of silvery-blue, patterned abstractly") that made her feel closed in. One snake swallows the other in this subtly predatory tale, but it will be a fate hard for both of them to digest.

"The Egg Race" is vintage Updike, focusing on a middle-aged male protagonist, divorced and remarried, on a sentimental return to his boyhood home. It also concerns fathers and sons and is full of finely designed metaphoric patterns. Ferguson, the central character, is an archaeologist, and the tropes of exploration into the stratified past are dominant. Ferguson is undergoing a delayed reaction to the death of his father, a much admired high-school teacher, five years earlier and to the loss of his son through the divorce and the boy's growing up. Ferguson's dream of travelling with his father, and his recollection of a good trip with his own son represent important fragments in his unconscious and in his memory that need to be excavated for him to understand, this late in life, what great "unstated sorrow" his father had kept from him. Similarly, his hospital visits to his senior colleague, a surrogate father dying of cancer, cause him to relive, in quick and concentrated form, his life's stages thus far.

"A seeker of lost cities," Ferguson in his middle-age crisis (his "problem") accepts an invitation to return to his boyhood town for a twenty-fifth high-school class reunion. The drunken and melancholy celebration there teases him into digging for more of his past, and in the act he uncovers shards of memory that instruct him, interpreted as they are through his profession, in how he already belongs to history and exists as a fixed entity in the memories of others.

The archaeologist destroys in order to preserve, but Ferguson is far more cautious in his personal life. The memory of the egg race from his adolescence stands as a reminder of how conservative he has been. He never won the race as a child, intent on saving his egg on its spoon, and throughout life he has avoided risks in the interest of safety: "to this day he crouched within his life as within a fragile shell." The shards of ancient cultures that the archaeologist uncovers, and the shattered shells that result when one ventures out from safety merge, then, in Updike's imagery, and these symbols of death and birth come together in the concept of crisis. Ferguson's ritual trip into his literal past, his memory, and his unconscious may help him to meet the critical juncture of middle age, and mature into equanimity regarding death's inevitability. An archaeologist of all persons should be able to recognize the dimensions of a grave and be able to project one's own dimensions for it, but Ferguson is still not ready to look into this "unstated sorrow." Like so many of Updike's males, he lives in fear of the void.

"Atlantises," the final story, deals with an earlier life in a different way. In it Farnham and his second wife, living in what must be Iowa, recall their younger and always (seen from this distance) festive lives in coastal New England. Farnham, landlocked in the midwest, thinks nostalgically, "with a sinking feeling," of this vanished Atlantis. Quotations from Plato's *Critias* interspersed with the modern narrative and referring to human sacrifice teach that change and growth are built upon loss. If the Farnhams are reasonably content in their present life, they still long, however unreasonably, for their mythicized past. The new life, elsewhere, with the new partner, must constantly be validated in order to compete with the immense pull of idealized memory and old desire.

"Atlantises" and hence the *Problems* collection concludes with the memorable image of the frogman hanging in a tower full of water, poised to help novice submariners practicing emergency escapes and stopping those who risk embolisms by rising too fast from the bottom. Most of Updike's characters, trying to surface from some lost Atlantis, need such succor, someone at midpoint to slow them down, calm their panic, and show them the discipline of survival.

Too Far to Go: Getting There

Ten of the seventeen Maple stories comprising *Too Far to Go* appeared earlier in other of Updike's collections, but the publication of all of them in this format amounts, as a reviewer observed, to "an inspired piece of editing."[1] Like the Bech collections, the stories of *Too Far to Go* together are "noveloid" in scope and complexity of plot. They follow the Maples from young, already threatened marriage in "Snowing in Greenwich Village" (1956) to their divorce in middle age in "Here Come the Maples" (1976). The stories take the couple during these two decades through child rearing; the social-political events and fashions of the sixties and seventies; through lovers, estrangement, attempted reconciliation, and the final rituals of ending the union. The stories together, and particularly the last four, form some of the most poignant prose Updike has ever written. He has the Maples, paradoxically while betraying each other and separating, discovering the depth of their affection, of their mutual caring that they feel and can express now that they are giving each other up.

"Marching through Boston," however, collected earlier in *Museums and Women,* catches the Maples at a prior stage, at the point where Joan breaks out of the traditional wifely role and engages in the civil rights action of the 1960s. The striving of blacks for justice and greater freedom becomes a conduit for Joan's own efforts toward independence. And Richard's literally and symbolically feverish response is intended, perhaps unconsciously, to keep her "in her place." His imitation of a black civil rights leader's rhetoric, which degenerates further into a tasteless parody of black plantation dialect, is a compulsive performance that reveals his insecurity in the face of his wife's activism and self-reliance. Richard has used illness before (in "Twin Beds in Rome") to get his way in the marriage. Here it becomes the context for a demonstration of egocentric nastiness that does not bode well for the Maples' common future.

"The Taste of Metal," the next story, might have been excluded from *Too Far to Go,* not because it is not good fiction but because it does little to aid the momentum of the collection. Its account of Richard using an automobile accident as an opportunity to fondle

another woman (injured) while Joan goes for help adds further insight into Richard's capriciousness, but it does not otherwise contribute to the plot of the Maples' mutual life disintegrating. "Your
Lover Just Called," on the other hand, is a key story toward this
end, for it shows the couple now sparring in earnest, and with a
sense of the marriage at stake. Yet the suspicion and accusations
that poison their domesticity have another motivation, according
to Joan, who says that Richard's charge of her having a lover, and
then identifying him as a mutual friend, is an attempt "to make
her more interesting than she is." This could be dissembling on
Joan's part, but Richard indeed is fascinated, during a voyeuristic
moment, by the sight of Joan and their friend Mack kissing—by
this revelation of unfamiliar behavior by his wife. The lure of the
unknown (Who calls and hangs up? Is Mack really Joan's lover?)
occupies him more than the challenge to nurture the familiar, and
this preference suggests that Richard, at least, already has taken a
lover, even if Joan has not. Possibly, too, Richard is pushing his
wife toward finding a lover because he has, and wishes to have his
guilt lessened. The story teases the reader toward such speculation
about the truth of the Maples' liaisons, and thus creates for the
reader the mood of uncertainty and frustration that the characters
suffer.

"Eros Rampant," told for strong dramatic effect in the present
tense, presents an overcharged sexual ambiance in destructive conflict with domesticity. It begins with "The Maples' house is full of
love," but the ominous complexities of that pervasive emotion soon
become evident in this pivotal story in which Joan reveals *her* infidelity to Richard and abruptly changes their lives. The stress is
placed mainly on the nature of Richard's reaction; he is excited by
Joan's confession, apparently because it lends her the allure of something new, and the story employs a language of concealment to
describe her (she is "an abyss of secrecy"). Yet the news also becomes
a critical element in what emerges more and more as a power struggle
in the marriage. Joan's revelation is, among other things, her attempt to gain the upper hand, and Richard tries to wrest it back
by forcing further confidences from her—which both pain and arouse
him. These tactics are a sign of the marriage's degeneration: each
seeks control because each no longer trusts the other as the rules of
the relationship blur. Richard's dream, in which Joan tells him of
still other lovers, terrifies him not least because that sort of wan-

tonness by his wife would signal her independence from him and his lack of control over her.

The title, a phrase which one would expect to convey vigorous sexuality, represented by a tumescent penis, has additional connotations. It labels the story as an account of the consequences of the couple's adulteries on the whole family—how these generate anxiety and insecurity among the children and disturb the very atmosphere.

"Plumbing," a quiet and reflective tale, is placed to good contrasting advantage just after the high-energy "Eros Rampant." Its meditative description of the Maples' (who are not mentioned by surname) move to a new house, rife with birth and death imagery (the Easter season, clogged pipes that remind one of the blocked arteries leading to the heart), surrounds a central ghostly scene (the narrator watches from a distance, in his mind's eye) in which the fighting husband and wife come to blows as the cowering children look on. "I feel a tenderness toward my characters that forbids making violent use of them," Updike remarked in his 1968 interview, and it is typical that he should place violent scenes at such a remove as in this tale.[2] The ghost imagery, at any rate, is prominent and prepares well for the specter of divorce now taking form.

Divorce becomes an active option in "The Red Herring Theory." In the late-night, postparty discussion here Joan declares sarcastically to Richard, "The properly equipped suburban man . . . has a wife, a mistress, and a red herring." The red herring is the person with whom one pretends an affair in order to divert attention from the real lover. The Maples' conversation rapidly turns into a clash of wills and a discordant rhythm of concealment and breaking through the other's deceptions. The situation is, like the aftermath of the party, "a mess," and one way of clearing it up is to divorce.

That decision is postponed in "Sublimating" in favor of an experiment in celibacy. The Maples decide to abstain from sex, "since sex was the only sore point in their marriage." One expects this to be a comic tale—especially when Richard at the start comes home with a cabbage, erotically described, and proceeds to eat it raw, reliving a childhood experience—but it is not. It is not clear what the continence is supposed to accomplish, but it mainly aggravates the tension already corroding the marriage and intensifies the conflict of wills. Images of violence permeate the story: the guillotine that their son builds, Richard vigorously pruning vines, Richard thinking of punching Joan in the face, the "cleansing" energy of the

Crusades. These hint that the sublimation is really just a suppressing of hostility, and that the Maples are fooling themselves. Sex is by no means the main problem in their marriage; their sexual difficulties are symptomatic of other things radically wrong that this game of celibacy will not cure.

There is only one hint that "Nakedness," the next tale, belongs to this narrative sequence tracing the dissolution of the Maples' marriage: at the end, when Joan, bare and desirable, faces Richard equally unclothed, and says the one word "no." It may be that she is continuing their sexual abstinence, although the action takes place three years after "Sublimating"—a long time for the experiment and the marriage still to endure. It may be a strategic refusal after the couple's return to intimacy. The tale in any case is more of a contemplation of the naked human body's beauty, full of references to painterly nudes, than it is a description of the next stage of the Maples' domestic decline. Perhaps the references to the expulsion of Adam and Eve from Eden, and to the phenomenon of human shame, foreshadow the loss of integrity where innocence is long gone, and the hardness of life outside of the protective family circle.

"Separating" is a masterpiece of itself and in the context of this collection. The Maples' plan to divulge their impending separation (at last) as painlessly as possible to their children is botched, predictably, and the description of the resultant, barely controlled hysteria, particularly as the younger son expresses it, is excellent crafting of affectivity in fiction. Updike, seldom one to overwrite, chooses disciplined understatement to articulate this highly emotional moment. The final passage, in which the oldest son betrays his agony over his parents' choice, is a moving scene that shines with authenticity out of cynical surroundings.

"Separating" is the first of the final quartet of stories in *Too Far to Go* that together constitute as compelling and unique a depiction of a marriage ending as exists in modern American fiction. Of the four, "Gesturing" is possibly the best. After twenty years of marriage and both now with lovers, the Maples separate in earnest—which means that Richard at Joan's request moves to Boston and out of comfortable distance for daily visits to wife and children. As the title advertises, gestures are the significant language of this tale. Gestures of the hand, the face, or other parts of the body are both a surplus of expression and a substitute for speech. They add meaning to the already-said, or they convey that for which the mind has no words. Repeated, they become the intimate, if only half-recognized language of people close to each other.

Related to the motif of gesturing is the overwhelming presence of the John Hancock Tower in Boston (Updike does not name it), the "beautiful disaster," always within Richard's purview in his city apartment, with its windows constantly falling out and crashing below. The glass monolith functions like a huge flawed mirror that reflects the motions—the mean and grand gestures—of the metropolis, including Richard's solo performances (as he himself see them) that constitute his new state of bachelorhood. To that macroimage Updike contrasts a tiny, related one: that of the words "With this ring / I thee wed" etched into Richard's apartment window by former tenants—a perhaps banal but withal moving gesture toward desired permanence.

The glass imagery combined with that of gesturing connotes both the fragility and durability of human bonds. They can be formally shattered, yet they somehow endure even in the fragments. In the final meeting between Richard and Joan in this story, a window metaphor introduces the awesome words on marital permanence that Richard hears beyond what Joan (who is "giddy amid the spinning mirrors of her betrayals") actually says: "He saw through her words to what she was saying—that these lovers, however we love them, are not us, are not sacred as reality is sacred. We are reality. We have made children. We gave each other our young bodies. We promised to grow old together." Against this sobering recognition the two will, nonetheless, separate. Yet Joan chooses this moment to confide to Richard intimate details of her life with her lover, and this act causes Richard to realize that the reflexes of their two-decade-old marriage will survive divorce, that even if the union is destroyed the separation can never be total: "Though a decree come between them, even death, her gestures would endure, cut into glass."

"Divorcing: A Fragment" is, as Updike says in his foreword, "a fragment that cried off completion," but the mere three-and-one-half pages shape a cogent narration of the suffering that the broken relationship entails. Richard in a brief visit catches Joan in a depressed and even suicidal state that causes both to wonder at the rightness of their intention. But the momentum is now clearly toward divorce: "no way out, no way but a numb marching forward." "Here Come the Maples," the final story, is in contrast an oddly cheerful, although bittersweet narrative of the divorce itself. Richard travelling about Boston to secure the proper documents for the actual divorce recalls the wedding and honeymoon years ago and thus compares the beginning and ending of this long alliance. He also reads from a pamphlet on physics, passages of which are quoted in the text, and seems to recognize that he rather than Joan is the "weak force" in the marriage, like the weak force in nature, who contributes most to its dissolution. Indeed, a telephone conversation between him and Joan demonstrates her toughness and his vulnerability; now that she is almost free of the marriage constraints, her natural strength asserts itself again.

The end of the quick, "no-fault" divorce (like Updike's own) ceremony provides a neat denouement to the suspended state of the Maples' marriage, to the tale, and to the collection. Having forgotten to kiss his bride at the wedding those many years ago, Richard now, following the divorce decree, remembers to do so. One takes it as an affectionate, peaceful gesture of parting.

Updike, Josephine Hendin writes, "is one of the few writers to take from modern discord the gift of reconciliation, to find even in unhappy marriages necessary harmonies."[3] That the Maples' stories conclude on a reconciliatory note should not, however, obscure the fact that they are above all fictions of emotional and even spiritual anguish. As much as in *Museums and Women,* metaphors of the void permeate these tales: "the abysmal loss of . . . the other" in "Waiting Up," the featureless darkness at the end of "Separating," the "black hole" of "Gesturing," and "the chasm of lost life" in "Here Come the Maples" are a few of these. They connect the personal trauma of broken bonds of love to something deeply wrong with the human condition and even to a sense of universal chaos. The reader is made to experience this disorder even as the ordering power of expert narrative writing subdues and channels it.

Chapter Fourteen
Rabbit Is Rich and *Bech Is Back:* Sequels and Success

I think, *There must be more than this.*

—from "Dream and Reality"

Rabbit Is Rich: Coffins and Safe Deposits

Rabbit Is Rich (1981) is a novel of entropy and renewal, of lost opportunities and second chances, of falling and recovery, of ghosts and new life; and from the tensions of these related opposites a stasis, an equilibrium, a coming-to-terms takes form. "In the vacuum of the heart love falls forever," the voice half Updike's and half his protagonist's muses in mid-novel, and that sentence could well stand as an epigram for the book, for this is a narrative of tenacious love, of family members and outsiders suspended in postures of clumsy and often vulgar affection as they drift toward death. "Running out of gas" is the first phrase of the novel, "Another nail in his coffin" the last. These call to mind exhaustion and the end, yet they contain hope. Harry Angstrom, now forty-six in 1979 and part owner of a Brewer, Pennsylvania, Toyota agency, profits through small-car sales during the global energy crisis; and the "nail in his coffin" is in actuality the baby granddaughter in his lap, a child at last to take the place of his own infant daughter drowned so many years earlier. Such a redoubling conveys the vast weight of the past in the last book to date of what has become Updike's Rabbit trilogy, but it is just as much a novel of the next generations. It is significantly about Nelson, twenty-two-year-old erratic son of Rabbit and Janice, to the extent that at a few critical points Nelson assumes the role of the narrator's consciousness from his father. It is about others of Nelson's generation, and the birth of Nelson's daughter makes it at the end about the generation beyond his as well.

Rabbit Is Rich as much as *The Centaur* (with which it shares a powerful father-son relationship) is concerned with time, and a network of images carries the peculiar qualities of past, present, and future. Ghost imagery, familiar to readers of the earlier Rabbit books, is continued here to evoke memories of the dead and of half-buried events. Rabbit in an eerie passage thinks of his daughter as a phantom teen-ager ("with her leggy pallor and calm round face she glows like a ghost") who thrives in water, the element that killed her, and he hears his dead mother calling him at night: "Mom's voice clear as a whisper from the corner of the room saying *Hassy,* a name as dead as the boy that was called that is dead." Jill and Skeeter, his dead counter-culture comrades from *Rabbit Redux,* are ghostly recollections, and the spray-painted message SKEETER LIVES on various walls about Brewer haunts him. When he meets Ruth, his lover from *Rabbit, Run,* the encounter's description includes the spectral: "having risen together their ghosts feel their inflated flesh fall away"—a passage that resonates with resurrection as well as decay. These are all, of course, restless and unassimilated memories, kept alive by a guilt that throbs less painfully than it might both because Rabbit is a relatively unreflective person (even though he often has to serve as Updike's meditating voice) and because time has dulled the harshest sensations.

An admirably achieved combination of image and literal action that Updike develops to move Rabbit from past to present has to do with running. Rabbit takes up jogging, in a fairly fruitless effort to regain physical fitness, and runs first on holiday in the Pocono Mountains of northeastern Pennsylvania and then back home in Brewer ("a kind of ghost town"). The old familiar activity also allows his mind to run free, and in the two semi-stream-of-consciousness passages on Rabbit's exertion he muses on dead loved ones, the still lively past, his own mortality, and vaguely connects these to the problems of his complicated present. It seems to him that he is running above the buried dead, that his movement creates the necessary distinction between past and present but also the transition from the one to the other. Whereas in the first novel of the trilogy, however, Rabbit ran mindlessly to flee an unbearable present, here his nerves do not demand escape. He has become calmer, resigned, baffled by the conditions of life (especially his aging), but he copes—exactly what he did not do in his earlier years. Thanks to good luck long overdue, he is even moderately successful, he and Janice having reconciled and inherited part ownership of Spring Motors, a Toyota franchise, from her father. A parvenu of sorts, a golfer and Rotarian, he enjoys the symbols of middle-class status. The situation is now the obverse of what it was: in the first two Rabbit novels the world was getting along but Rabbit was a failure in it; now Rabbit has learned how to survive but the world is winding down. There seems to be little he can do but construct his fragile refuges against that final time and practice his private rituals of renewal.

Most galling to Rabbit—and herein is the substance of the novel's plot—is that failure has not left him altogether but has merely moved down a generation and attached itself to his son. It is an understatement to call Nelson accident prone; he is, as the saying goes, an accident waiting to happen, and throughout the novel he triggers a succession of minor catastrophes like a string of small explosives popping off. Nelson's mishaps involve automobiles and sex; he wrecks his father's cars and impregnates Pru, the girl he eventually marries. In this last he proves to be his parents' child, for they, too, have perpetrated accidents with children, Rabbit making Ruth pregnant in the first novel (the foetus may or may not have been aborted—Ruth will not tell him), and Janice drowning the baby Becky. It is apt that Nelson's little disasters should concern cars and sex, for automobiles have long been considered sexual (both phallic and vaginal) symbols in American popular culture (one thinks, for example, of Faulkner's treatment of the subject in *Intruder in the Dust*). It is plausible, at any rate, to interpret Nelson's destructiveness with Rabbit's cars as displaced sexual aggression against his father, with whom he is in constant conflict, and his impregnating of Pru as an unconscious imitation of his father and an attempt to usurp his place.

Rabbit, then, has "run" from past to present, from failure to a measure of success, but in the process he has also "run into" a new set of problems associated with entropy, aging, and the awareness of death closing in, while his son, who literally runs into things with cars, begins the irresponsibility and bad luck cycle that his parents suffered through as young adults. Imagery of falling works to express this aspect of the country's atmosphere and the family's mood: Skylab is falling, the satellite disintegrating as it burns through the atmosphere; President Carter stumbles for the nation to see while pushing his age and running in a marathon—little could be more heavily and ironically symbolic; pregnant Pru falls down the stairs (possibly helped by Nelson—another accident?) while leaving a party, and there is fear for a time that her baby may be harmed; Nelson recalls his grandmother's German dialect song about the falling horseback rider. These fallings, and others, do not have grim results. They are, rather, indicative of the nation's and the family's disposition: things seem ominous, although nothing is in immediate crisis; people are uneasy but still hopeful. It is, of course, the temper of the late twentieth century in the West that Updike knows how to project so well.

It is obviously the future that one fears. Rabbit challenges the future by running too hard for his years, courting a heart attack—the personal disaster that worries him. Death is always behind the anxiety about the future, and in an era in which a religious belief in a personal immortality suffers the same attrition as other aging phenomena, the characters conceive death as a void. That void, in turn, threatening from the future, haunts the present as an existential emptiness that humans try to fill with objects and actions, in *Rabbit Is Rich* above all with material goods and sexual involvement. Consumerism is in fact the main topic of this novel, in conjunction with sex, just as *A Month of Sundays* links sex and religion and *The Coup* blends sex and politics. It is fitting that *Consumer Reports* has become Rabbit's Bible and that he thinks of it (inspired by a tube of toothpaste!) just before a night of extramarital sex on a Caribbean holiday.

Updike makes the void/sex/consumerism triangle work effectively for him in *Rabbit Is Rich.* Contemplating his pregnant wife, Nelson thinks: "Women. They are holes you put one thing in after another and it's never enough, you stuff your entire life in there and they smile that crooked little sad smile and are sorry you couldn't have done better." Here the female is the void that cannot be filled by the male's efforts. She makes him feel inadequate in all ways: he is not a good provider, not in any sense a good husband. This standard metaphor of the greedy and devouring female is unusual for Updike. Generally, for his men, women are not representative of the void but as desirable sexual beings are a sort of mystery that occupies the males and distracts them from intimations of death, the ultimate void. But in *Rabbit Is Rich,* by conjoining imagery of women (as a rule both symbols and objects of sexual opportunity in Updike's fiction), the void, and possessions, and in a sense collapsing these into each other, Updike complicates his portrayal of spiritual and social strategies. Sex no longer necessarily helps one to elude the consciousness of the void but sometimes instead leads directly to it. Faced with this dilemma, Updike's protagonist turns to acquisition and consumption: to material goods, possessions, wealth as another kind of hoped-for tangible hedge against death.

This psychological maneuver is illustrated dramatically in the scene with the thirty gold coins, surely one of the most accomplished set pieces in all of Updike's fiction. Updike draws attention to death first by describing Rabbit stretched out on the bed, corpselike, amidst the Krugerrands with a coin over each eye. The gold arouses both Rabbit and Janice and excites them to sexual coupling—after Janice prevents Rabbit from putting a coin into her vagina. It is, of course, an erotically playful gesture but also an intensely symbolic one: "Harry holds a Krugerrand by the edge as if to insert it in a slot." Implied is that the woman, in touch with the void, has some power over death, and that she can be bought and manipulated by the male to use that power and postpone the inevitable encounter with nothingness. This reading might seem heavy-handed, were it not that Updike loads the passage himself with Classical myth (Janice as Danaë visited by Zeus as a shower of gold, suggested by the coins that "spill between her legs"; Janice and Rabbit in sexual embrace among the coins as "Gods bedded among stars") and biblical allusion (the missing gold piece reminds one of the parable of the lost coin in the Gospel of Luke 15:8–10). Later when they sell the gold for the eight hundred eighty-eight silver pieces and struggle with their weight and bulk as they try to fit them into the insufficient bank deposit box, they become excited again, and the language is rife with sex and death. When Rabbit returns laden to the bank teller, "She lets him slide his long box into the empty rectangle. R.I.P.," an image of sexual intercourse and of placing a coffin in a burial vault. If Rabbit appears incessantly and incorrigibly lustful, he also, now in middle age, cannot help perceiving women more and more as channels toward death and seeks to block that passage with his inflated sense of worth. Sexual intercourse for him, the tumescent penis aroused by the power of wealth and filling the vagina, becomes a denial of death in a virtually ritualistic way: he occupies the void.

The prefatory quotation from Sinclair Lewis's *Babbitt* (rhymes with Rabbit) alerts the reader to look for the common and the vulgar among the middle-class citizenry, but the Babbitts of Zenith would be shocked by the Angstroms of Brewer and their friends. Rabbit, Janice, and their circle are not merely tasteless; they are often gross in language and behavior. Their obscenity has led one reviewer to write, "I *think* it's pornography," but this judgment is extreme.[1] *Rabbit Is Rich* may be offensive to anyone who considers its characters offensive, as indeed they are, but that offensiveness is not pornographic. The depersonalizing of the body by focusing on genitalia and on the mechanics of sexual acts, generally said to constitute pornographic writing, occurs in this novel, but it is consonant with Updike's effort to explore instructively the sex/wealth/death configuration as it affects his characters' struggles with temporality. In what is probably the most objectionable sexual scene, where Rabbit on Caribbean holiday has anal intercourse with one of the wives of the Brewer circle, Updike develops significantly the juncture of sex and death. The key sensation for Rabbit is "no sensation: a void, a pure black box, a casket of perfect nothingness." And later he thinks: "That void, inside her. He can't take his mind from what he's discovered, that nothingness seen by his single eye." Rabbit is clearly fascinated because this is a novel act even for a sexual veteran like himself, but it must also strike him as matching the tenebrous condition he feels and wishes to overcome. In sexual union, in what should provide most intimate contact, he experiences the classical *horror vacui*. It is a less terrifying moment than the one David Kern suffers when, perched in the outhouse above the cloaca in "Pigeon Feathers," he has a vision of the abyss, but it has the same quality. The explicit descriptive detail of the passage, then, akin to pornographic depiction, actually conveys aptly the protagonist's emotional state, and one could say that Updike borrows the pornographic style to expose what pornography generally disguises: the emptiness of human relations determined by the glands.

The component of material goods, indirectly active in this passage on sex and the void (the couples, because of their material well-being, can afford the Caribbean interlude), is present in direct relation to pornography in the earlier scene where Rabbit finds the photos of his friends the Murketts. Technology, here in the form of the Polaroid camera, enhances salaciousness, for the wealthy Murketts have acquired the latest equipment to record, in imitation of the pornographic magazines, their genital play. Yet however tasteless the photos may be, they are the private possessions of the married couple, and it is Rabbit's licentious curiosity that transforms them, for him alone, into a pornographic event. This scene, which leaves Rabbit suspended in desire, is extended ironically in the Caribbean vacation incident. There Rabbit, lusting for Cindy Murkett, is dealt Thelma Harrison instead, who initiates him into anal sex and the sobering sense of nothingness.

Rabbit must leave the island, with Janice, before he has the chance to bed Cindy, but that frustration is offset by the effects of the emergency that calls them home. Nelson has run away (shades of his father), abandoning the highly pregnant Pru, and the baby arrives just before Rabbit and Janice return. That event, marred as it is by Nelson's irresponsibility, projects a dimension of hope to conclude the novel. Here, at least, is evidence of sex that does not mainly suggest the void—although Rabbit thinks of the child as "another nail in his coffin." "But as with dying there is a moment that must be pushed through," Rabbit thinks earlier as he forces himself to seek out Ruth his old lover. That is a birth image as well, and by the end of *Rabbit Is Rich,* in all the turmoil, the Angstroms have "pushed through" to a bit more humanity.

Updike has also delivered himself of a fine novel. If sequels can be of this quality and value, one can look forward to meeting Rabbit again in his mid-fifties.

Bech Is Back: The Hunger Artist as Best Seller

"D'you ever get the feeling everything these days is sequels?" the protagonist asks in *Rabbit Is Rich.* This half-derisive remark directed by Updike against himself announces the artist's risk undertaken in that novel: to revive an unattractive fictional character—too weak even to function as an antihero—a second time and make him embody the complex temper of the age. *Bech Is Back,* published in 1982, extends that risk. It, too, is a sequel, continuing in seven (like *Bech: A Book*) stories the literary-erotic world-wide adventures of the famous but unprolific author, and the euphonious title, like the earlier one, hints that this will also be a *"jeu"* of a book. This collection/quasi-novel deals more thoroughly than *Bech: A Book* with the complications of success, a problem that has come increasingly to preoccupy Updike—not surprisingly—and connects it at least as consistently to sexuality.

In a talk given at the Smithsonian Institution in the fall of 1976, Updike speaking on "The Cultural Situation of the American Writer" (also the title of a Bech lecture in Ghana in "Bech Third-Worlds It") states, "And let us say he is one of the dozen or two dozen who are beyond financial insecurity; he is rich. Royalties tumble in on him from his classics; the glamorous men of the media press luncheon invitations and rustling dollars upon him. But is he rich enough? Many sons of manufacturers, just by condescending to be born, are ten times richer. Can the writer, in a land that consumes wealth as rapidly as it bestows it, rest easy with his portion? . . . The writer's greed for money, however, is perhaps less damaging than his greed for greatness."[2] These remarks can be construed as Updike's both defensive and self-satisfied public reflection on his own wealth and fame, and it is reasonable to assume that the reappearance of Henry Bech has been stimulated by Updike's wish to explore, via fiction, the implications of success for an author and his/her career. *Rabbit Is Rich,* to be sure, examined the dynamics of success, but it focused on an unadmirable and decidedly nonintellectual character of only middling accomplishment. Bech, on the other hand, has earned a reputation as a talented novelist even if he has long been unproductive and has undergone the metamorphosis (and degeneration) from vital artist to literary personality. But when he "cranks out" (the term used disparagingly by his ex-mistress) a best seller and attains celebrity status, the glamour and tribulations of large-scale success take hold. Updike has remarked, "I think what's most disturbing about success is that it's very hazardous to your health as well as to your daily routine. . . . There is a kind of corrosion of your own humility and sense of necessary workmanship."[3] Bech manages to retain much of his humility—he has a sound attitude on his own worth—but the novel with which he triumphs lacks integrity, and the signs are that he will not, in the future, return to quality.

The stories are as much about Bech's relations with women as about success, and in fact his success as a writer exists in some sort of proportion to his success with women. The initial story, with the grandiose title of "Three Illuminations in the Life of an American

Author," shows Bech still living on his laurels (by now fairly faded) and in comic decline. All three "illuminations" treat the impinging of practical reality upon the imagination, and all produce a more or less painful disillusion. The first occurs when Bech on generous impulse stops off to visit an avid collector of his works and discovers that the dour old Pennsylvanian, far from valuing the presence of the author himself, is interested only in his texts (among those of many others) as objects to possess and takes the visit as an intrusion. Such experiences help to keep Bech humble. The second disclosure emerges from the interplay between a female character Bech invents for his novel in progress and her real-life double who materializes at his public performances. The inevitable affair between Bech and the woman destroys, predictably, the romantic attraction (nurtured on Bech's side by thoughts of Poe's ethereal and passionate heroines), for she cannot match the creatures of Bech's heated fantasy, and he does not live up to her idealized expectation of what a writer should be. The third revelation grows from Bech's journey to "San Poco" in the Caribbean, where with the help of Norma, his ex-mistress, he will autograph twenty-eight thousand five hundred sheets to be inserted into a new edition of an old novella—Updike himself once did something similar, signing twenty thousand copies of *Rabbit, Run* in the Virgin Islands. What looks for Bech to be an idyllic time, with a comfortable old lover in a luxurious holiday setting, becomes a nightmare. The signing turns into an enormous chore, Bech and Norma clash as a result of the tension, and Bech is afflicted literally with writer's cramp. His inability, finally, even to write his signature stands as a sign of the sorry state that he and his career have come to.

The second story, "Bech Third-Worlds It," consists of twelve scenes from Bech's government-sponsored tour through seven "underdeveloped" nations: Egypt, Ghana, Kenya, Korea, Nigeria, Tanzania, and Venezuela. The vignettes do not follow the sequence of Bech's itinerary but bounce back and forth among the various countries, reflecting the confusion of mind Bech feels from the surfeit of quick impressions that high-speed travel produces. The story is populated with the stereotypes of the international cultural lecture circuit: the arrogant American ambassador who despises the citizens of his assigned country, the hostile students who ask belligerent questions, the awed schoolgirls who practice their charming English on the visitor, the desperately poor seen only from a distance. Since they are sketched with deft and sometimes comic freshness (such as the Japanese poet in Seoul who has, he announces proudly to Bech, produced "one hunnert twelve" poems on "flogs"), they are as believable as anything else in the often surreal world of cultural exchange. It is surreal, among other reasons, because the people participating in the exchange perform the motions of interaction but seldom really connect; their radical otherness prevents it. Hence the places of encounter are full of mediators—ambassadors, guides, translators, attachés—who mediate poorly. People observe each other suspiciously or condescendingly or enviously, and confrontation substitutes for interchange.

Updike utilizes imagery of eyes and of whiteness to convey the difficulty of genuine rapport. "Alien blue eyes," "eyes . . . crossed in a fury of attention," "careful opaque eyes," "upturned, blind eyes" suggest how hard it is to see the foreigner through and beyond his/her differences. Whiteness, in turn (the U.S. ambassador's white suit, the Korean prostitutes' white dresses, Bech's acute consciousness of himself as a white man), especially as contrasted to the browns and blacks of the Third World nations Bech visits, is employed to track the shift away from "First World"dominance, where "white is right," toward realignments in which the old power structures and value systems are singled out for scrutiny and criticism by the rest of the human community.

This story of global disorder and misunderstanding has a compelling middle point. At the literal center of the narrative, in the seventh section, is the vignette of the young black madman in Nairobi who utters the sanest words of the tale and at the end of his elegant speech offers Bech peace. It is a gesture, even a blessing, that the embattled voyager, like his country, needs.

"Australia and Canada" is placed as the third story to contrast with "Bech Third-Worlds It." He flies to the orderly and "safe" (a key word in the tale) cities of Toronto and Sydney to appear on televised talk shows and functions far better in this urbane, efficiently organized electronic media environment, where only his transmitted image reaches people, than in the midst of the crowds in the poor countries he has visited. Bech's encounters in these two cities with three women and their improvised lives cause him to decide, at the end, to marry not Norma but her sister, the desperately patient Bea waiting for him in Ossining, New York: "to marry her, to be safe." In this story Updike continues his dependence on eye imagery and adds to it a motif of inflation. The eyes here, as is appropriate for a television context, are instruments of deception and secrecy even in what seems to be the cordial and open nature of these Commonwealth nations. The sensation of expanding that Bech feels when he is on-camera reflects not only the enormous range of television coverage but plays with the sense of threat that the United States presents as a powerful but clumsy culture-monger even to friendly countries: the vast emptiness of Canada and Australia could too easily be filled by commercialized American fare.

"The Holy Land" finds Bech recently married to Bea and visiting Jerusalem with her. A fitting image for interpreting this story is one not even mentioned in it: a palimpsest. Superimposition is central to the tale. Things with messages are articulated on top of other things: modern Jerusalem functions on a layer above the Christian shrines, which in turn cover an older stratum. The Israelis, having come here from elsewhere, are now making their mark upon the land and disguising the Arab influence which overlaid Hebrew history. Important for the plot of the whole collection is that Bea, so soon after the marriage, has begun to impose her style upon Bech, the naïve Episcopalian enthusiast's inscription over the cynical, somewhat world-weary Jew's signature—and as we learn in "Bech Wed," his best seller is in basic ways Bea's book.

Contrasted to this metaphor of overlay is the figure of Kafka's hunger artist mentioned three times in the story: the professional faster who, it turns out, wants no credit for his feats of starvation because, as he confesses, he has never found food to suit his appetite. Updike's strategy in evoking Kafka, along with using him to reinforce the Expressionistic description of Jerusalem's frenetic atmosphere, is to remark on a necessary is-ness of persons and things. Just as the hunger artist practices his art less by choice than by natural proclivity, so too is Bech *perforce* a Jewish storyteller—because he has no inclination to be anything else, and hence nothing heroic attaches to his "suffering" as a novelist. It appears as though Bea, ambitious for him, merely wants to confirm his hunger artist nature: "she had implied that his perfection lay nowhere but in a deepening of the qualities he already possessed. Since he was Jewish, the more Jewish he became in her Christian care, the better". Yet (in "Bech Wed") she manages to convert him for a time into a Protestant achiever, and his instinctive unease in Jerusalem, in contrast to Bea's enthusiasm, is for good reason. Following an argument with Bea, "some dim sense of what the words 'holy land' might mean dawned on him. The holy land was where you accepted being. Middle age was a holy land. Marriage." The hunger artist in Bech will not allow him to accept that view for long.

Whereas Bea is thrilled by "the Holy Land," her new husband is delighted by Scotland, the land of *her* heritage, that they visit after Israel to celebrate her fortieth birthday. This trip is the substance of "Macbech," a slight tale that is as much travelogue as dramatic fiction. Much of Bech's pleasure on his tour of the Highlands is malicious and derives from reciting for his wife the cruelties the Scots visited on each other throughout history. When at the end he torments her into pronouncing their marriage "a horrible mistake" and of turning her into one of his fictive characters, one sees that he manipulates her just as she, not so subtly, works her will on him. The marriage images here of monsters swimming in murky depths (borrowed from Loch Ness lore) and of the pair precariously at cliff's edge are omens of the threats to domesticity rising so quickly in this union.

"Bech Wed" is the centerpiece of the whole collection, and here one learns that "Bech Is Back!" is the advertising slogan designed to sell *Think Big,* the novel he writes in the course of this tale. The scope and length (seventy-five pages) of "Bech Wed" virtually qualify it as a novella, and in fact a novel is compressed into its pages— a novel of Bech writing a novel. Living now with Bea and her three children in the rambling and deteriorating house in Ossining, Bech is cajoled and bullied by his wife into writing, over a period of almost two years, the book that renews his fame and brings him wealth. It is, however, a compromised endeavor, for Bech produces a large and sloppy novel on the television industry that cannibalizes intimate relationships—and hence people close to him—in his life, and that otherwise both imitates soap opera and indulges undisciplined sexual fantasy. *Think Big* is engineered from the start to be a best seller, but it is also a major factor in the dissolution of Bech's and Bea's short marriage. Not only does he compose the novel inspired by deep resentment of Bea; he also does it as a catharsis of sorts, as an act that purges her and her suburban gentile life style from his Manhattan Jewish system. When Norma shows up unexpectedly one afternoon in Bea's absence, first chastises Bech for writing "lousy" and "slapdash" fiction and submitting to manipulation by her sister ("how does it feel," she asks Bech, "being a sow's ear somebody's turned into a silk purse?"), and then makes love with him, it is clear that the marriage is essentially over.

The story is a masterpiece of ambiguity and ambivalence. Bech ensconced in his upstate suburban retreat enjoys the rhythms of the seasons, nature's small revelations, even his stepson (but not Bea's late-pubescent twin daughters), but he misses the city, and he is never happy with the trivialities and empty rituals of this home-owners' neighborhood into which he has been dropped. Ossining, former site of Sing Sing penitentiary, seems to Bech to hold him captive, and, in another metaphor, he feels besieged and isolated in his third-floor improvised writer's studio. Yet the city, when he is back in it, does not satisfy him either, much as he is charmed by its tough sensuality. What is clear, at the story's close, is that he has outgrown this suburban interlude—having indeed never fully accepted it—and is empowered by the very success he bought from it to leave it.

The real price that Bech has paid for success becomes apparent in "White on White," the final story. Now separated from Bea, living alone back in Manhattan, and lionized as a literary celebrity, Bech attends a party in honor of an old photographer acquaintance and finds himself in the midst of a tawdry and ostentatious cele-bration carried off with affected heartiness by the guests. *White on White* is the title of the photographer's latest book and also the party's theme. As he says, it has to do with "the idea . . . of exploring how little contrast you could have and still have a pho-tograph. . . . Of taking something to the limit." Even though the execution of the concept results mainly in a *nouveau chic* display, it reveals more discipline than Bech has been able to muster for *Think Big* and stands in judgmental contravention to that slipshod novel.

Bech himself has arrived at disorder, although he now possesses fame and wealth. He expects (with some apprehension) to go off at the end of the party with a prostitute and television mud wrestler named Lorna. The name reminds one of Lenore, Bech's idealized fantasy woman in "Three Illuminations" and of how his standards have declined. When he pronounces to himself at the very end, *"Treyf,"* Yiddish for unclean (non-Kosher) food, he must be thinking not only of the defilement that marks modern America, and to which he has contributed, but to his own taste as well. It is a verdict that the hunger artist should find hard to swallow.

Conclusion: Craftsmanship, Nostalgia, and the Literary Tradition

Looking at Updike and his achievement, after assessing a quarter-century of productivity, one wishes to echo Henry Bech in "Bech Enters Heaven": "Now what?" Updike has become, like Bech, a literary celebrity and a wealthy man. His accomplishments have made him an embodiment of the American dream he dramatizes and criticizes in his art. But unlike Bech, he has not sold out to any forces which could exploit him, and he has not compromised his standards in any way. The key feature in his success and influence is craftsmanship. Immensely gifted from the start, he has shaped his talents into skilled artistry, and even now his writing continues to mature: his fiction has become more taut and efficient, as evocative as ever with less verbiage, the metaphors as brilliant yet more disciplined toward the comprehensive effects he desires. At the same time, his prose is now more relaxed; he has loosened up in the last decade or so and has allowed wit and humor to show through.

Hardly less important than his devotion to craftsmanship is the commitment to work. He is industrious and prolific, and because he is he has given his craft the chance to deepen and evolve subtlety. He has, at the same time, developed scope. Never an experimentalist but always more adventuresome than his negative critics would grant, he takes artistic and intellectual risks in all of his novels and tests constantly, if gently, the capacities of narrative to see what it can do.

As a fairly traditional storyteller, Updike represents a continuity with the heritage of the American novel and is evidence either that literary "postmodernism" is not as revolutionary and encompassing as it appeared to be in the seventies, when it was the term chosen to designate alternatives to the "exhausted" novel form—or that the term must be expanded to include powerful (in every respect) traditional writers such as himself. His subject matter and his mode of expressing it, on the other hand, are not always part of the mainstream American literary tradition. The most pervasive mood of his fiction has been nostalgia, and that has effected thematic treatments both inside and outside of the tradition. The nostalgic mood has been brought to bear on childhood, on small-town life, on sex, on marriage and family. Insofar as these treatments stress a loss of innocence, as they often do, they participate in and extend a tradition at least as old as Hawthorne. Updike declared in the late sixties that he was "kind of elegaically concerned with the Protestant middle class"—an expression of nostalgia, regret, and concern that suggests how he wishes to mark both the fulfillment and waning of the tradition.

But he has also remarked frequently on his interest in exploring the bases and ramifications of contemporary sexuality, and the ways in which he does so (even within the constraints of conventional storytelling), characterized by extremely frank language and explicit description, take him outside the mainstream.[4] He is by no means the only novelist of stature writing in this mode nowadays (one thinks also, for example, of John Barth, Robert Coover, John Fowles, Edna O'Brien, Philip Roth, Patrick White), and he may in fact be one of a number of serious writers addressing themselves to themes of sexuality and in the process broadening the American and whole English-language literary tradition to include, and even to emphasize, this dimension.

What next, then, for Updike? One has the sense that he can do virtually anything he wants with the language of narrative. He is, simply, one of the most accomplished stylists of the English language, and he continues to get better. There is reason to hope that his discipline, wedded to his awesome talent, will generate still more compelling fictions of human intimacy to sustain us above the void.

Notes and References

Chapter One

1. The poetry introducing Chapters 1, 12, 13, 14 appears in John Updike, *Tossing and Turning* (New York, 1977); the poetry introducing Chapters 2–7 and 11 appears in John Updike, *Telephone Poles and Other Poems* (New York, 1963); the poetry introducing Chapters 8 and 9 appears in John Updike, *The Carpentered Hen and Other Tame Creatures* (New York, 1958); the poetry introducing Chapter 10 appears in John Updike, *Midpoint and Other Poems* (New York, 1969).

2. "John Updike Breaks Out of Suburbia," *New York Times Magazine* (10 December 1978), pp. 60–65.

3. Michiko Kakutani, "Turning Sex and Guilt Into an American Epic," *Saturday Review* 8 (October 1981): pp. 14–22; Paul Gray, "Perennial Promises Kept," *Time* 120 (18 October 1982): pp. 72–81.

Chapter Two

1. *Olinger Stories* (New York, 1964), p. vii. The eleven stories in this collection appear also in *The Same Door, Pigeon Feathers,* and *The Music School*. The only new material in *Olinger Stories* is Updike's brief introduction.

Chapter Three

1. *Assorted Prose.* (New York, 1965), p. 156.
2. Ibid.

Chapter Four

1. Updike has said that he passed through an acute religious crisis during the time he was writing *Rabbit, Run,* and some of that crisis is reflected in the novel. Cf. "View from the Catacombs," *Time* 91 (26 April 1968): 74.

Chapter Five

1. *Olinger Stories,* p. ix.
2. Ibid.

Chapter Six

1. Arthur Mizener, *The Sense of Life in the Modern Novel* (Boston, 1964), pp. 264ff.

2. Wylie Sypher, *Rococo to Cubism in Art and Literature* (New York: Vintage Books, 1960), pp. 295ff.

3. Ibid., p. 301.

4. Philip Rieff, *The Triumph of the Therapeutic* (New York: Harper & Row, 1966).

5. Mircea Eliade, *Cosmos and History: The Myth of the Eternal Return* (New York: Harper & Row, 1959). Cf. chapter four, "The Terror of History."

Chapter Seven

1. John Thompson, "Matthiessen and Updike," *New York Review of Books* 7 (23 December 1965): 23.

Chapter Nine

1. Representative reviews of *Couples* are William H. Gass, "Cock-a-doodle-doo," *New York Review of Books* 10 (11 April 1968): 3; Alfred Kazin, "Updike: Novelist of the New, Post-pill America," *Washington Post Book World* 2 (7 April 1968): 1, 3.

2. "View from the Catacombs," p. 66.

3. A church did burn down in Updike's town of Ipswich prior to his composition of *Couples;* the destruction of the Congregational Church in Tarbox is not a tenuous symbolic event but is inspired by an actual occurrence.

4. "More Love in the Western World," *Assorted Prose,* pp. 283–300.

5. Ibid., p. 298.

6. Ibid., p. 286.

7. Ibid., p. 291.

8. Ibid., p. 299.

Chapter Eleven

1. Sections of the first chapter of *Rabbit Redux* were published as "Pop/Mom/Moon" in *Atlantic* 228 (August 1971): 48–51, 54–63; and as "Rabbit's Evening Out" in *Esquire* 76 (September 1971): 109–12, 191–96. The novel itself was published in November 1971.

2. Anatole Broyard, "Updike Goes All Out at Last," *New York Times,* 5 November 1971, p. 40.

Chapter Twelve

1. *Buchanan Dying,* pp. 251–52.

2. Peter Straub, "Wise Women," *New Statesman* 89 (10 January 1975):50.

3. For a thorough treatment of *Buchanan Dying,* and one more sympathetic than mine, cf. Donald J. Greiner, *The Other John Updike* (Athens: Ohio University Press, 1981), pp. 243–60.

4. For a fine short essay on the relationship of Updike's later fiction to sexuality, cf. Jerome Klinkowitz, "John Updike's America," *North American Review* 265 (September 1980):68–71.

5. "One Big Interview," in *Picked-Up Pieces,* p. 497. This piece is a composite of interviews Updike gave over the years to Charles Thomas Samuels et al.

6. Victor W. Turner, "Betwixt and Between: The Liminal Period in *Rites de Passage,*" in *The Proceedings of the American Ethnological Society* (Seattle: University of Washington Press, 1964), pp. 4–20.

7. Greiner, *The Other John Updike,* p. 194. Greiner, in his individual chapters on Updike's story collections through *Museums and Women,* provides a sampling of the reviewers' and critics' responses to the tales.

8. George Hunt has an imaginative chapter on *A Month of Sundays* in his *John Updike and the Three Great Secret Things* (Grand Rapids: Eerdmans, 1980). Cf. also my "Updike's *A Month of Sundays* and the Language of the Unconscious," *Journal of the American Academy of Religion* 47 (December 1979):609–25.

9. Cf. my "Updike's Sermons," in Klaus Lanzinger, ed., *Americana-Austriaca V: Beiträge zur Amerikakunde* (Vienna: Wilhelm Braumüller, 1980), pp. 11–26.

10. Hunt, *John Updike and the Three Great Secret Things,* p. 190.

11. A representative positive review is Robert Towers's "Updike in Africa," *New York Times Book Review* 83 (10 December 1978):1,55. One more critical is Harold Hayes's "Updike's African Dream," *Esquire* 90 (19 December 1978):27–29. Hayes thinks that Updike's imagination, "in its extravagance . . . has soared past the truth of his principal character."

12. Joyce B. Markle, however, doing her own detective work and drawing on an unpublished paper by Barry Amis, argues that "the country described in *The Coup* is a pastiche of inaccuracies." Her argument is made in *"The Coup:* Illusions and Insubstantial Impressions," in William R. Macnaughton, ed., *Critical Essays on John Updike* (Boston: G. K. Hall & Co., 1982), p. 283.

13. Ibid., p. 289.

14. Ibid., p. 300.

15. Ibid.

Chapter Thirteen

1. Anatole Broyard, "Falling into Love," *New York Times,* 17 March 1979, p. 17.

2. "One Big Interview," p. 482.

3. Josephine Hendin, *Vulnerable People: A View of American Fiction Since 1945* (New York: Oxford University Press, 1978), p. 88

Chapter Fourteen

1. Cynthia Propper Seton, "John Updike and His American Everyman," *Washington Post Book World,* 27 September 1982, pp. 1–2
2. *American Studies International* 15 (Spring 1977):24.
3. "Perennial Promises Kept," *Time,* 18 October 1982, p. 81.
4. In a thirty-nine page appendix to *Hugging the Shore* entitled "On One's Own Oeuvre" Updike comments on sexuality in his writing and offers interesting (if not particularly significant) information on other dimensions of his prose and verse. He says, for example, that a myth of sorts *does* inhabit *Rabbit Redux:* "The cost of the disruption of the social fabric was paid, as in the earlier novel, by a girl. Iphigenia is sacrificed and the fleet sails on, with its quarrelling crew" (pp. 858–59).

Selected Bibliography

PRIMARY SOURCES

1. Novels and Story-Cycles
Bech: A Book. New York: Alfred A. Knopf, 1970.
Bech Is Back. New York: Alfred A. Knopf, 1982.
The Centaur. New York: Alfred A. Knopf, 1965.
The Coup. New York: Alfred A. Knopf, 1978.
Couples. New York: Alfred A. Knopf, 1968.
Marry Me. New York: Alfred A. Knopf, 1976.
A Month of Sundays. New York: Alfred A. Knopf, 1975.
Of the Farm. New York: Alfred A. Knopf, 1965.
The Poorhouse Fair. New York: Alfred A. Knopf, 1958 (reprinted with
     an introduction by the author, 1977).
Rabbit Is Rich. New York: Alfred A. Knopf, 1981.
Rabbit Redux. New York: Alfred A. Knopf, 1971.
Rabbit, Run. New York: Alfred A. Knopf, 1960.

2. Short-Story Collections
Museums and Women. New York: Alfred A. Knopf, 1972.
The Music School. New York: Alfred A. Knopf, 1966.
Olinger Stories. New York: Alfred A. Knopf, 1964.
Pigeon Feathers. New York: Alfred A. Knopf, 1962.
Problems. New York: Alfred A. Knopf, 1979.
The Same Door. New York: Alfred A. Knopf, 1959.
Too Far to Go. New York: Fawcett Crest, 1979.

3. Poetry
The Carpentered Hen and Other Tame Creatures. New York: Harper &
     Row, 1958.
A Child's Calendar. New York: Alfred A. Knopf, 1965.
Midpoint and Other Poems. New York: Alfred A. Knopf, 1969.
Telephone Poles and Other Poems. New York: Alfred A. Knopf, 1963.
Tossing and Turning. New York: Alfred A. Knopf, 1977.
Verse. Greenwich, Conn.: Fawcett, 1965.

4. Drama
Buchanan Dying. New York: Alfred A. Knopf, 1974.

5. Collected Discursive Prose
Assorted Prose. New York: Alfred A. Knopf, 1965.
Hugging the Shore. New York: Alfred A. Knofp, 1983.
Picked-Up Pieces. New York: Alfred A. Knopf, 1975.

SECONDARY SOURCES

1. Bibliographies
Olivas, Michael A. *An Annotated Bibliography of John Updike Criticism,
1967–1973, and a Checklist of His Works.* New York: Garland
Publishing Co., 1975.
Sokloff, B. A., and **Aranson, David E.** *John Updike: A Comprehensive
Bibliography.* Darby, Pa.: Darby Press, 1970; Norwood, Pa.:
Norwood Press, 1973.
Taylor, Clarke C. *John Updike: A Bibliography.* Kent, Ohio: Kent State
University Press, 1968.
See also *Modern Fiction Studies* below.

2. Books
Because of the large number of writings about Updike and the
availability of several detailed bibliographies, this listing is
confined to book-length studies of the author. Other works used
here are described in "Notes and References."
Burchard, Rachel C. *John Updike: Yea Sayings.* Carbondale: Southern
Illinois University Press, 1971. Discusses Updike's dualisms of
love versus death, matter versus spirit., etc., in the context of
treating him as a writer of affirmation.
Galloway, David. *The Absurd Hero in American Fiction.* Austin:
University of Texas Press, 2d rev. ed., 1981. Sound discussion of
Updike's fiction published through 1976 in a chapter on Updike
entitled "The Absurd Man as Saint."
Greiner, Donald J. *The Other John Updike: Poems, Short Stories, Prose,
Play.* Athens: Ohio University Press, 1981. Thorough treatment of
Updike's writing other than his novels to show his artistic
development; much attention given to other Updike interpreters.
Hamilton, Alice, and **Hamilton, Kenneth.** *The Elements of John Updike.*
Grand Rapids: Wm. B. Eerdmans Publishing Co., 1970. Study of
Updike's fiction and poetry with much symbol hunting and
attention to religious allusions.

Harper, Howard M. Jr. *Desperate Faith: A Study of Bellow, Salinger, Mailer, Baldwin, and Updike.* Chapel Hill: University of North Carolina Press, 1967. Study of the spiritual effect of Updike's fiction in a secular world.

Hendin, Josephine. *Vulnerable People: A View of American Fiction Since 1945.* New York: Oxford University Press, 1978. Chapter entitled "The Victim Is a Hero" treats Updike, Bellow, and Heller; good discussion of sexuality in Updike's fiction.

Hicks, Granville. *Literary Horizons: A Quarter Century of American Fiction.* New York: New York University Press, 1970. Chapter consisting of Hicks's *Saturday Review* reviews of eight Updike books, plus an afterword.

Hunt, George W. *John Updike and the Three Great Secret Things: Sex, Religion, and Art.* Grand Rapids: Wm. B. Eerdmans Publishing Co., 1980. Employs Jungian, theological, and new critical approaches to argue that Updike's emphases have shifted from religion to sex to art.

Macnaughton, William R., ed. *Critical Essays on John Updike.* Boston: G. K. Hall & Co., 1982. Reprints of reviews by Anthony Burgess, Alfred Kazin et al.; original essays by Joyce Markle, Kathleen Verduin et al.

Markle, Joyce B. *Fighters and Lovers: Theme in the Novels of John Updike.* New York: New York University Press, 1973. Follows the progression of conflict in Updike's novels as far as *Rabbit Redux.*

Modern Fiction Studies 20 (Spring 1974). "John Updike Number" consisting of eight articles on Updike, reviews of Updike criticism, and a checklist of Updike criticism. A valuable source for Updike study.

Podhoretz, Norman. *Doings and Undoings.* New York: Farrar, Straus, 1964. Hostile evaluation of Updike in a chapter called "A Dissent on Updike." Says that Updike is immature, lacking in imagination, and unable to create credible characters.

Samuels, Charles Thomas. *John Updike.* Minneapolis: University of Minnesota Press, 1969. Valuable monograph that describes Updike as a skilled traditionalist.

Tanner, Tony. *City of Words: American Fiction 1950–1970.* Harper & Row, Publishers, 1971. Intelligent commentary on *The Poorhouse Fair, Rabbit, Run, The Centaur,* and *Couples* in a chapter entitled "A Compromised Environment."

Taylor, Larry E. *Pastoral and Anti-Pastoral Patterns in John Updike's Fiction.* Carbondale: Southern Illinois University Press, 1971. Study on the pastoral theme in Updike's writing, with emphasis on the symbolic importance of place.

Thorburn, David, and Eiland, Howard, eds. *John Updike: A Collection of Critical Essays*. Englewood Cliffs, N.J.: Prentice-Hall, 1979. Reprints of twenty-three essays on Updike's novels and stories by Richard Gilman, George Steiner, Arthur Mizener et al.

Vargo, Edward P. *Rainstorms and Fire: Ritual in the Novels of John Updike*. Port Washington, N.Y.: Kennikat Press, 1973. Studies Updike's novels to show centrality of ritual and celebration, places Updike in context of many other novelists.

Index